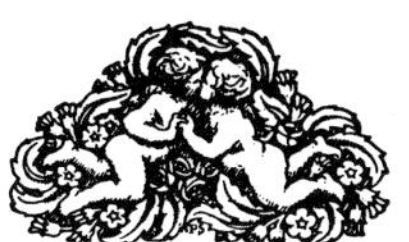

Men of Consequence

JANE BOWN

With a foreword by Snowdon

Chatto & Windus

LONDON

Prints by David Watkinson

Published in 1987 by Chatto & Windus Ltd
30 Bedford Square, London WC1B 3RP

British Library Cataloguing in Publication Data

Bown, Jane
Men of consequence
1. Photography of men
I. Title
779'.23'0924   TR681.M4

ISBN 0 7011 3181 0 (hardback)
ISBN 0 7011 3182 9 (paperback)

Photoset by Rowland Phototypesetting Ltd
Bury St Edmunds, Suffolk

Printed in Great Britain by
Butler & Tanner Ltd
Frome, Somerset

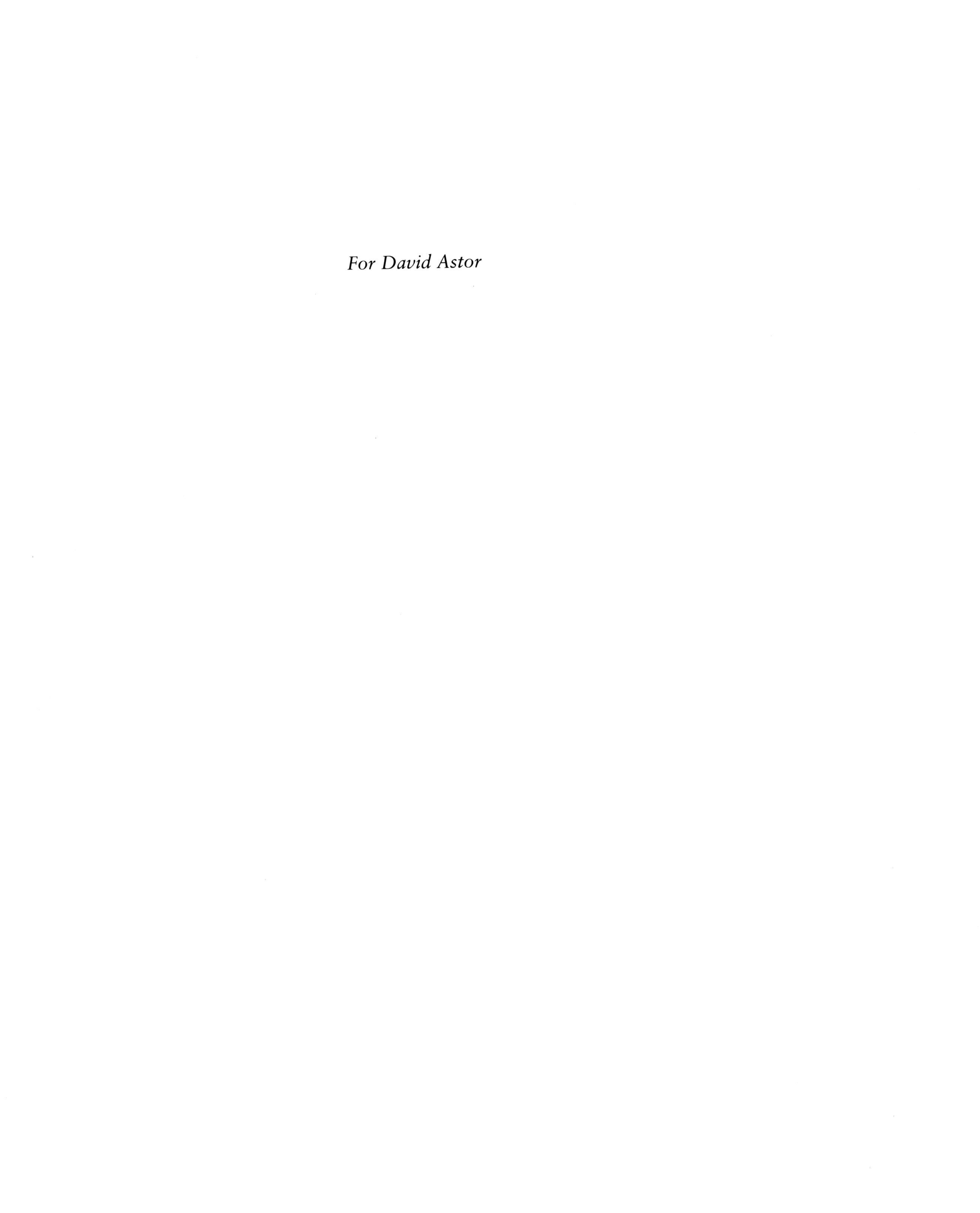

For David Astor

My early Rolleiflex portraits were backed up by the occasional
photoflood, but by the time I had graduated to the Olympus OM I
with 50mm and 85mm lenses I found everything was possible with
available light, and that 1/60th at f2.8 on Tri X film was the recipe
for the majority of the later portraits. These were mostly taken in-
doors with the sitter in the strongest possible pool of light by a
window.   J.B.

FOREWORD

I admire Jane Bown as a person as much as I admire her work as a photographer. She reminds me of an Oxford don, blending into the background, with no funny hats nor loud clothes. She is one of the great recorders of our time, a kind of English Cartier-Bresson. I imagine she works with very little equipment, probably no lights at all, and the result is photography at its best. She doesn't rely on gimmicks or tricks, just simple, honest recording, but with a shrewd and intellectual eye. That is surely what photography is about.

Over the years I have greatly admired her work in the *Observer*. It has always achieved a standard of quality that is stunningly good. I'd love to ask her if she considers photography to be an art form. I wonder if she would like her photographs framed, on a wall. I doubt it. I suspect she keeps them in folders. I wonder too whether she hates talking about photography as much as I do. I'm sure she never discusses speeds and stops and filters and which is the best camera to use — one that doesn't break down is the simple answer. Her chief concern is the use of light, especially daylight.

You can nearly always tell what the light source is in a photograph by looking into the subject's eyes. When you use complicated flash guns in the studio the eyes look wrong, almost too clear, with untypical, large pupils. Often the white umbrella is reflected in them. But look at Jane Bown's picture of Paul Getty and you see a little window reflected there and how his pupils have remained small. I think eyes are the most important thing in a picture. I'm sure Jane Bown would agree. Her sitters' eyes draw you into her pictures; for her, eye contact is clearly very important.

I have never had the honour of being photographed by her, so I don't know if she talks as she works or tries to get a reaction from her sitter. I imagine she goes quietly about her business. But underneath her simplicity and humility, she is probably just as nervous as the rest of us when we go on an assignment. Many people find being photographed an unpleasant experience; they want only to escape from the camera. It helps greatly if, like Jane Bown, the photographer has a one-to-one relationship with the sitter, without the distraction of an assistant or another person. Jane Bown is careful to tell the truth, not to distort. Her pictures are penetrating and informative, yet full of kindness.

There's so much nonsense talked about photographers. They are completely unimportant; it's the subject which is all-important and that's what Jane Bown captures so magnificently. She catches moments which are typical – Sir Harold Acton imitating himself with his book on the Medicis; Mr Scargill in front of his own portrait, which is very telling; Lord Shinwell's humour and inquisitiveness; the kindness and humour of Lord Denning, and that haunting academic seriousness of Enoch Powell. She has captured the charm of Lord Hailsham, plus the fact that he's not someone who will go down in history for his dress-sense but as one of the world's nicest and wittiest human beings. Mr Heath, very much 'being photographed'. I love the picture of John Betjeman in Cornwall, capturing his wonderful laugh and the shape of his suit, which was so typical of him and his poetry.

All her pictures prove that black and white is still a force to be reckoned with. She has managed to avoid working in colour for colour's sake. As a result her photographs — I prefer to call them photographs because I find the word portrait rather pretentious — have a unique quality. This book gives us a wonderful opportunity to see the seriousness of her work, as a whole, in a lasting way. I don't consider photography to be one of the fine arts, but Jane Bown is undoubtedly a great artist.

Snowdon

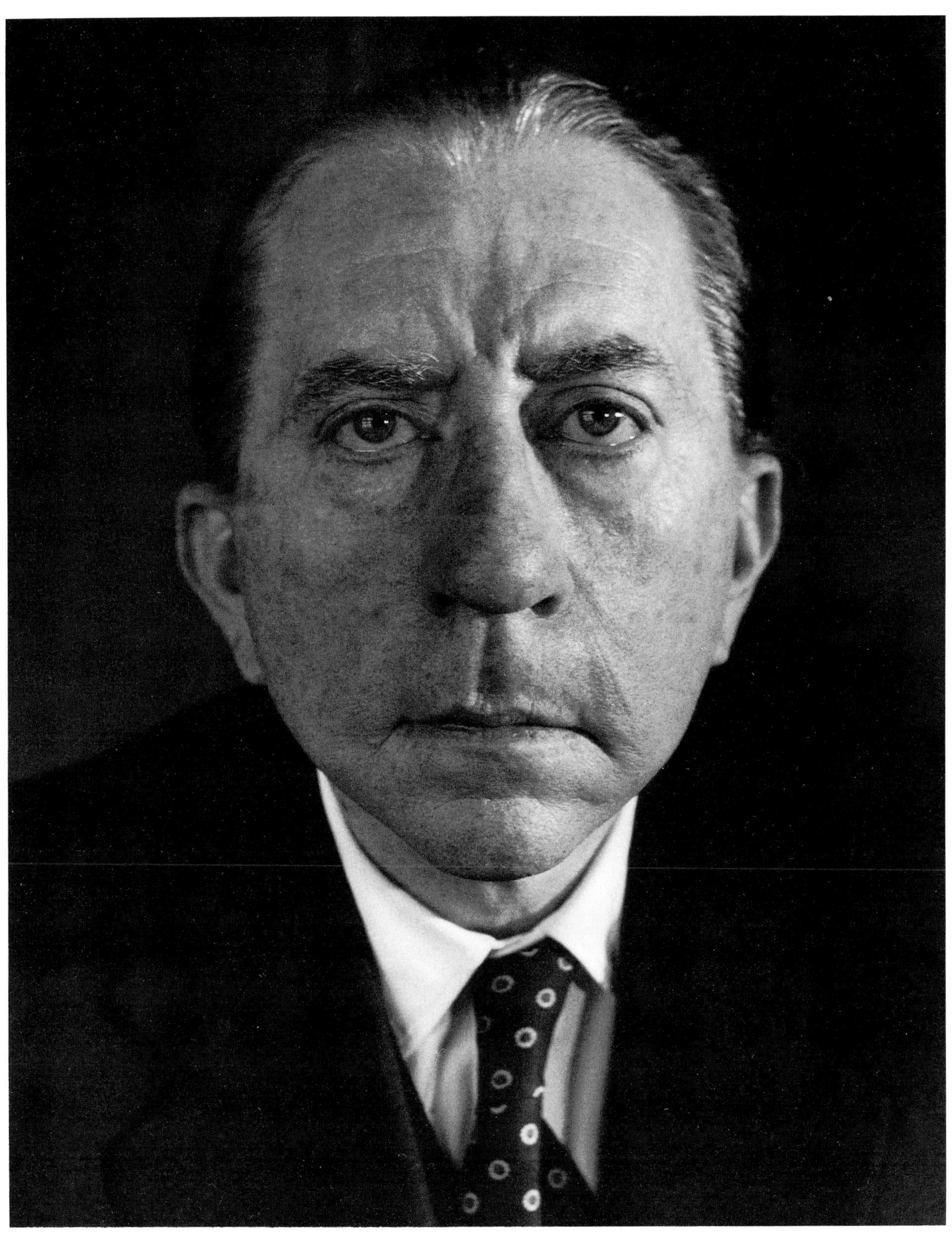

1 – Jean Paul Getty, 1957

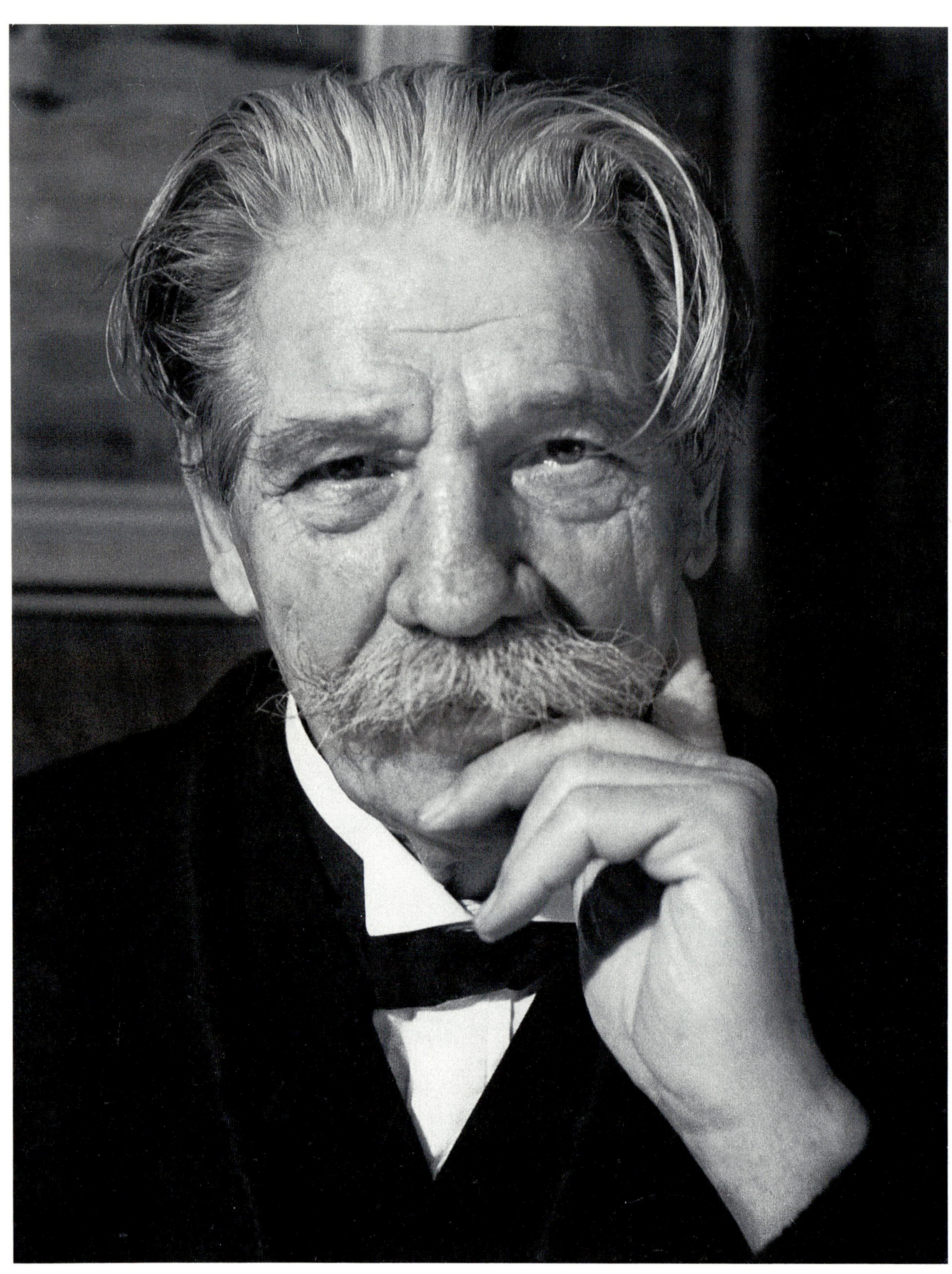

2 – Dr Albert Schweitzer, 1955

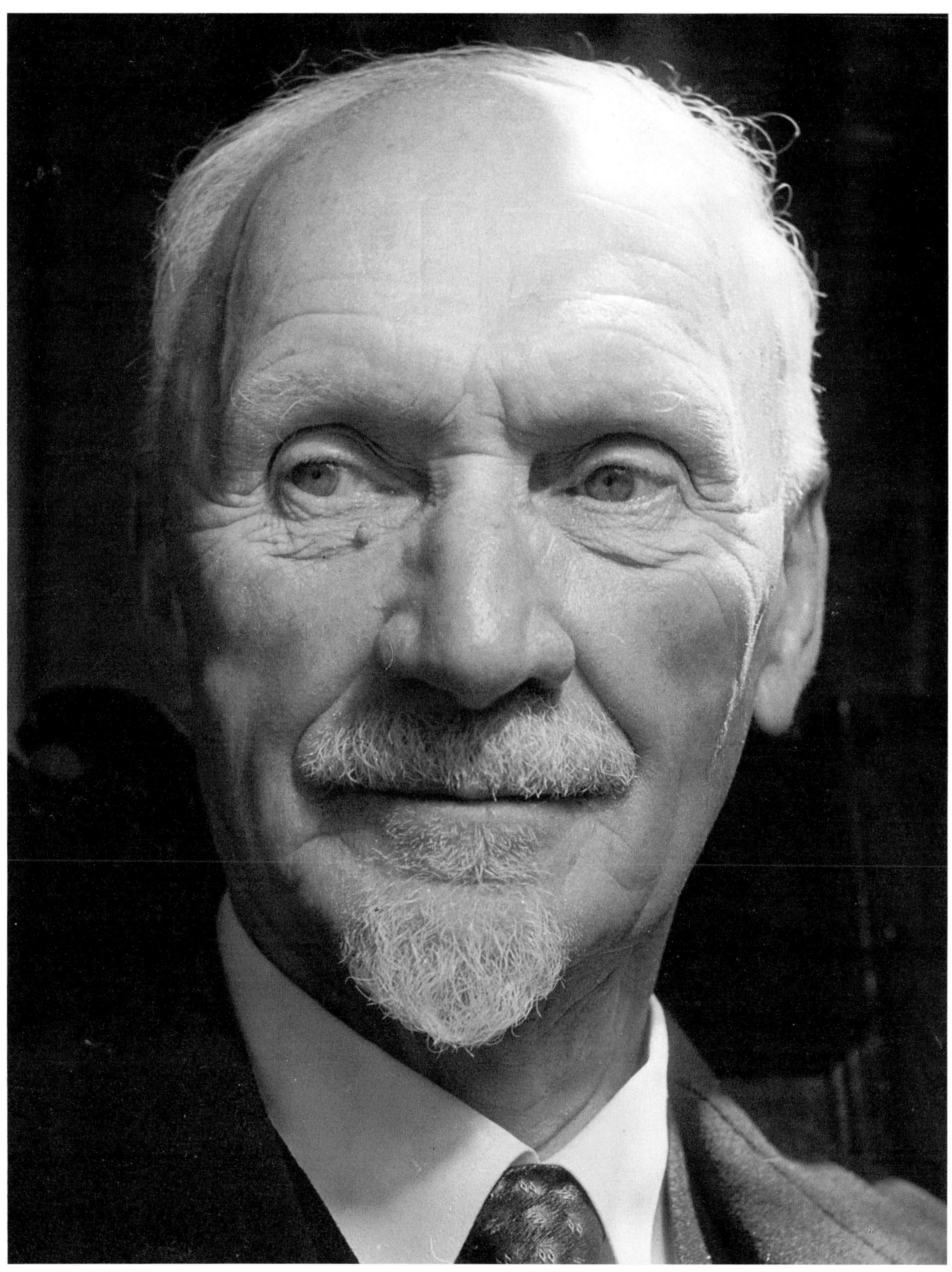

3 – General Jan Smuts, 1949

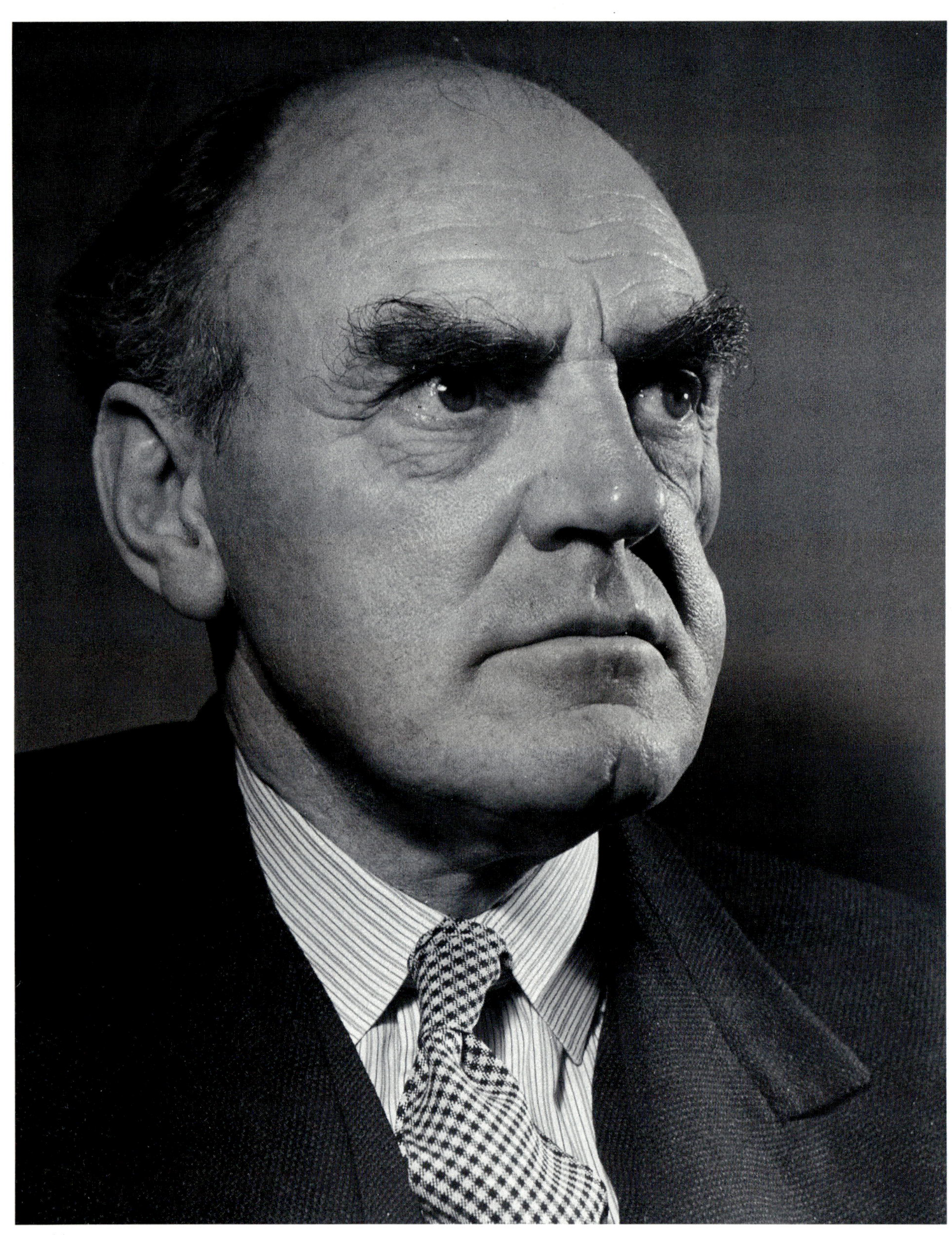

4 – Lord Reith, 1951

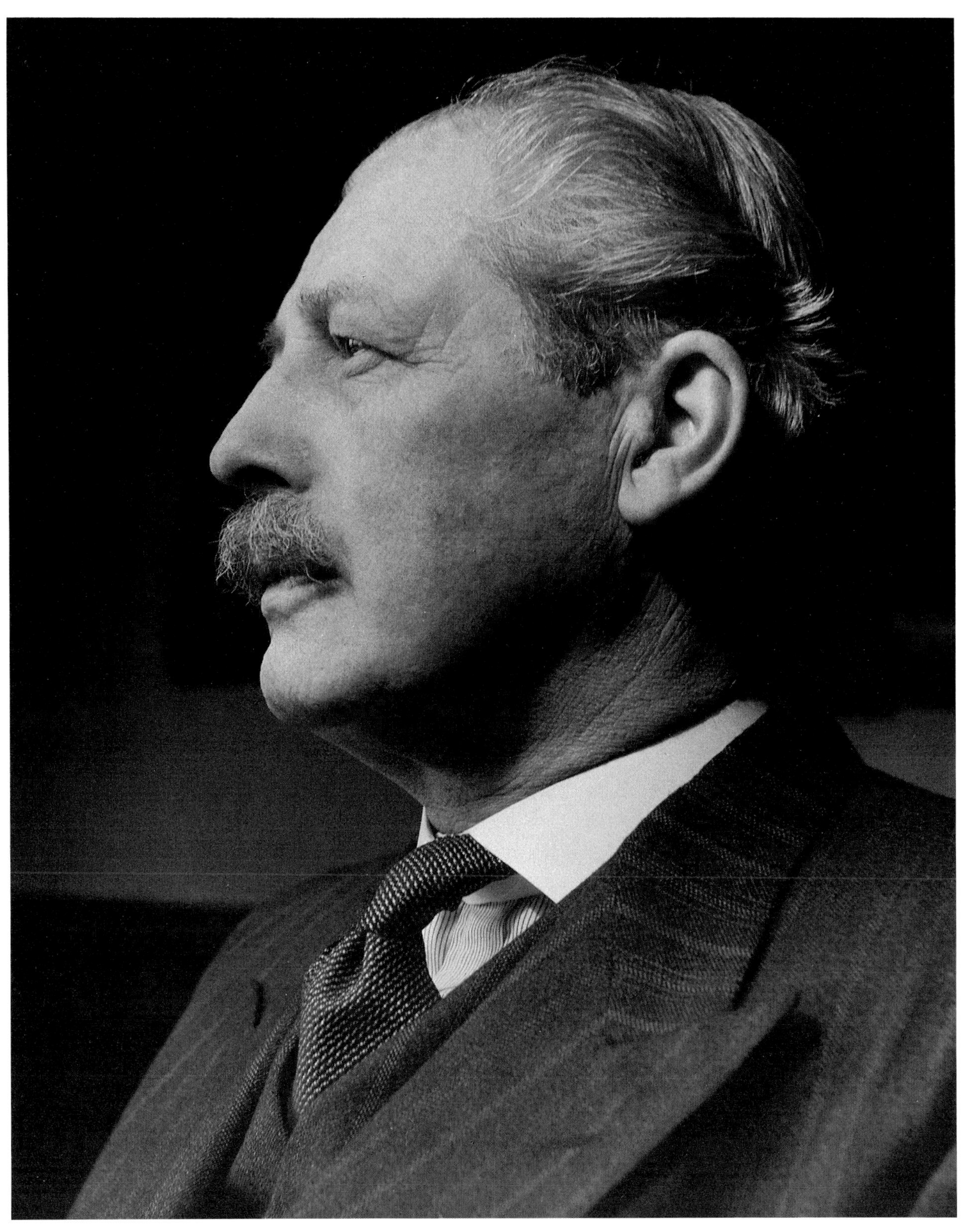

5 – Harold Macmillan, 1955

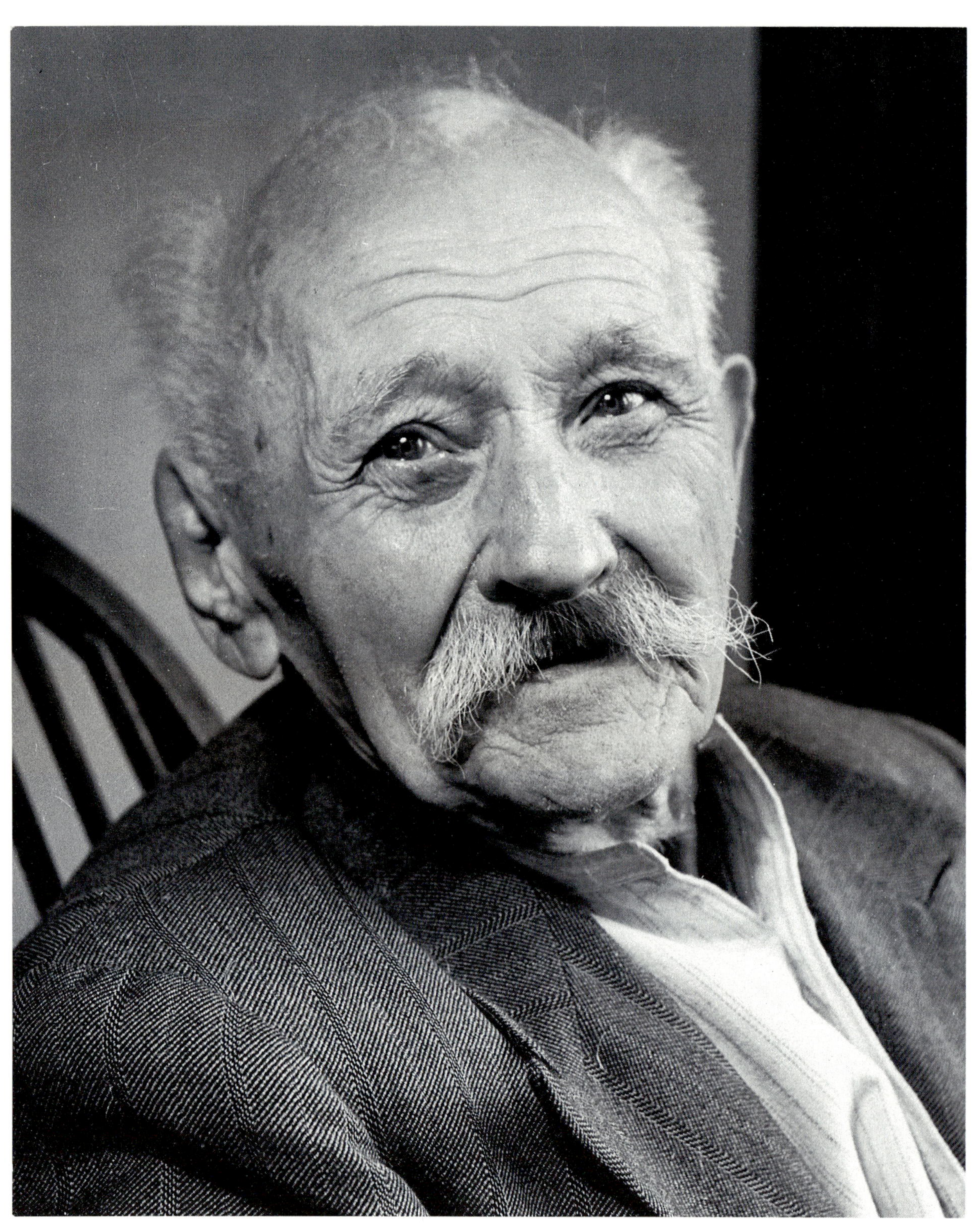

6 – William Russell, 1952

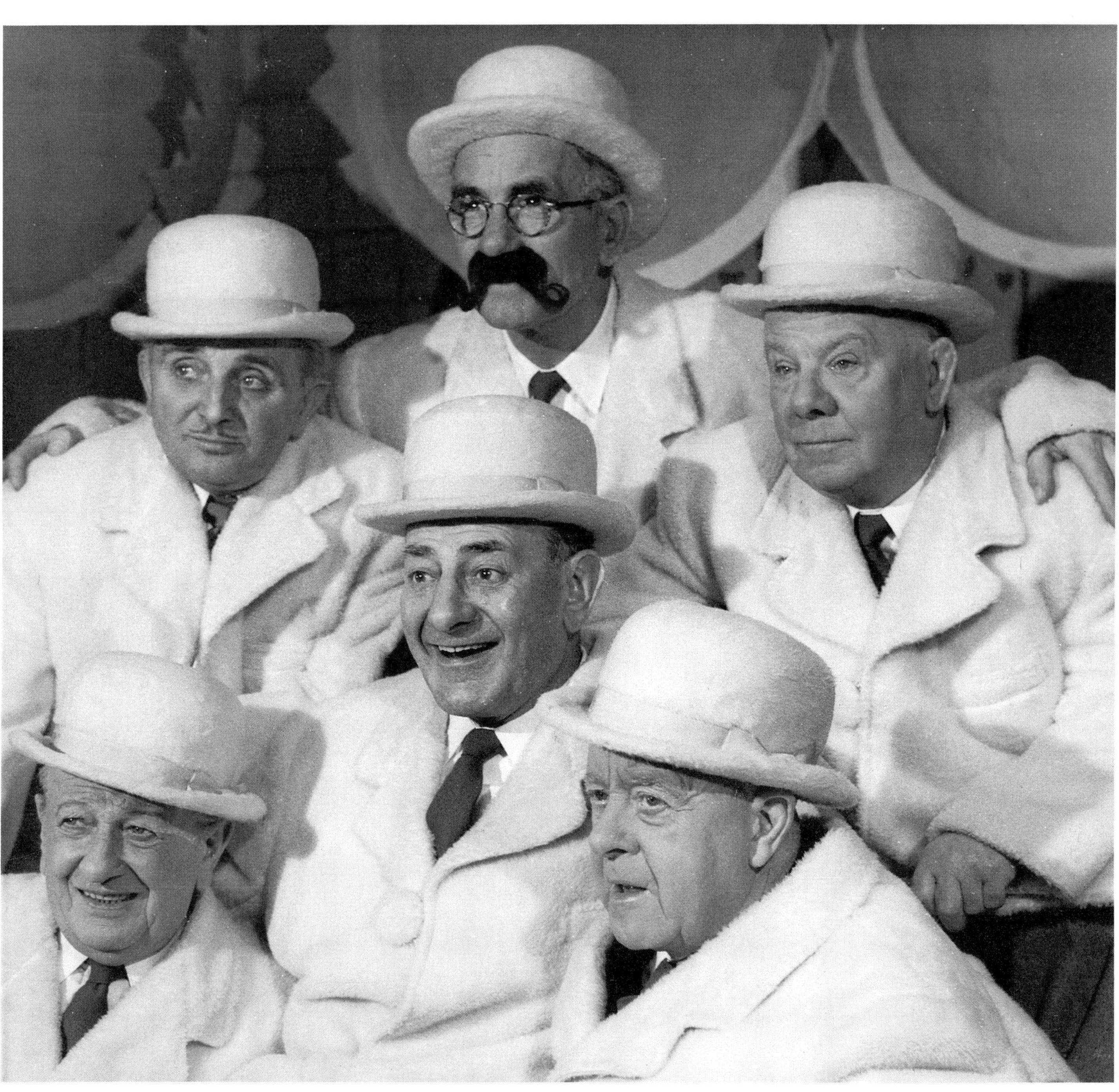

7 – The Crazy Gang, 1957

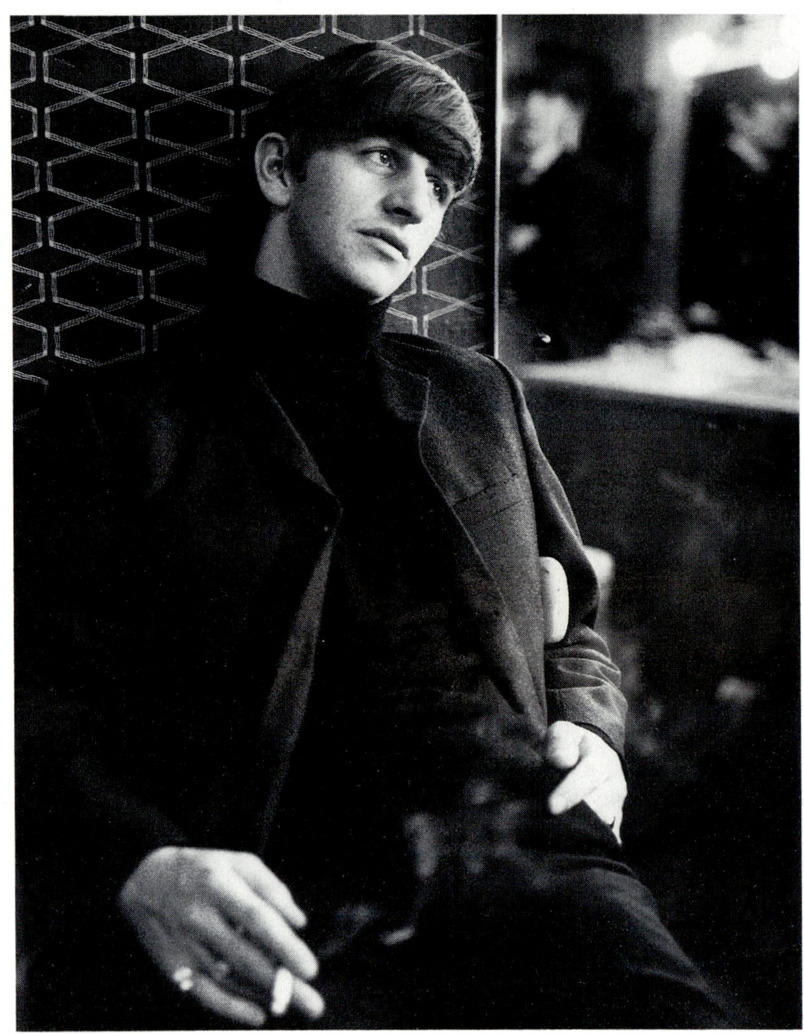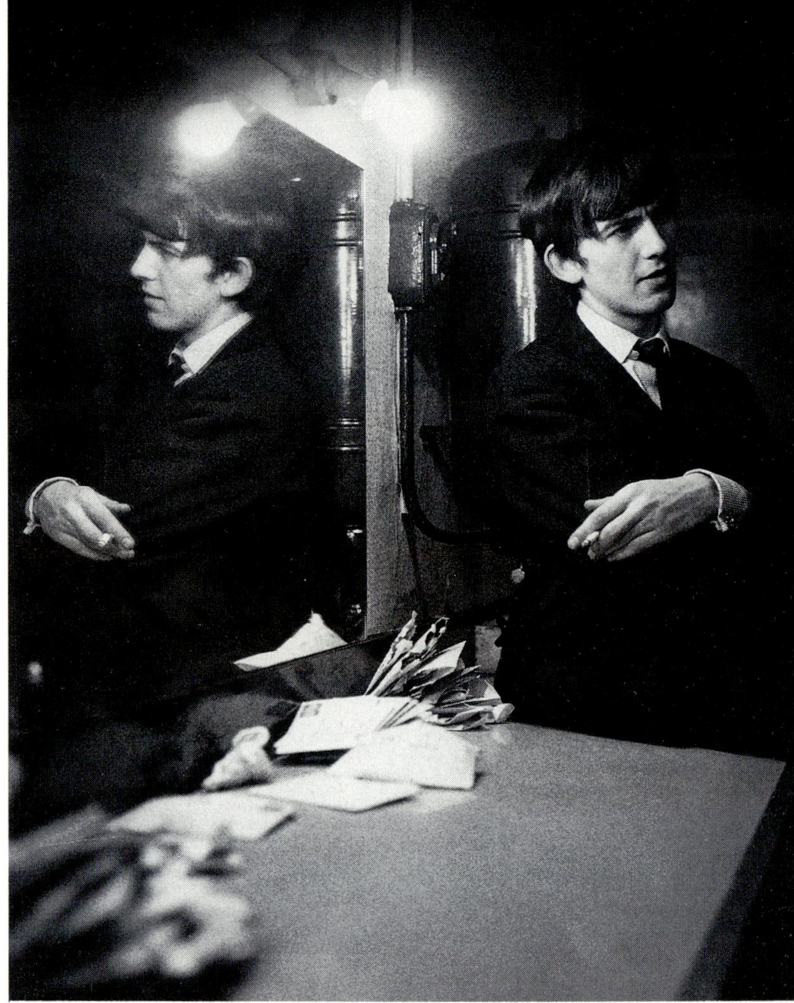

8, 9 – Ringo Starr and George Harrison, 1963

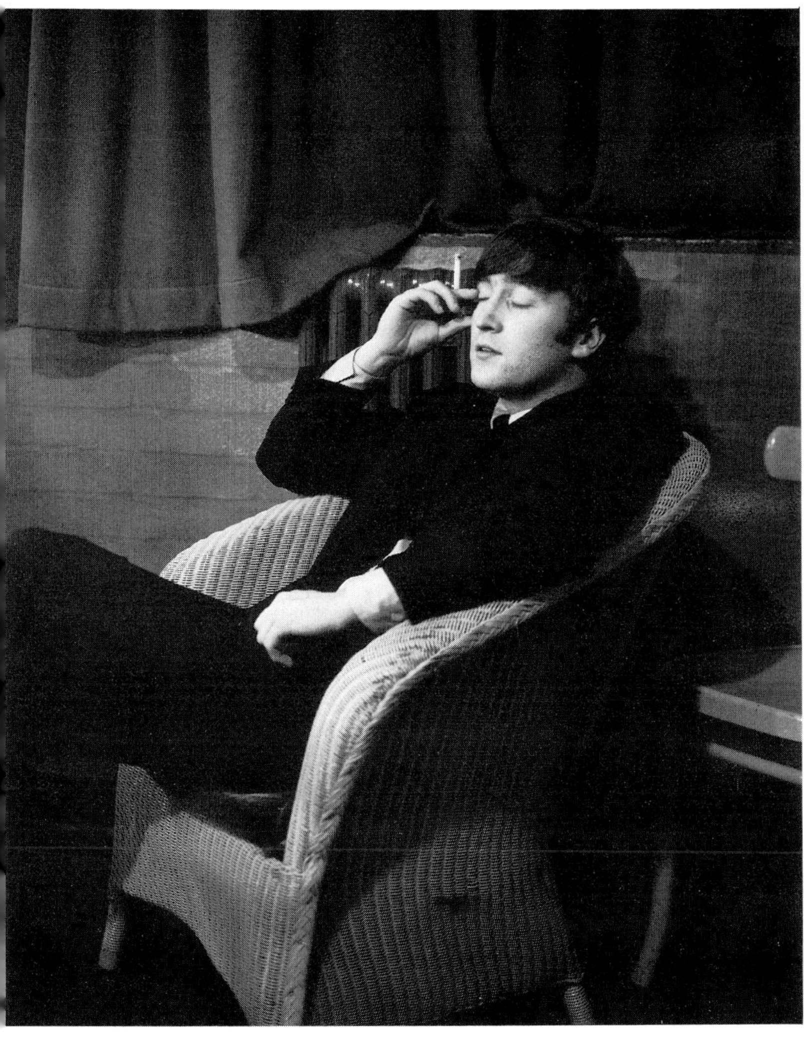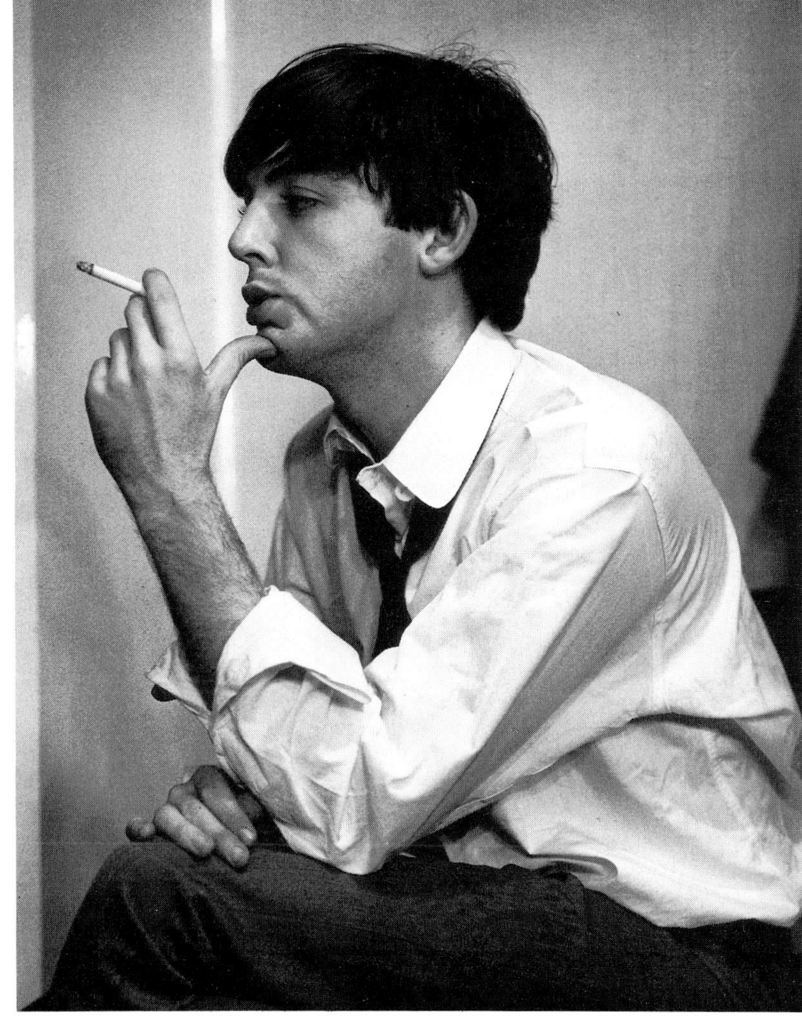

10, 11 – John Lennon and Paul McCartney, 1963

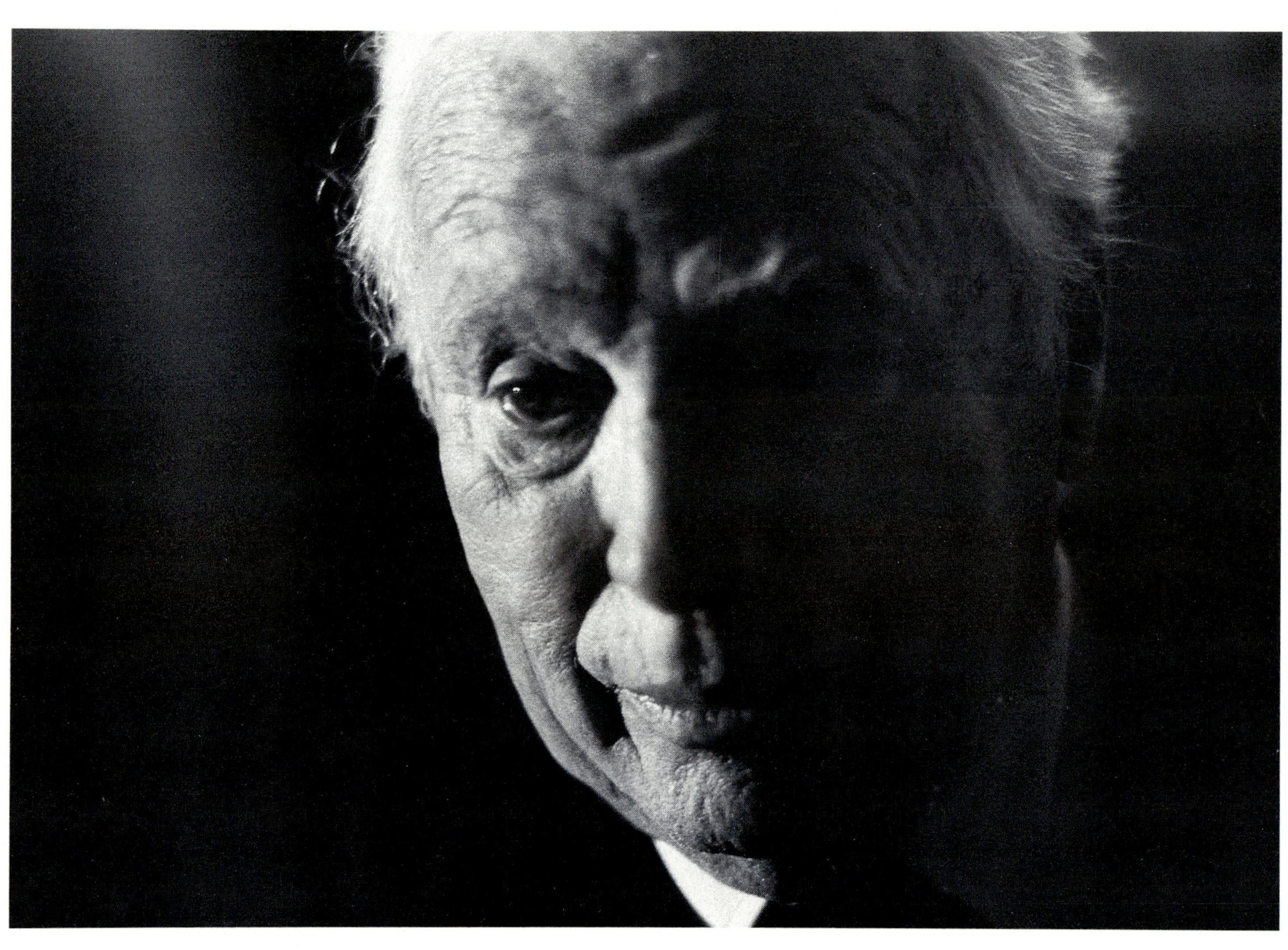

12 – Charlie Chaplin, 1969

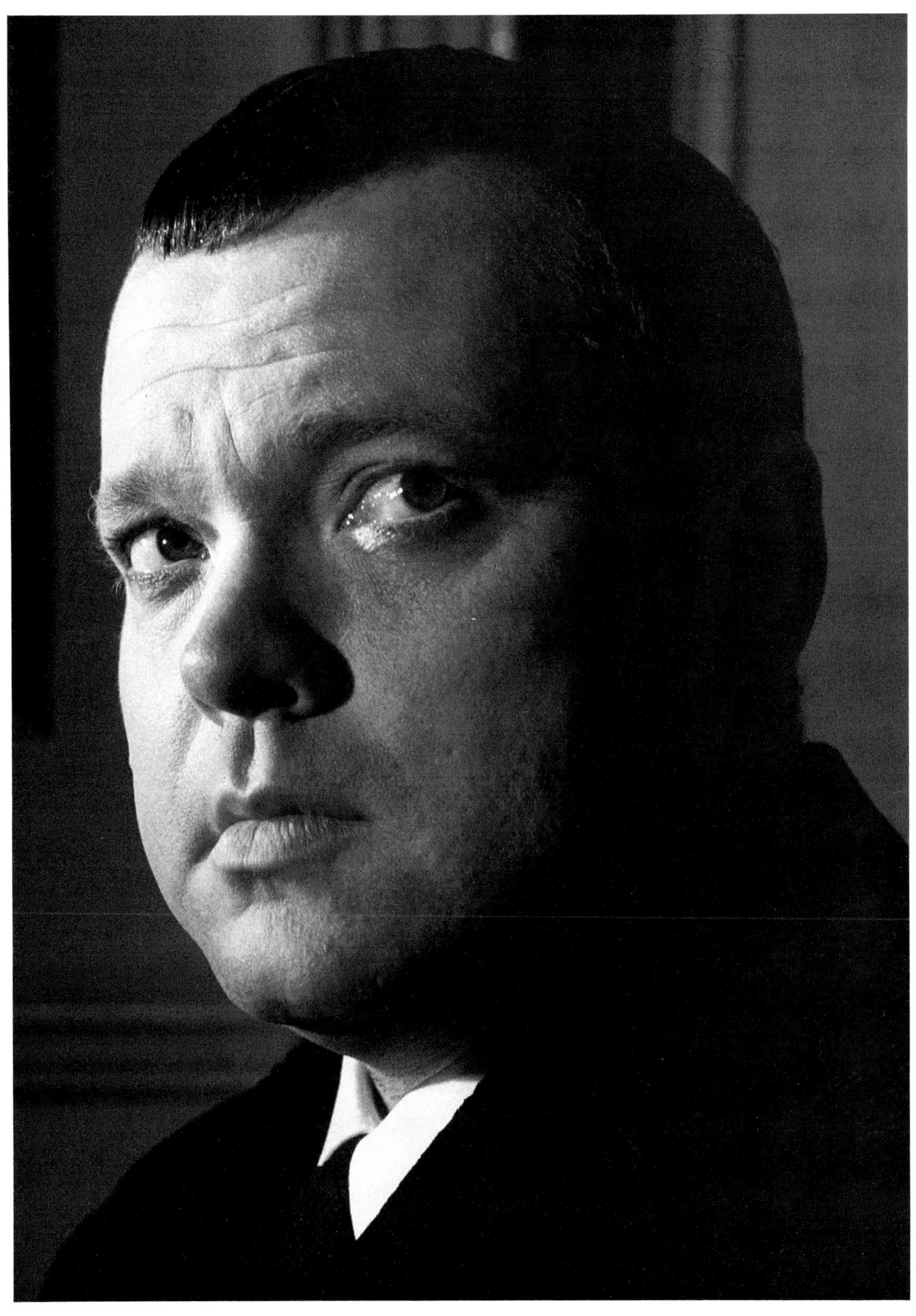

13 – Orson Welles, 1951

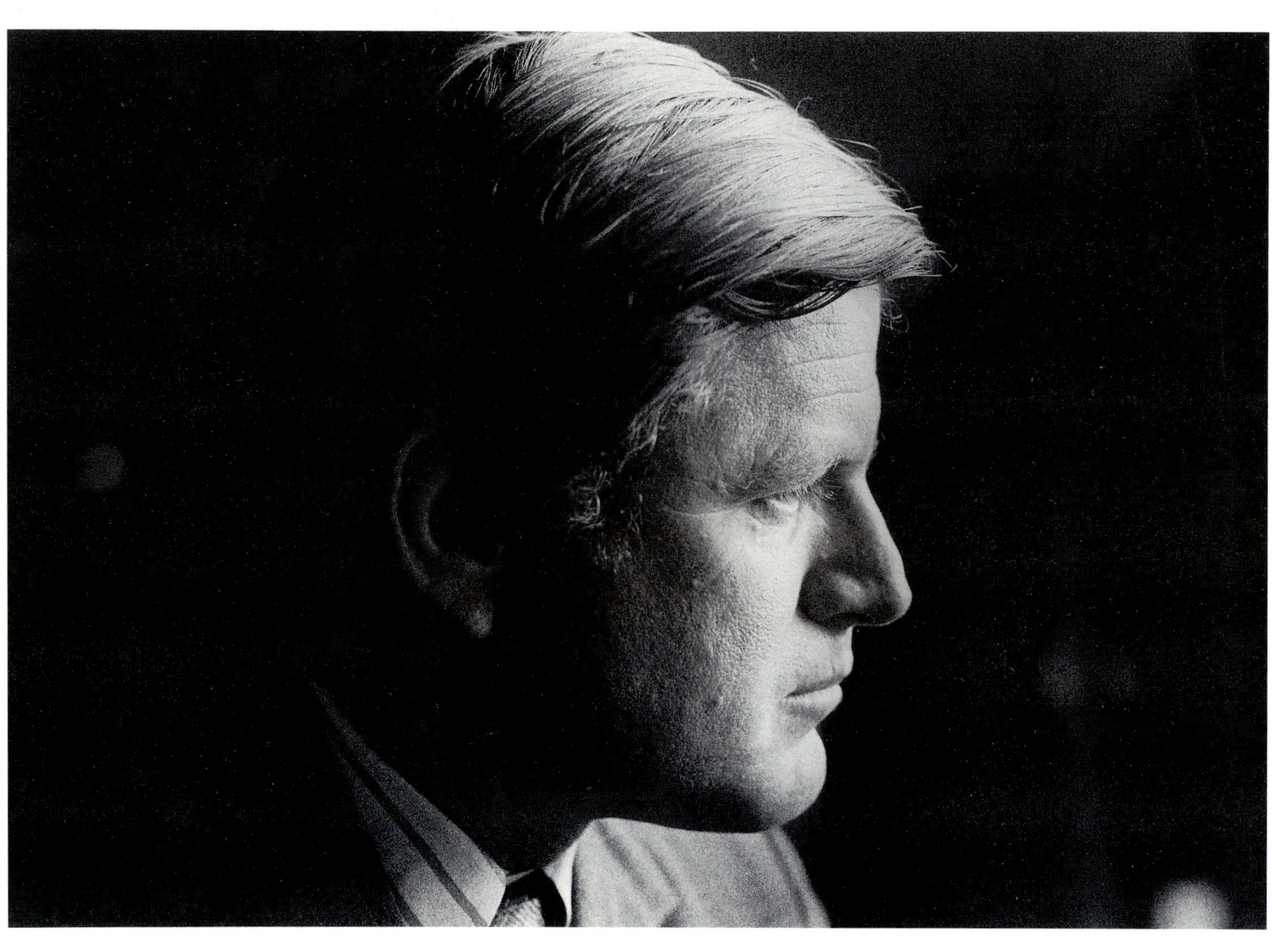

14 – Edward Kennedy, 1971

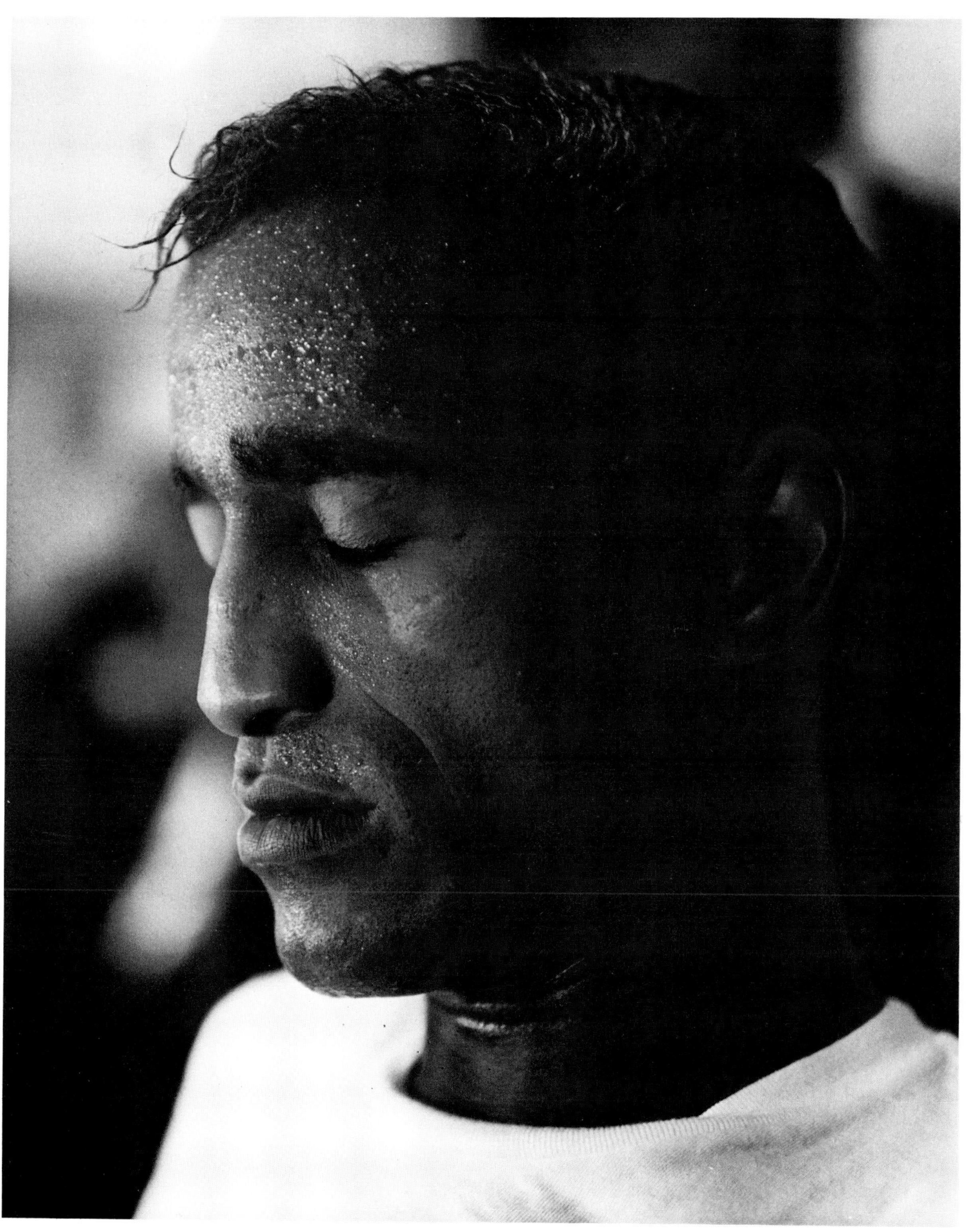

15 – Sammy Davis Jnr, 1961

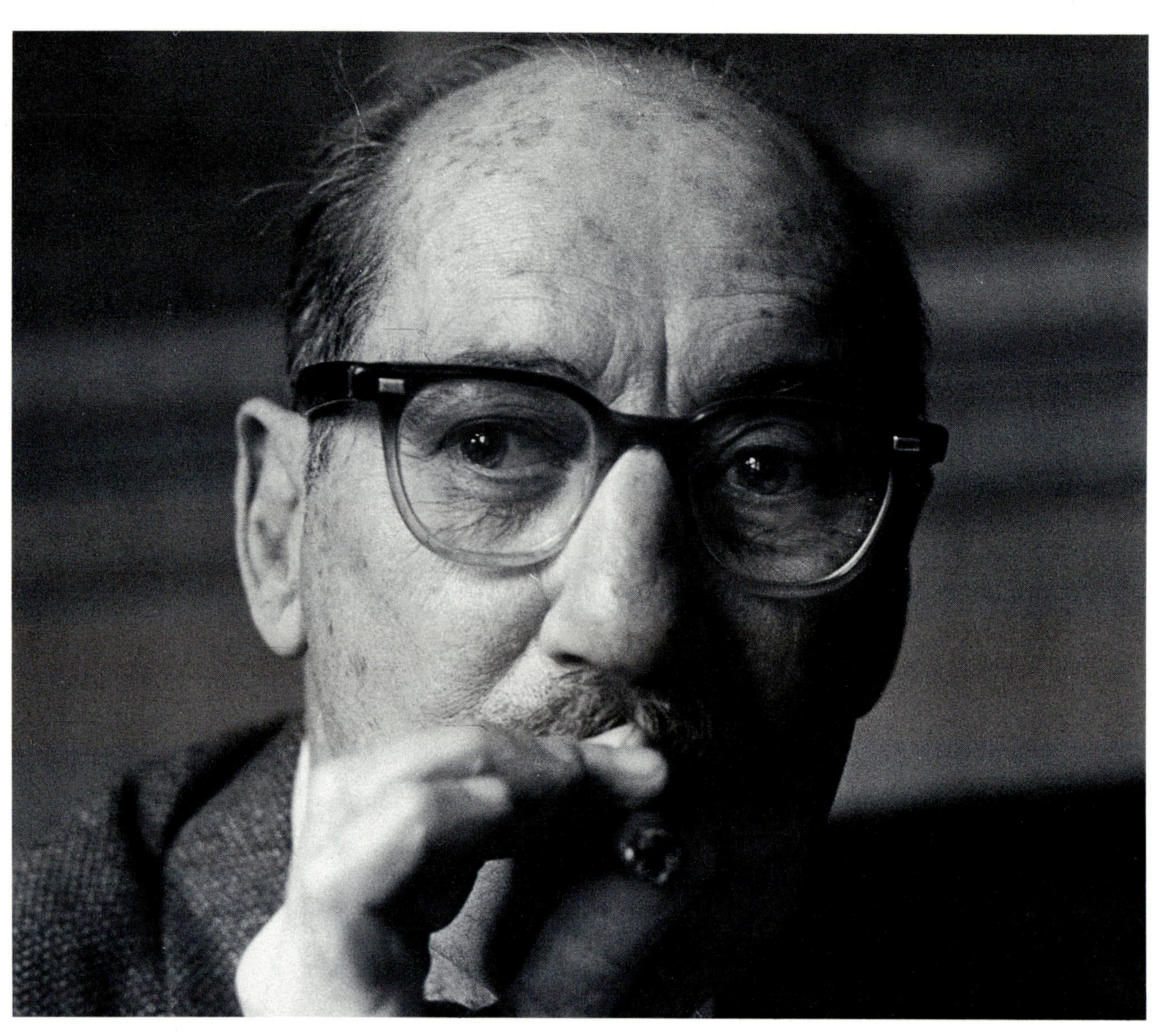

16 – Groucho Marx, 1964

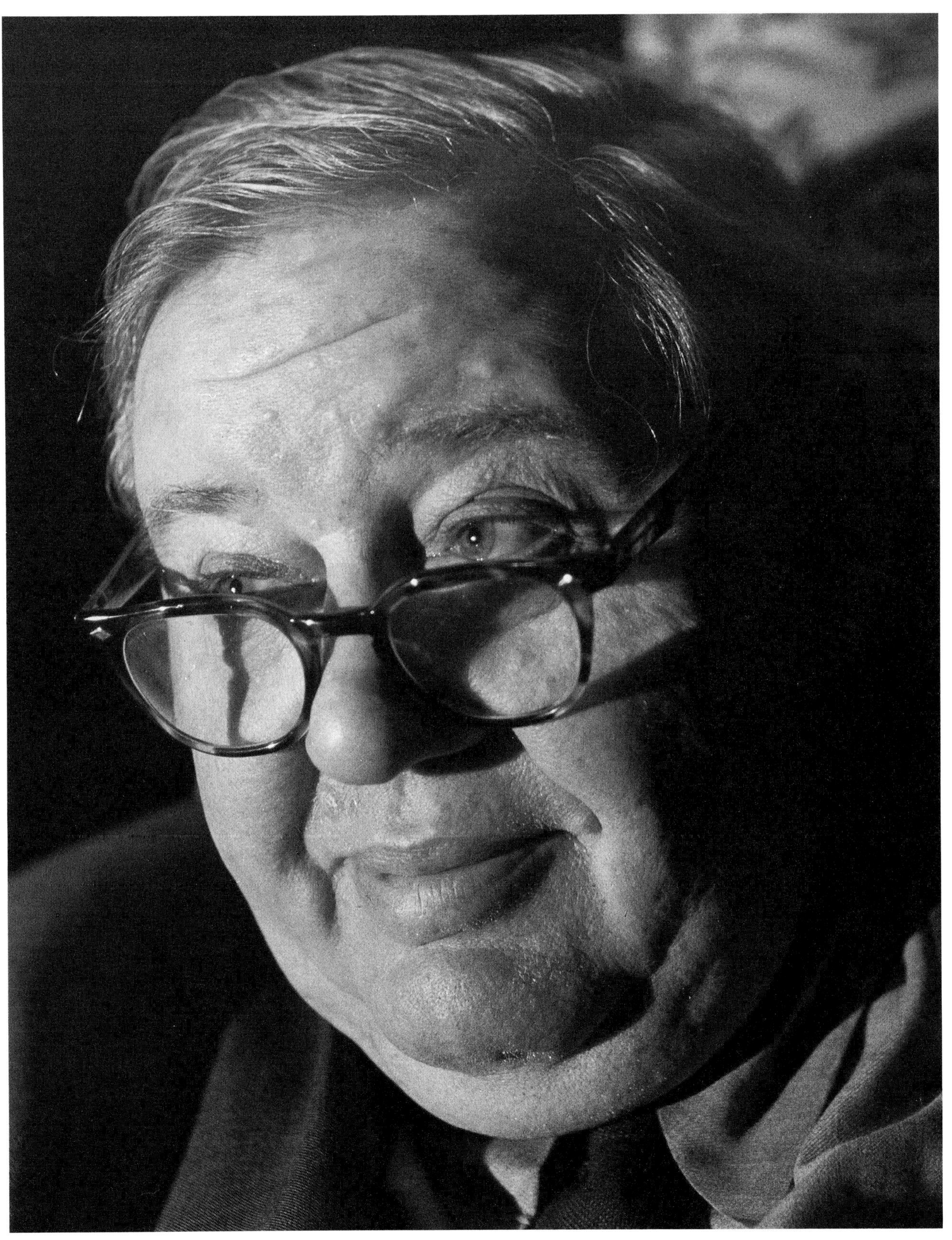

17 – Charles Laughton, 1958

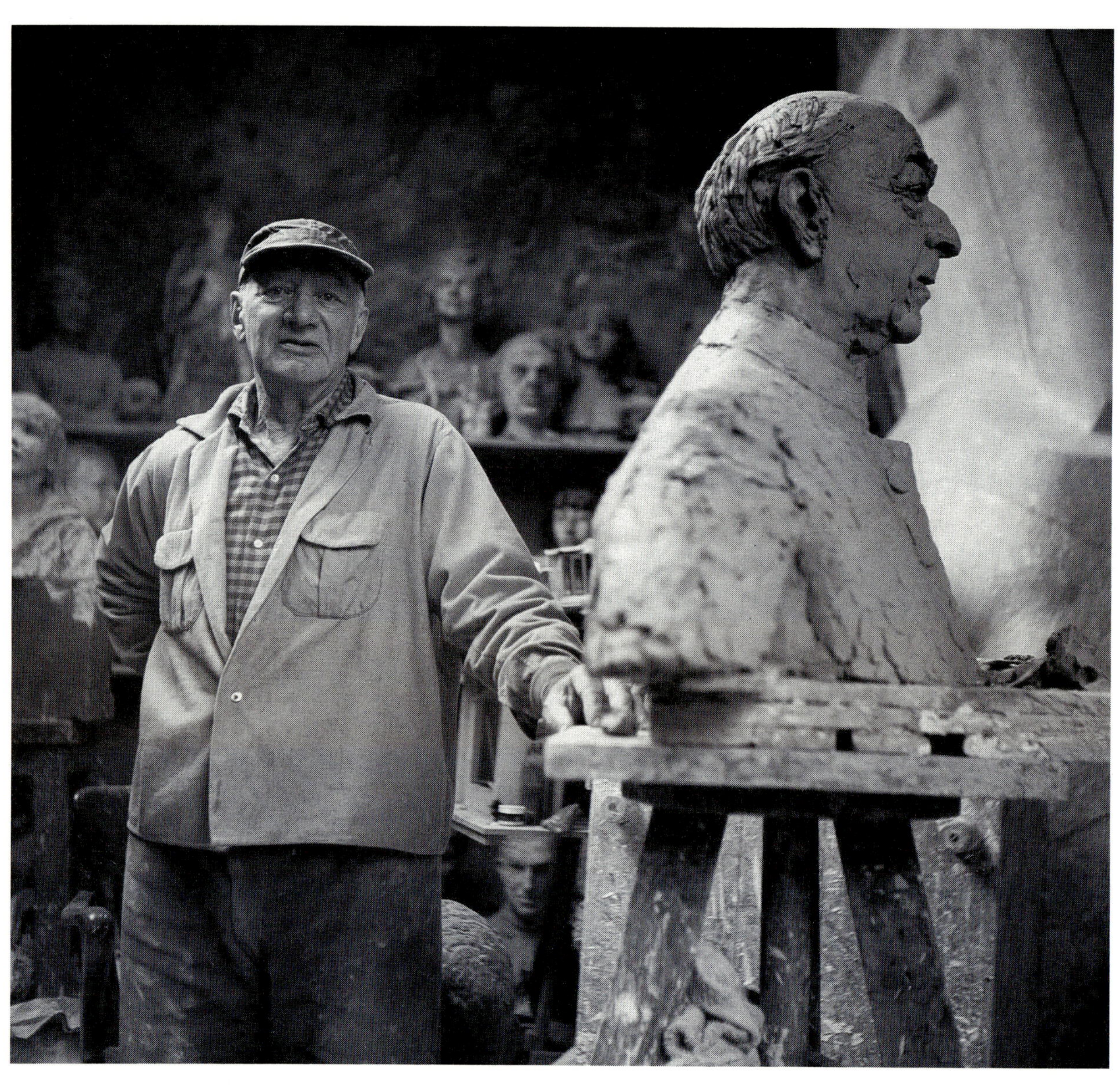

18 – Jacob Epstein, 1958

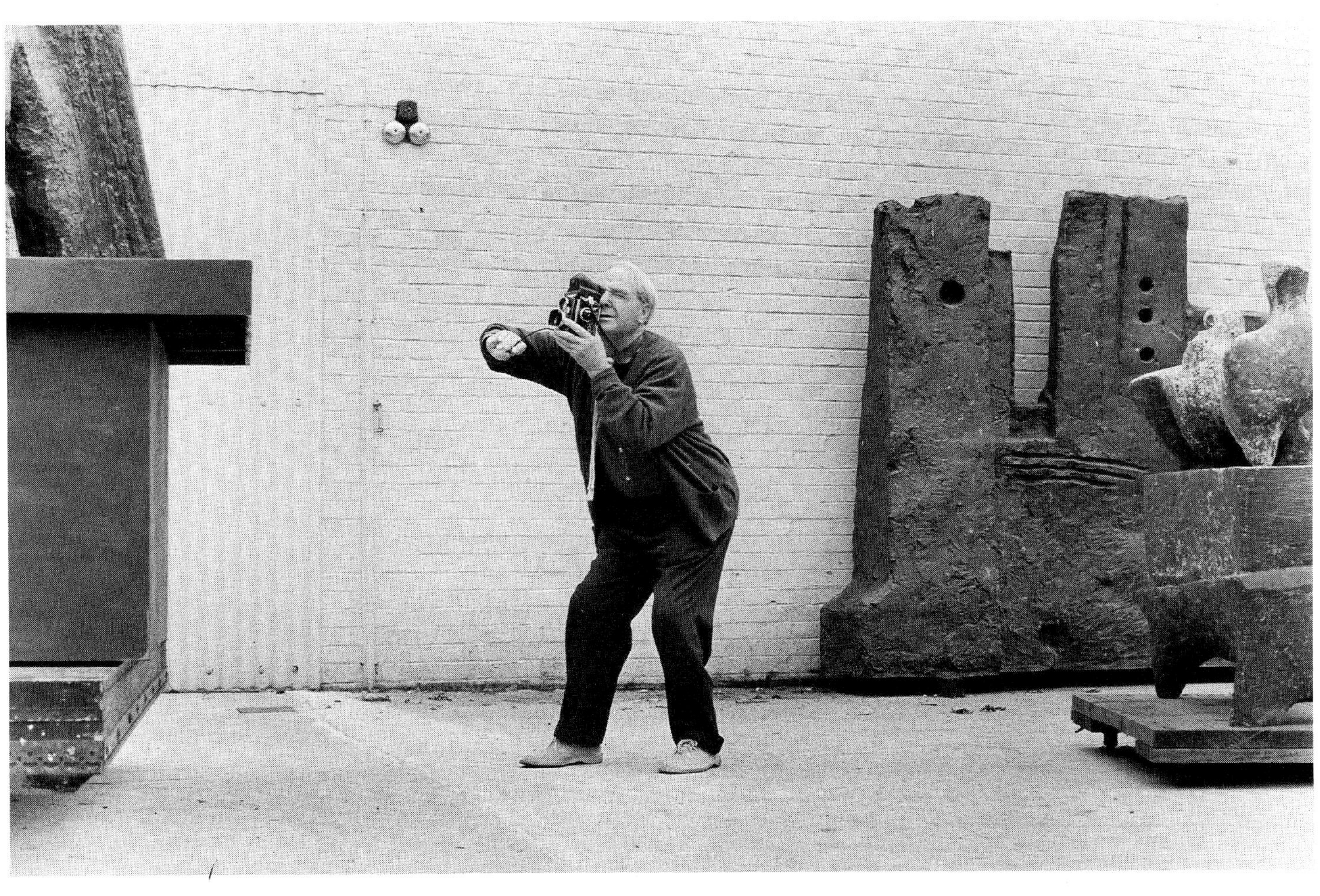

19 – Henry Moore, 1968

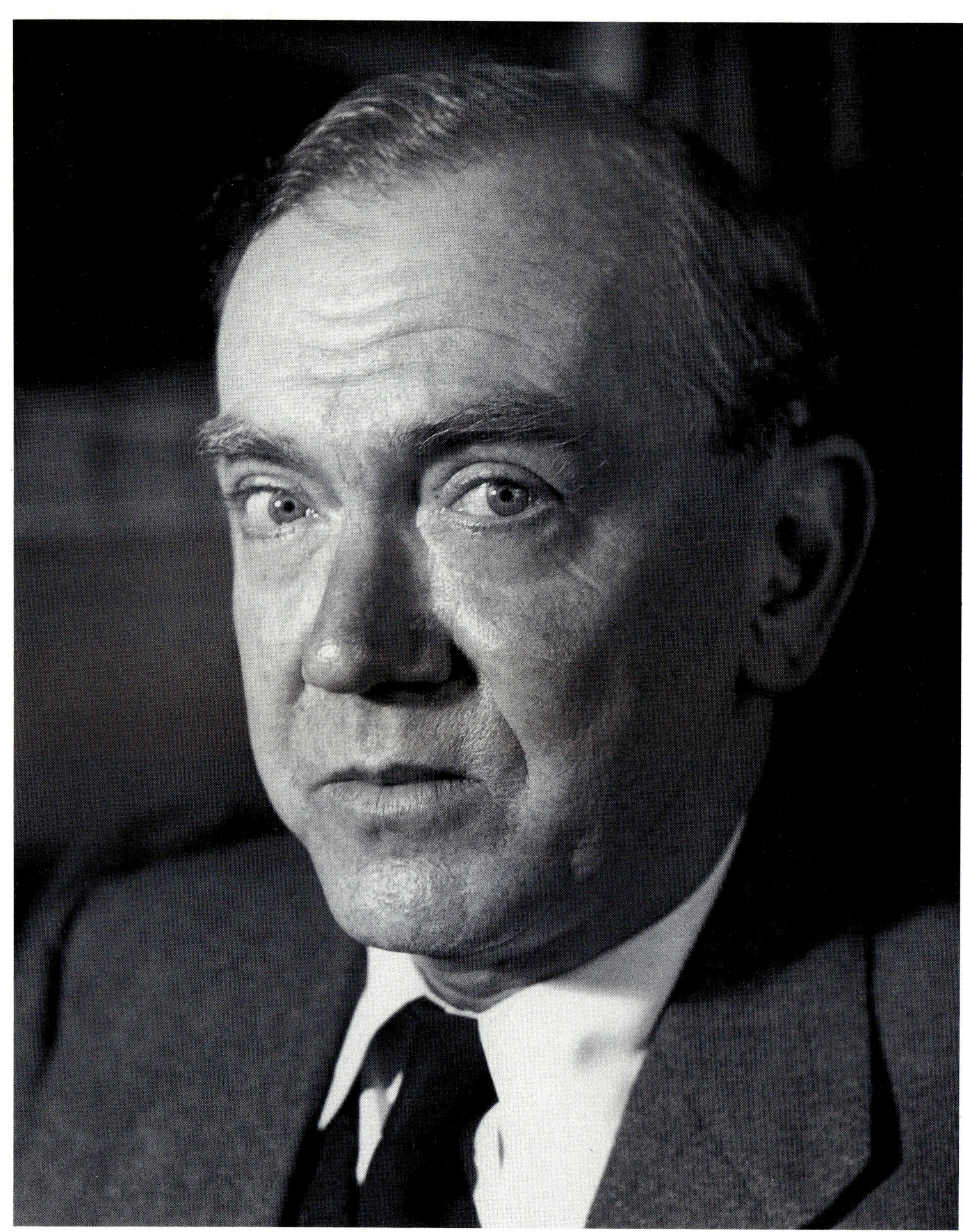

20 – Graham Greene, 1957

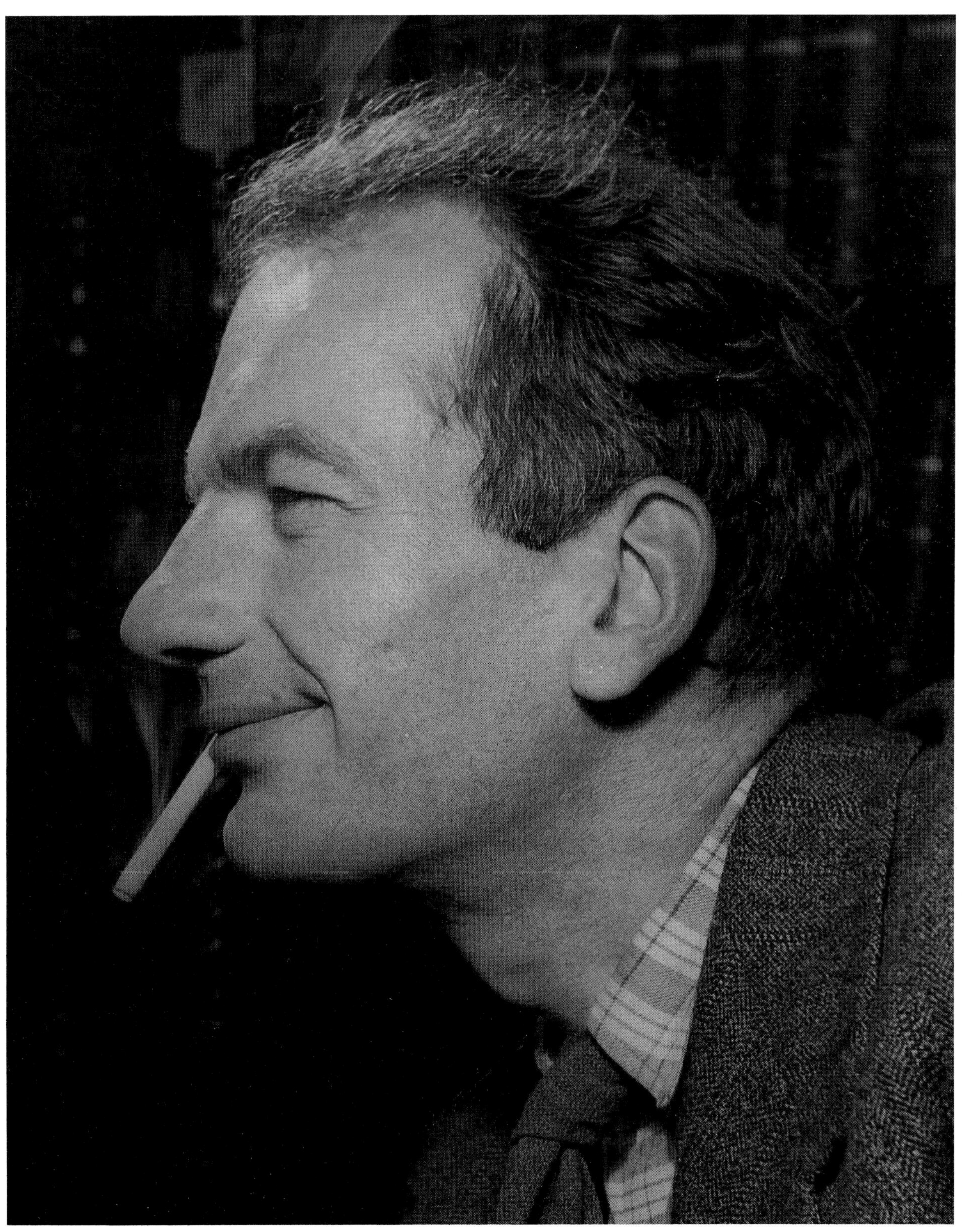

21 – Philip Toynbee, 1961

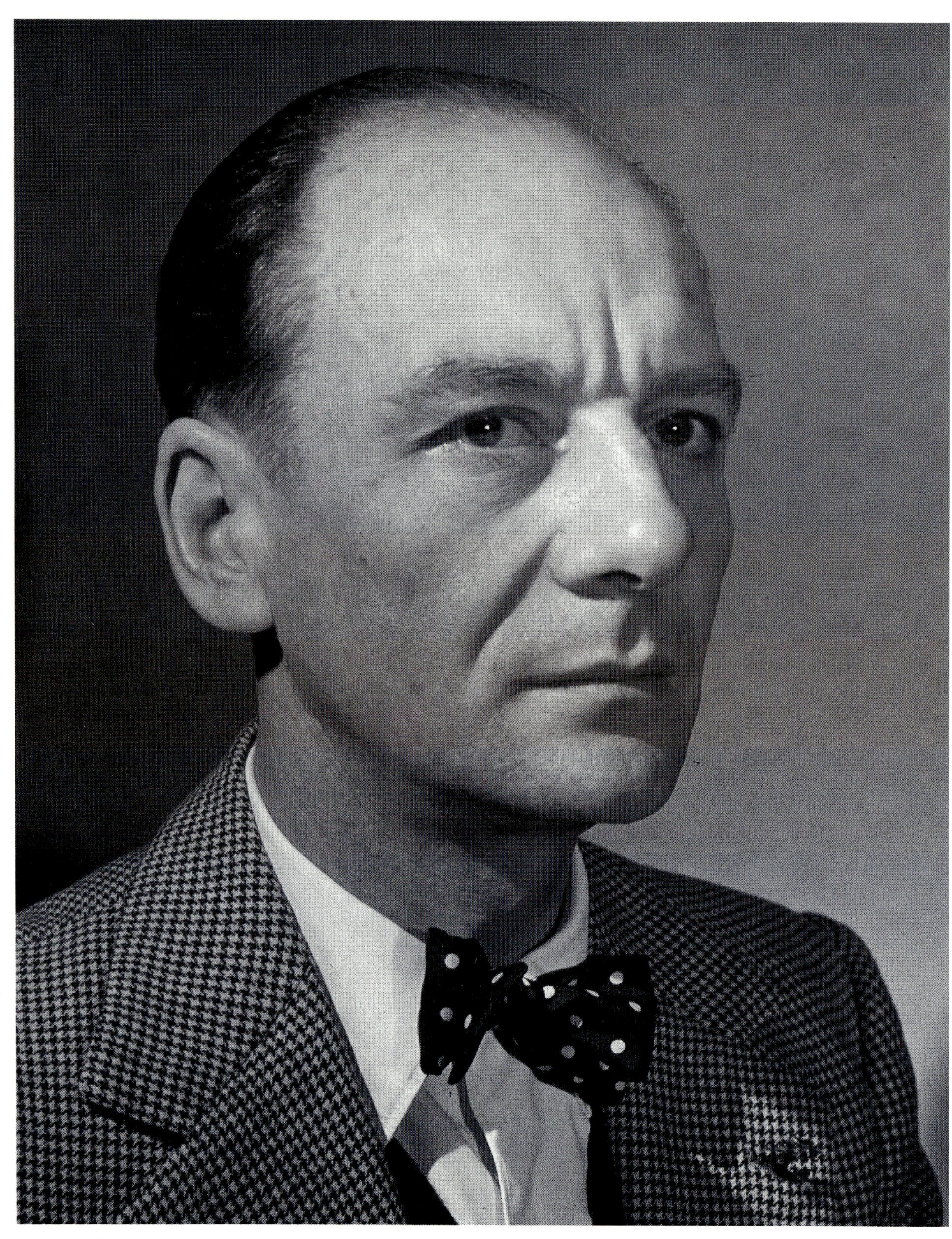

22 – Sir John Gielgud, 1950

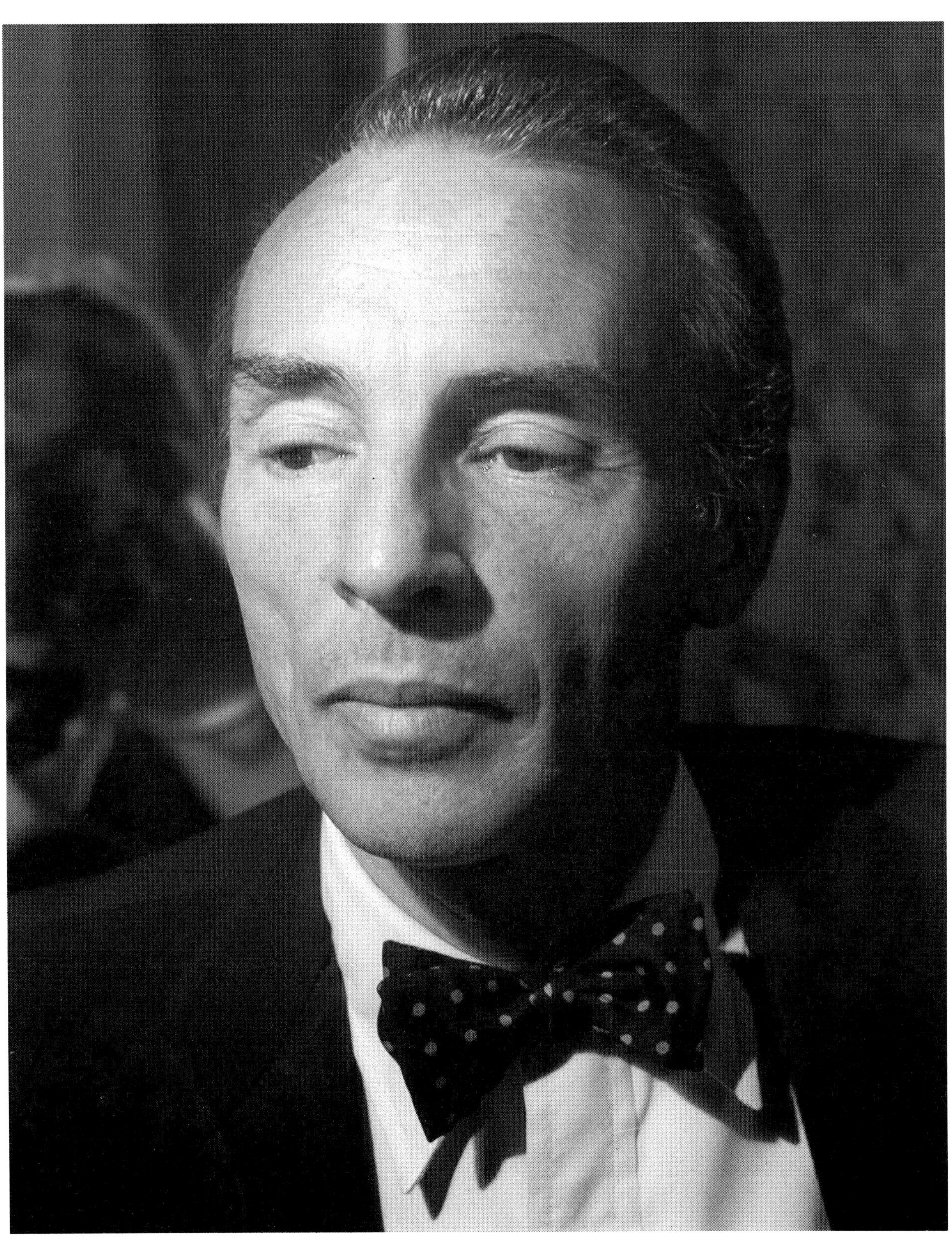

23 – George Balanchine, 1960

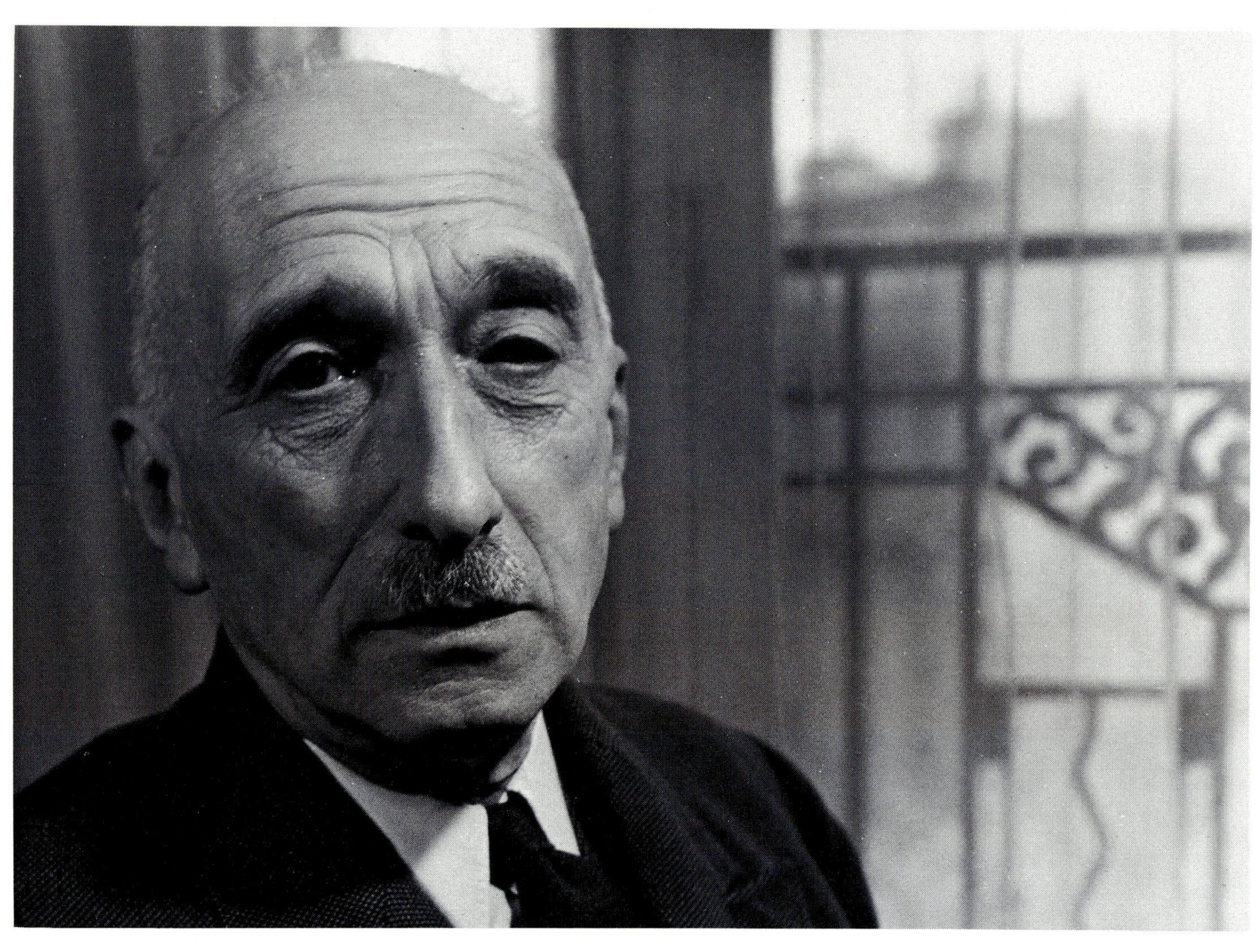

24 – François Mauriac, 1950

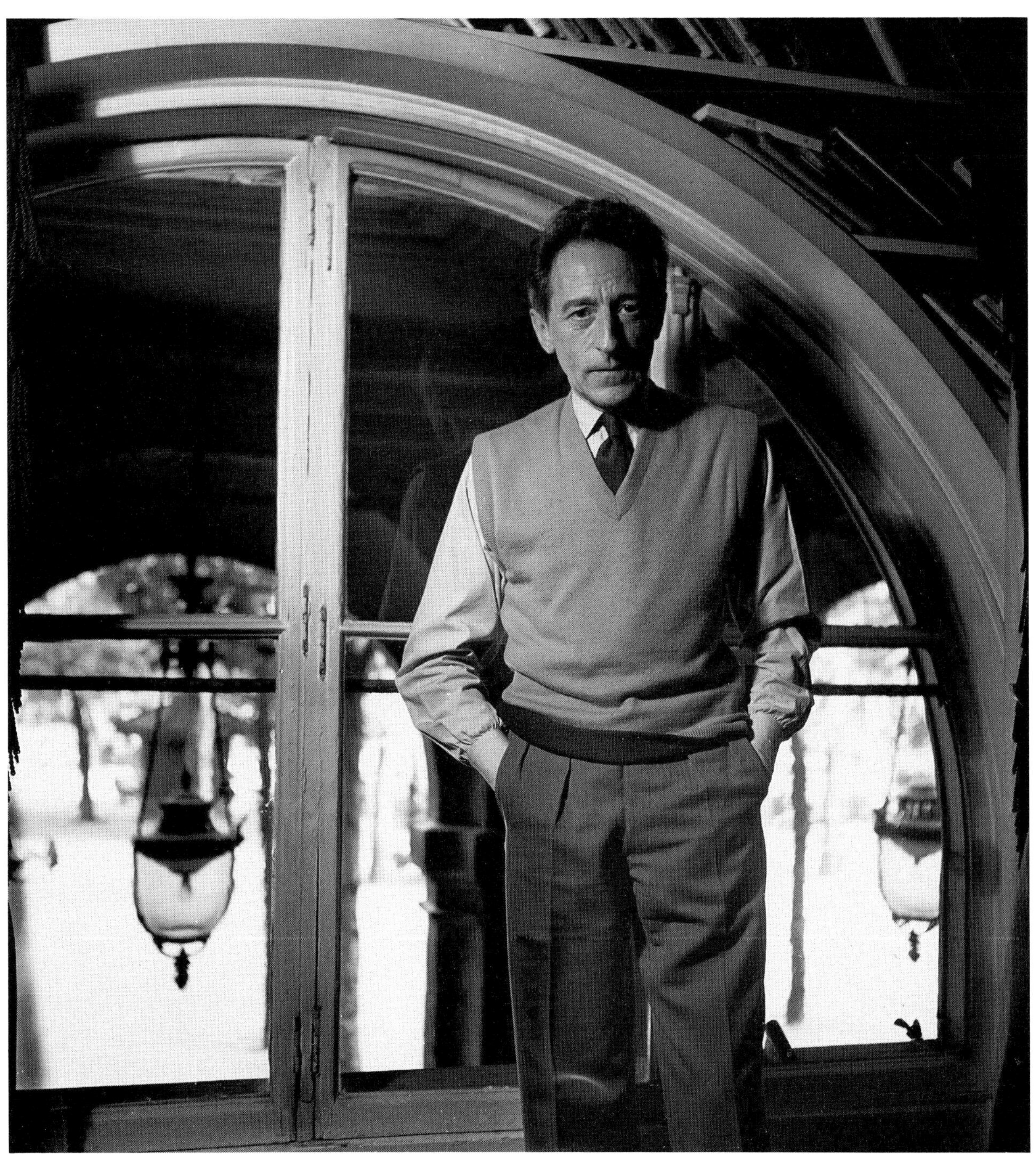

25 – Jean Cocteau, 1950

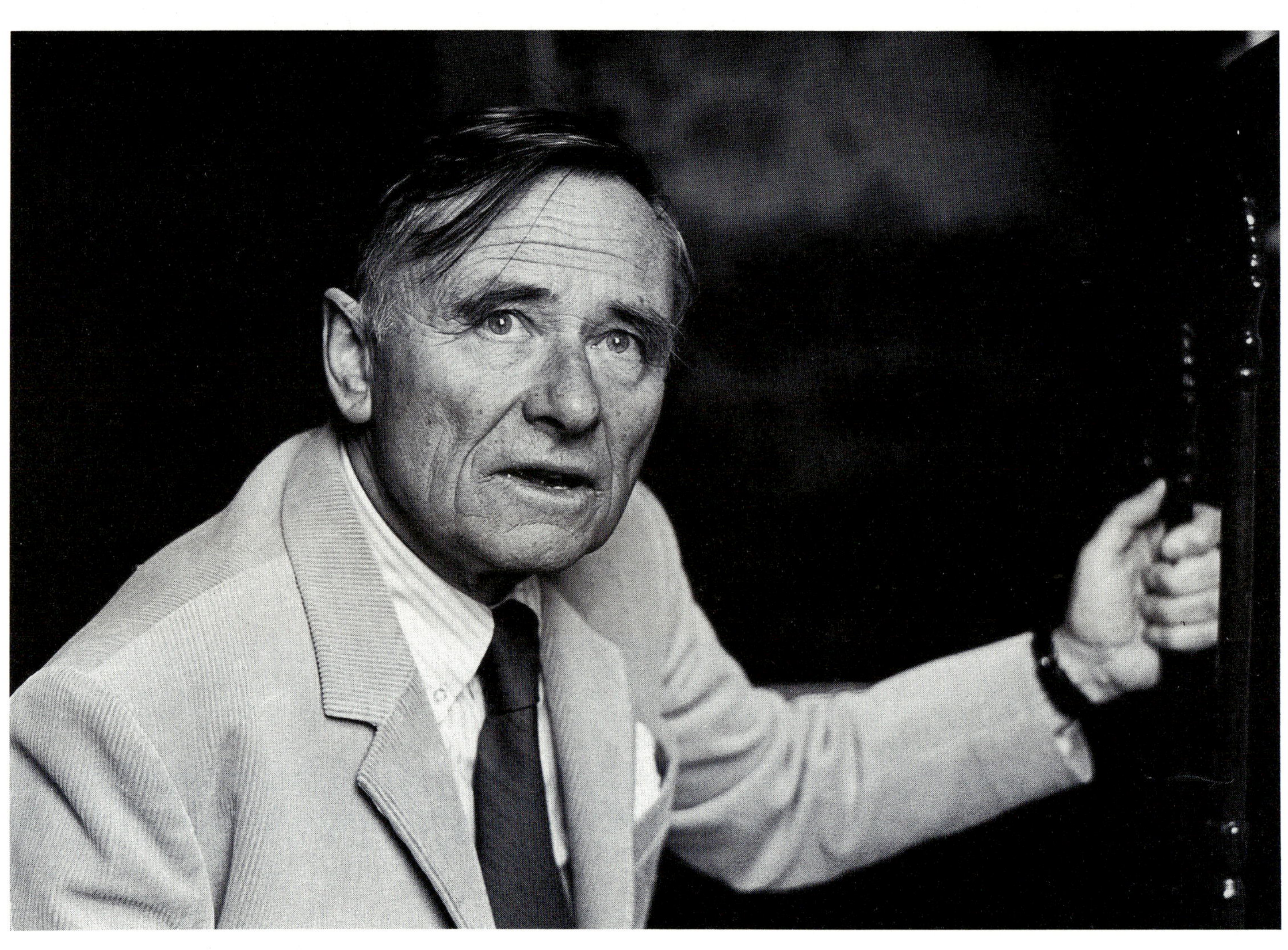

26 – Christopher Isherwood, 1970

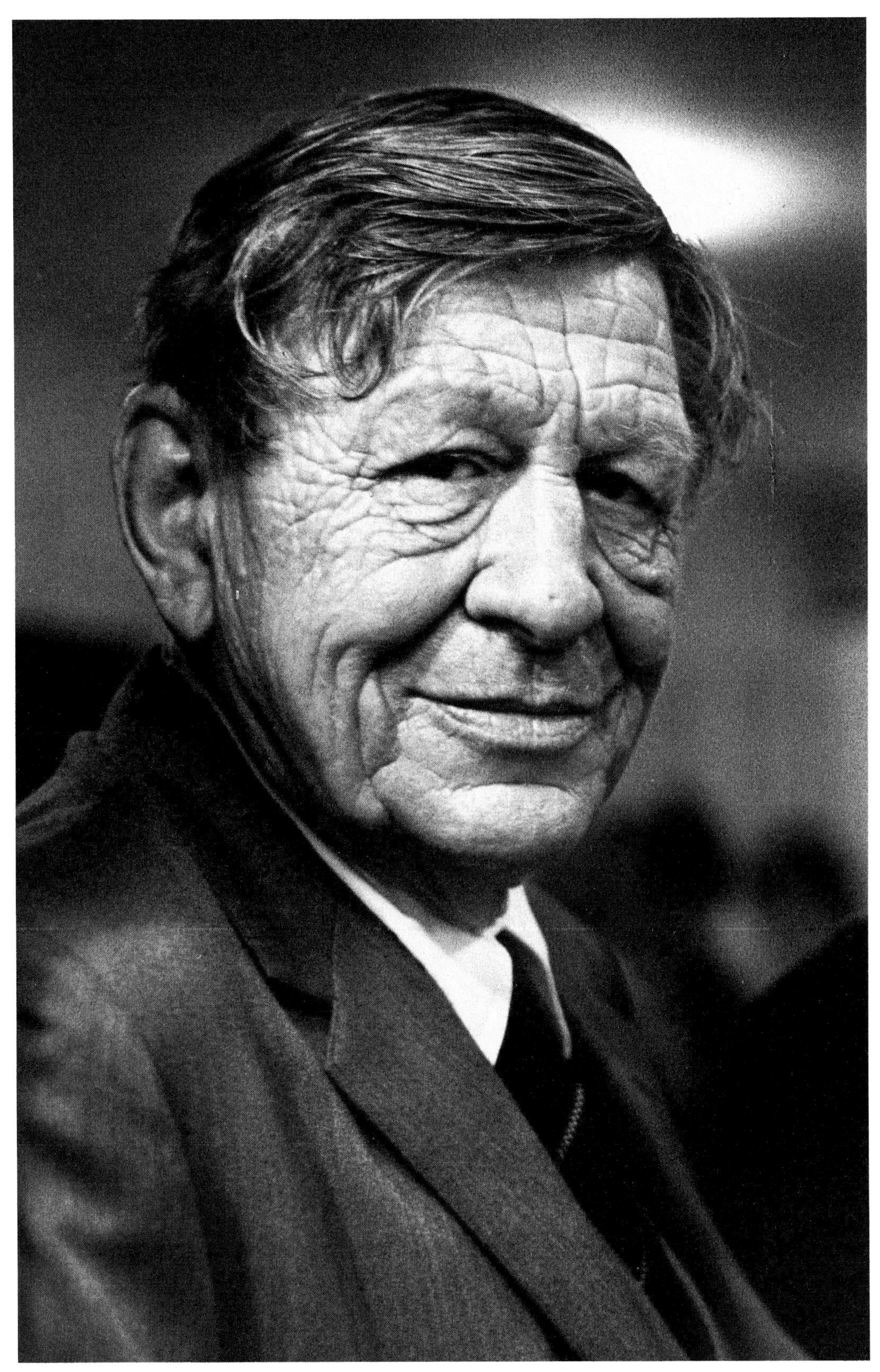

27 – W. H. Auden, 1970

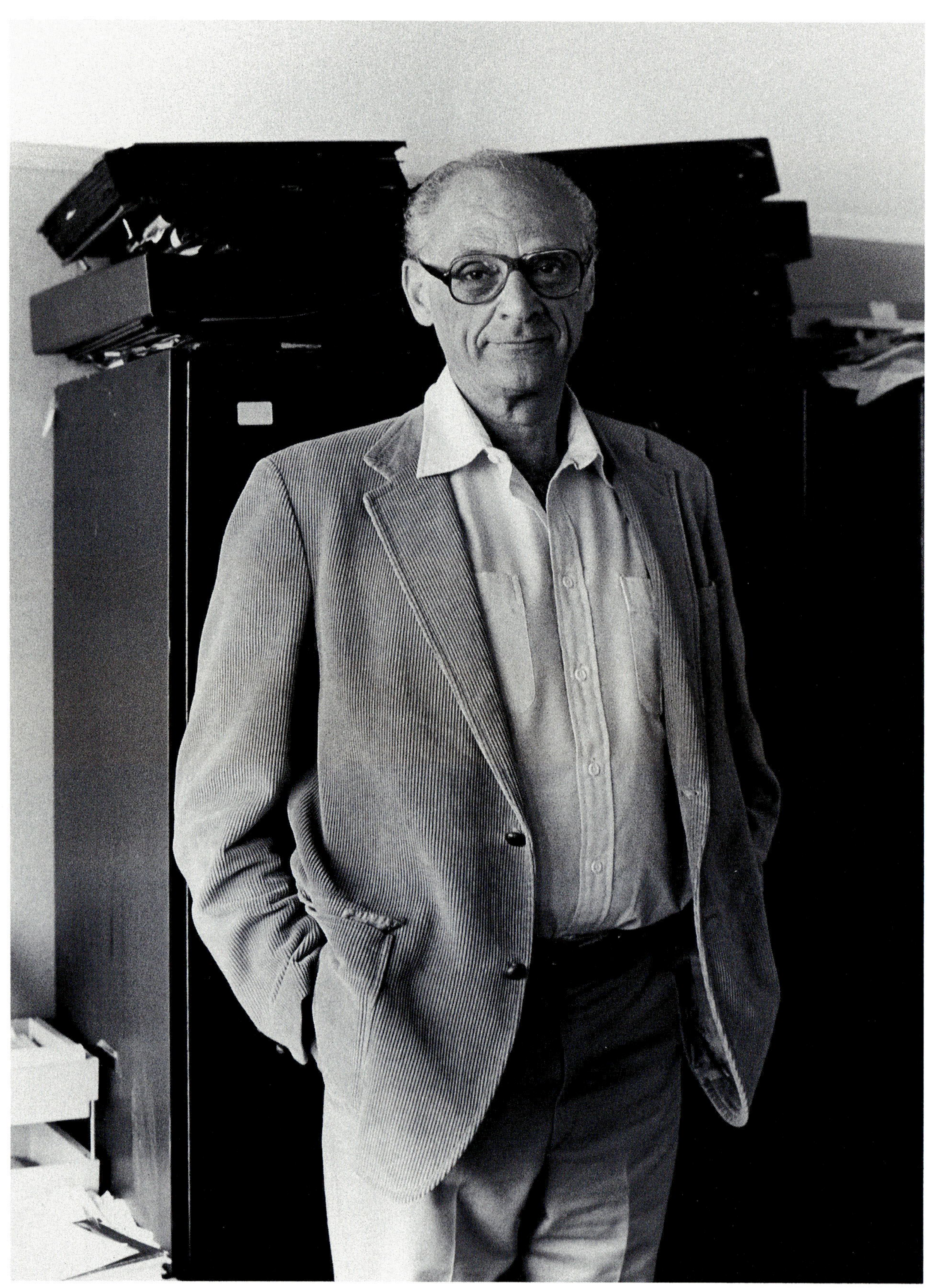

28 – Arthur Miller, 1979

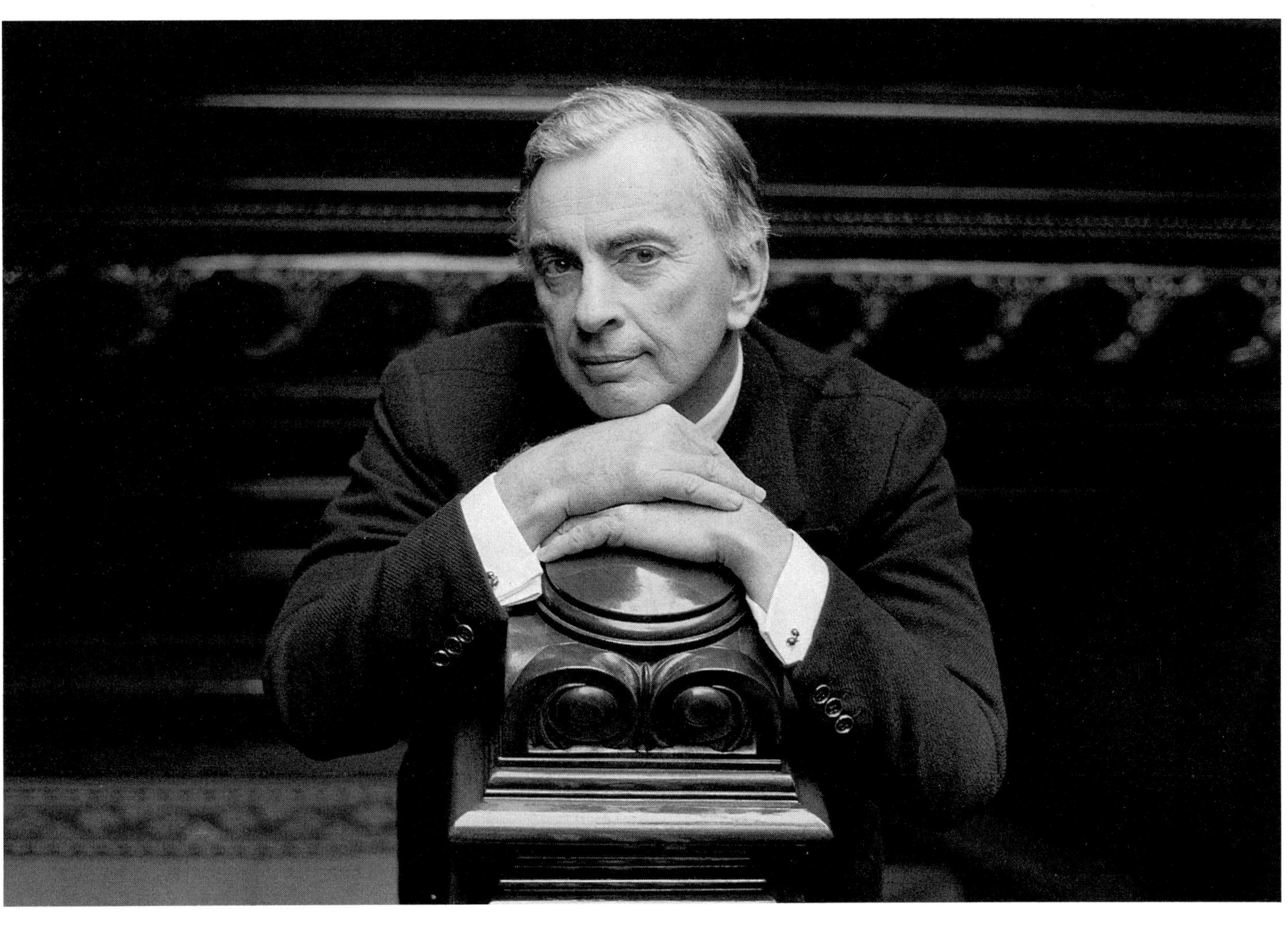

29 – Gore Vidal, 1981

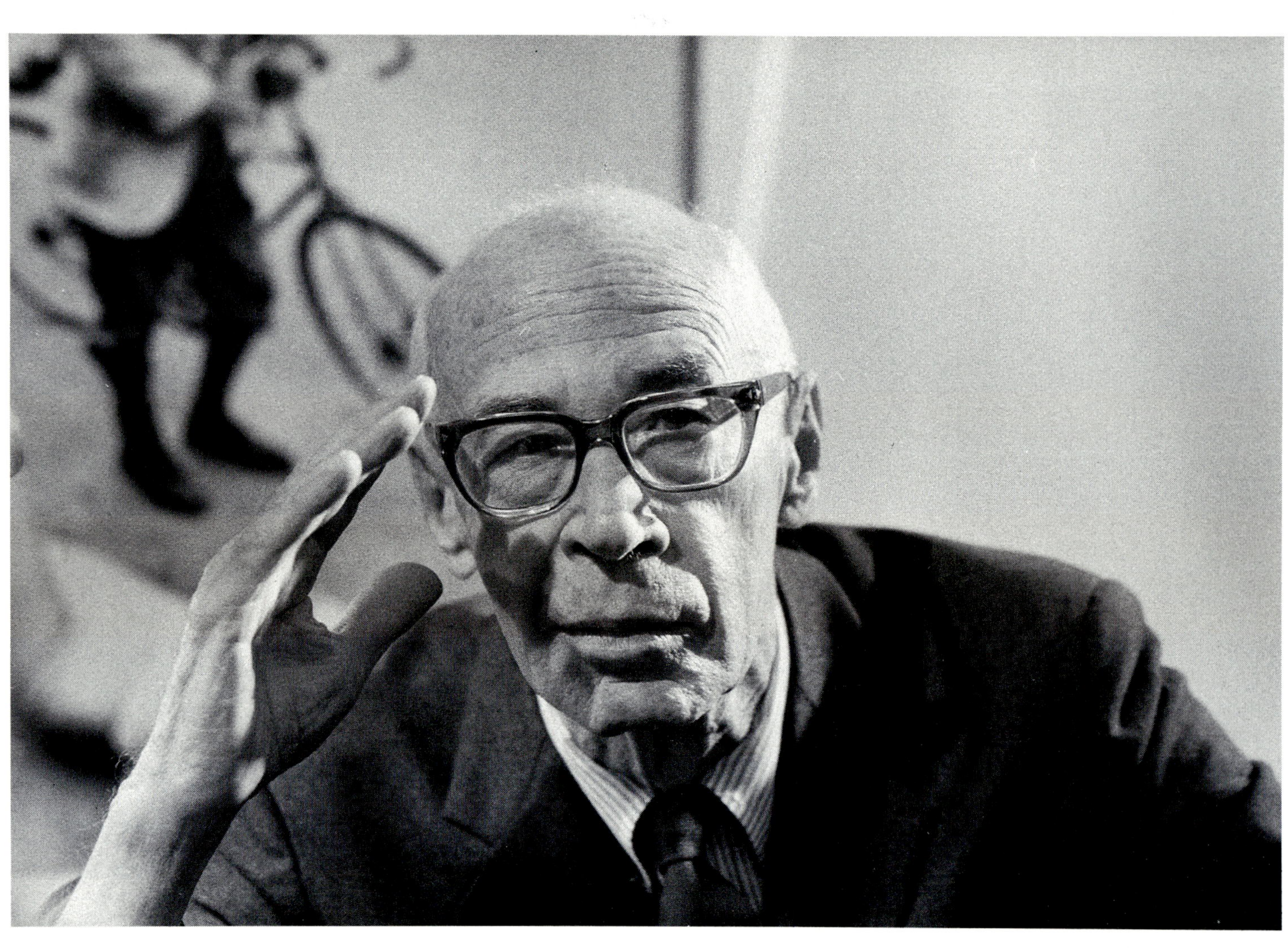

30 – Henry Miller, 1967

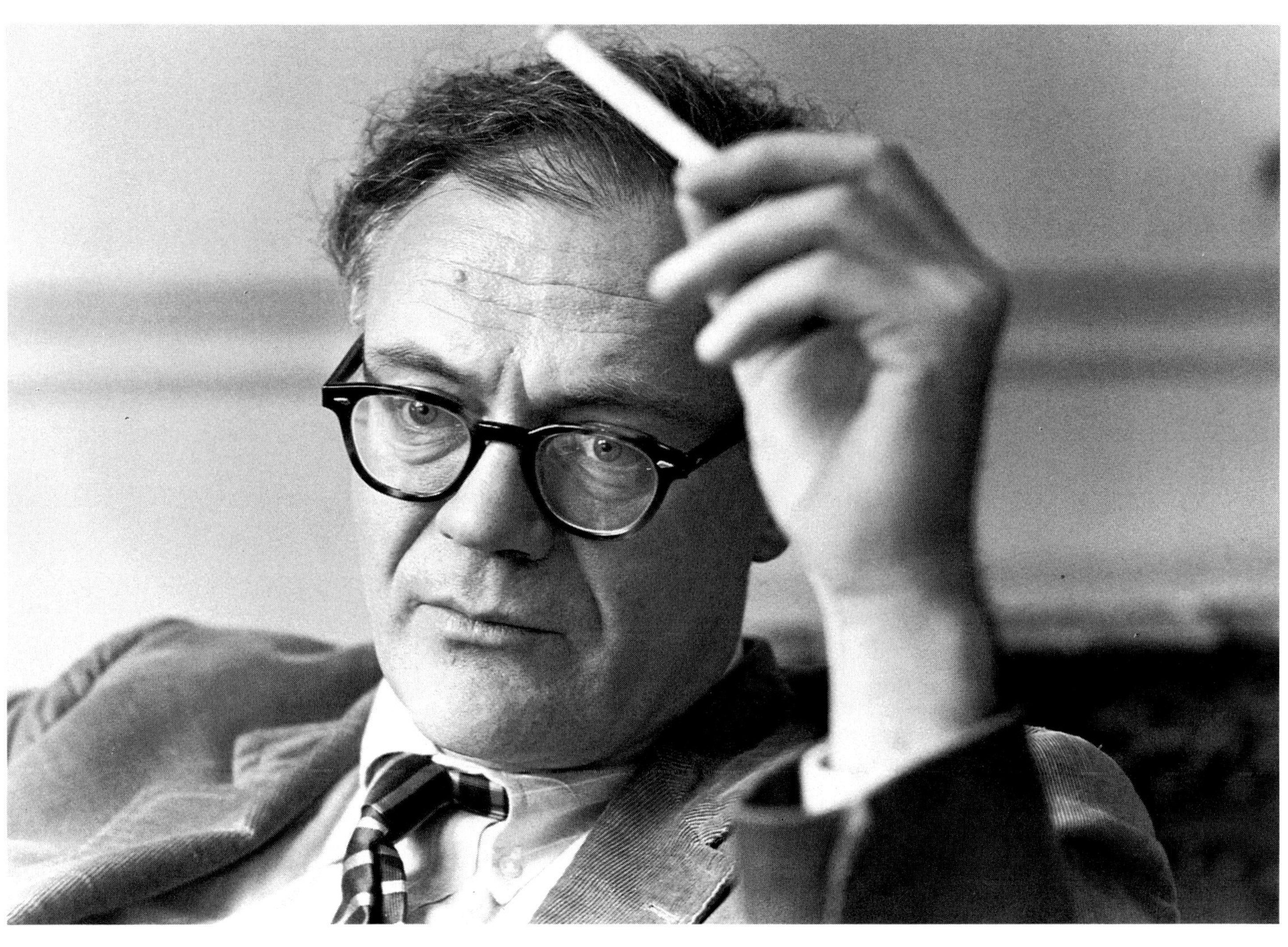

31 – Robert Lowell, 1967

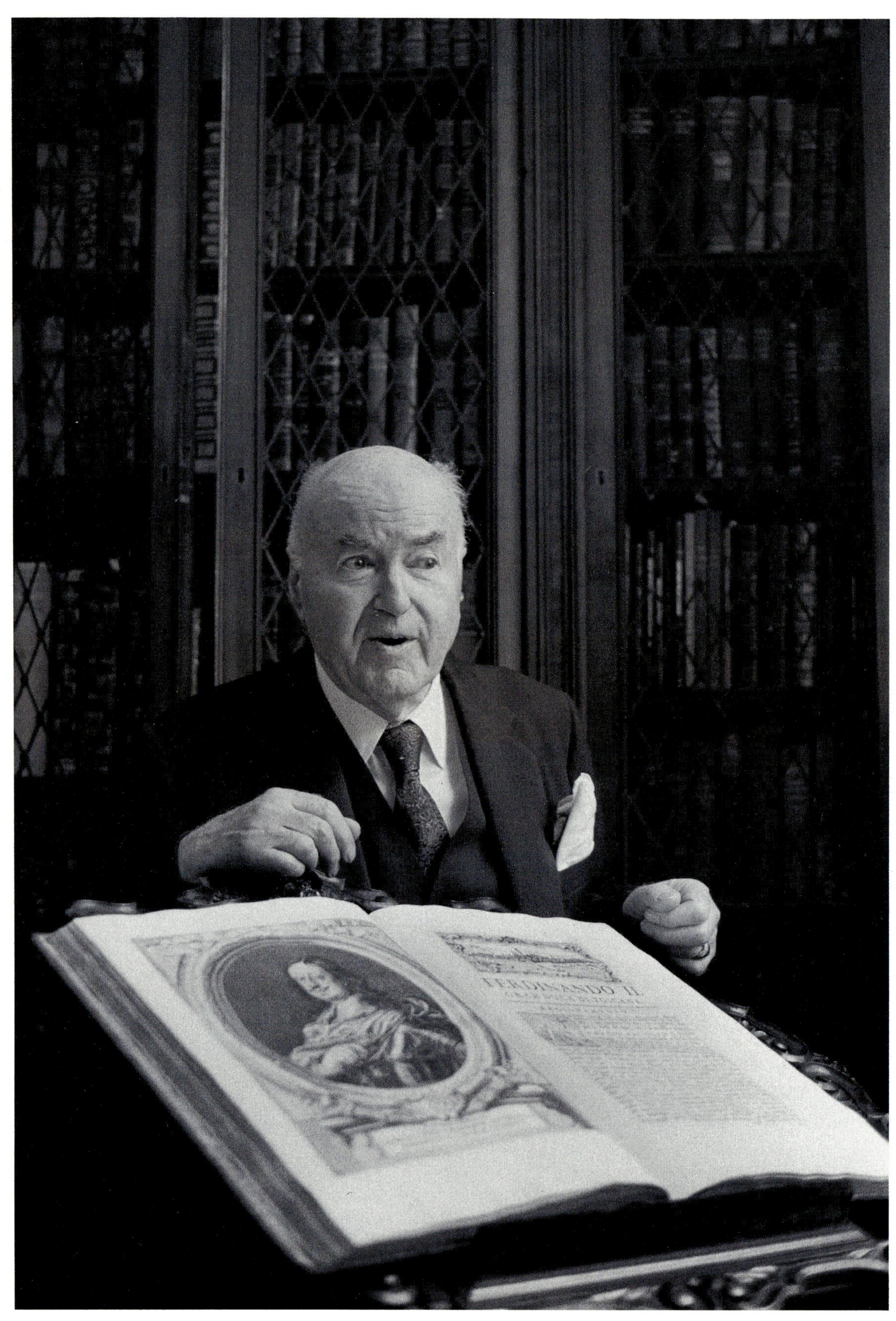

32 – Sir Harold Acton, 1982

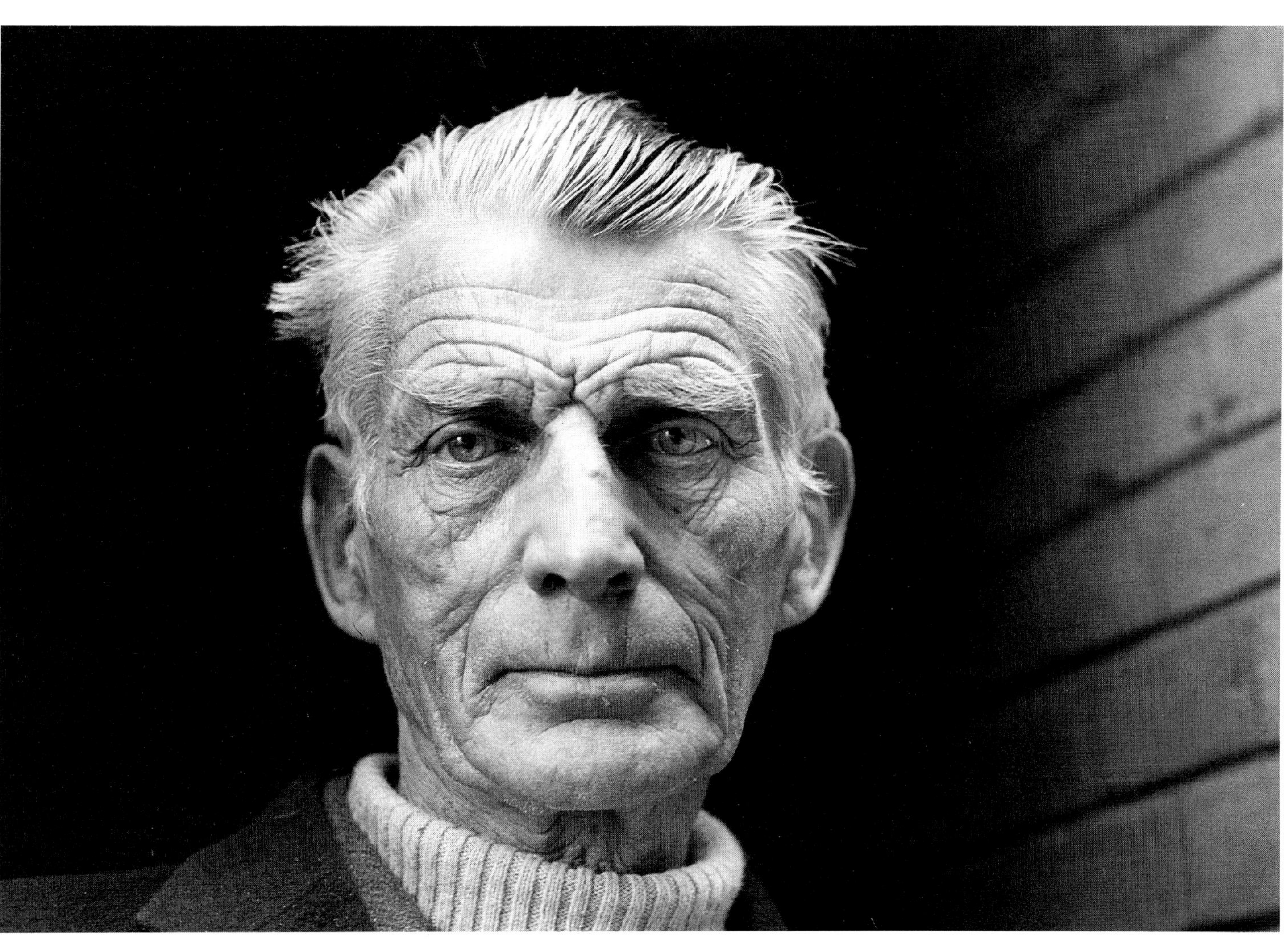

33 – Samuel Beckett, 1976

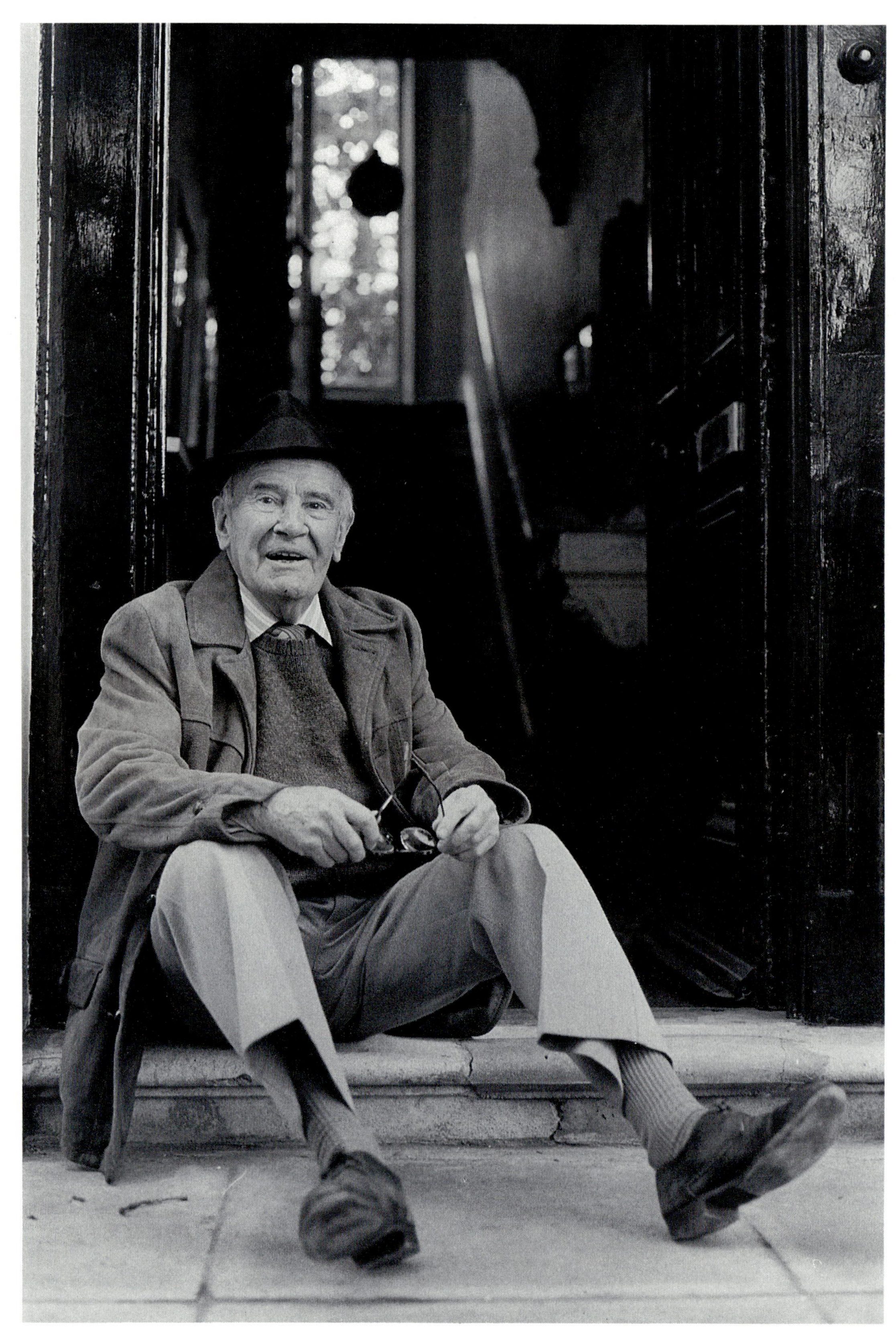

34 – V. S. Pritchett, 1980

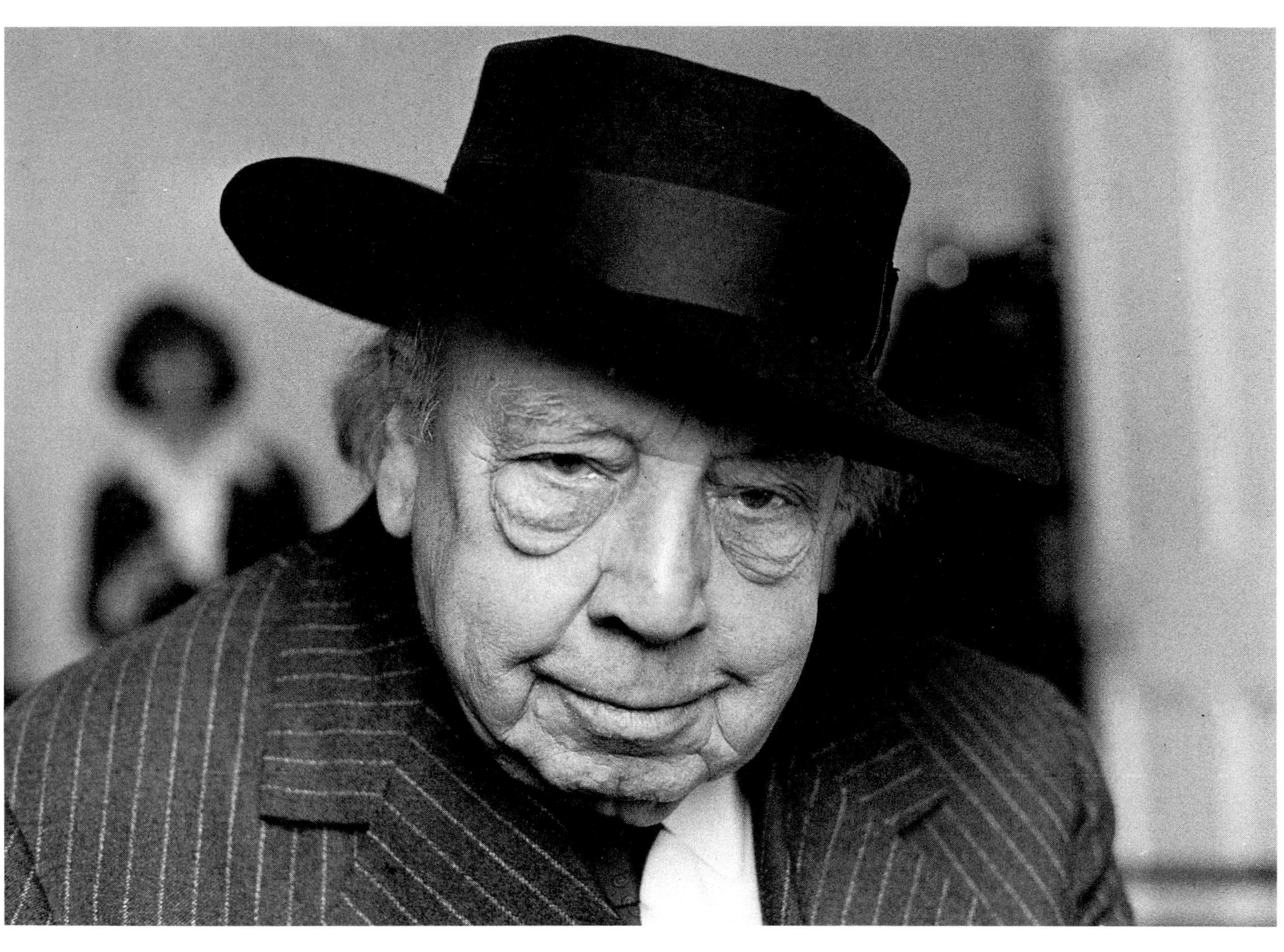

35 – J. B. Priestley, 1980

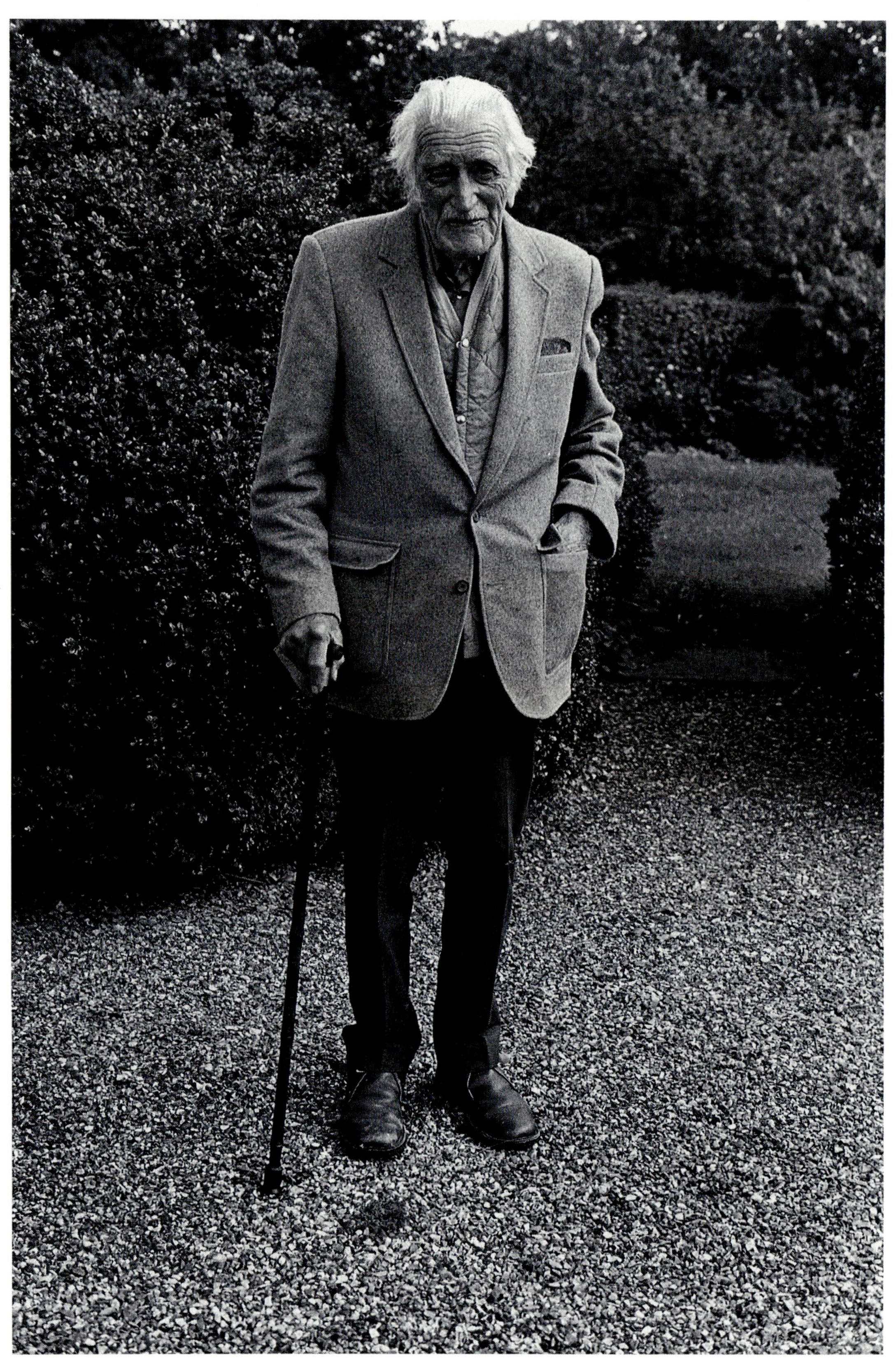

36 – Sir Geoffrey Keynes, 1981

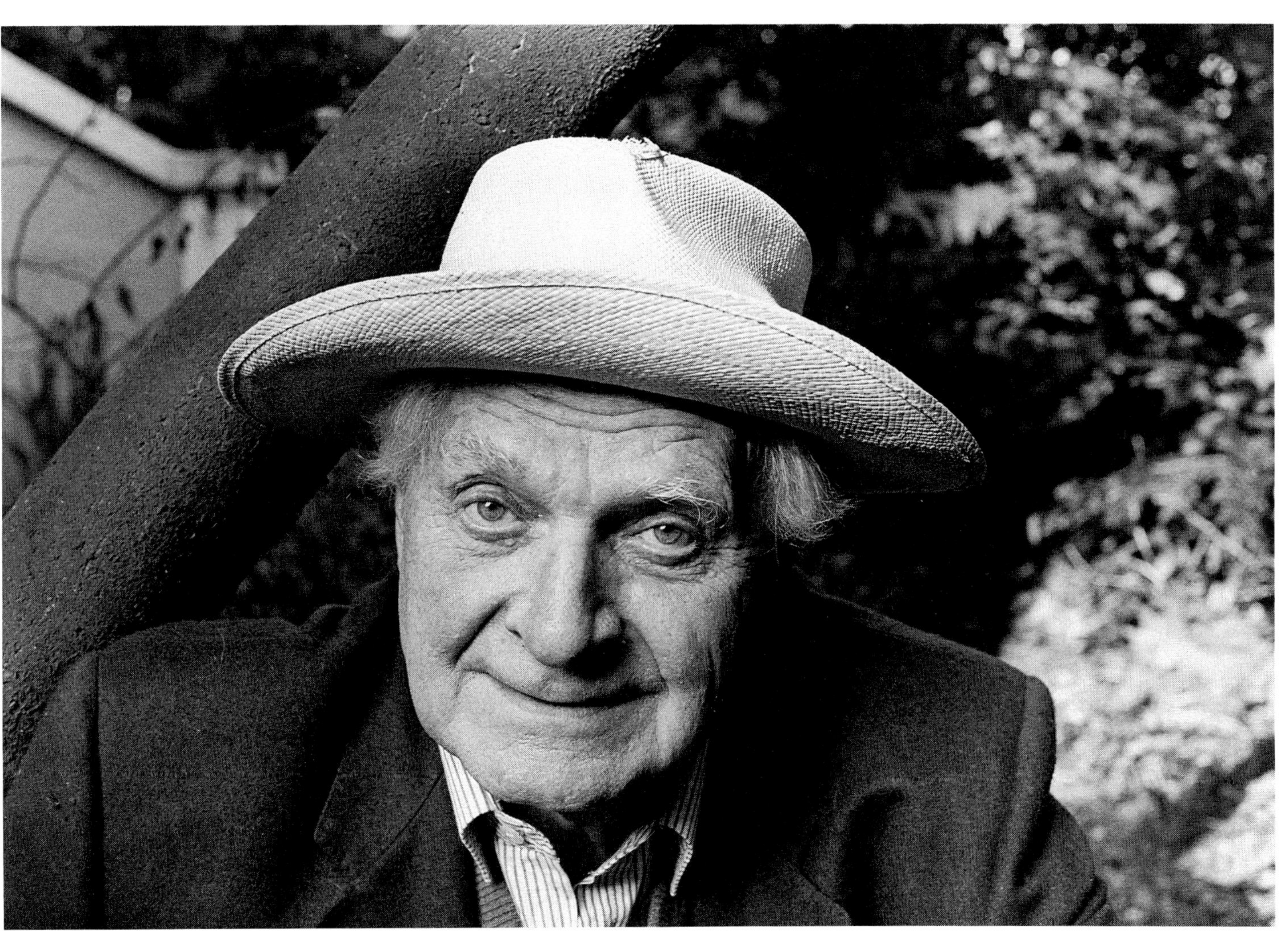

37 – Sir Stephen Spender, 1985

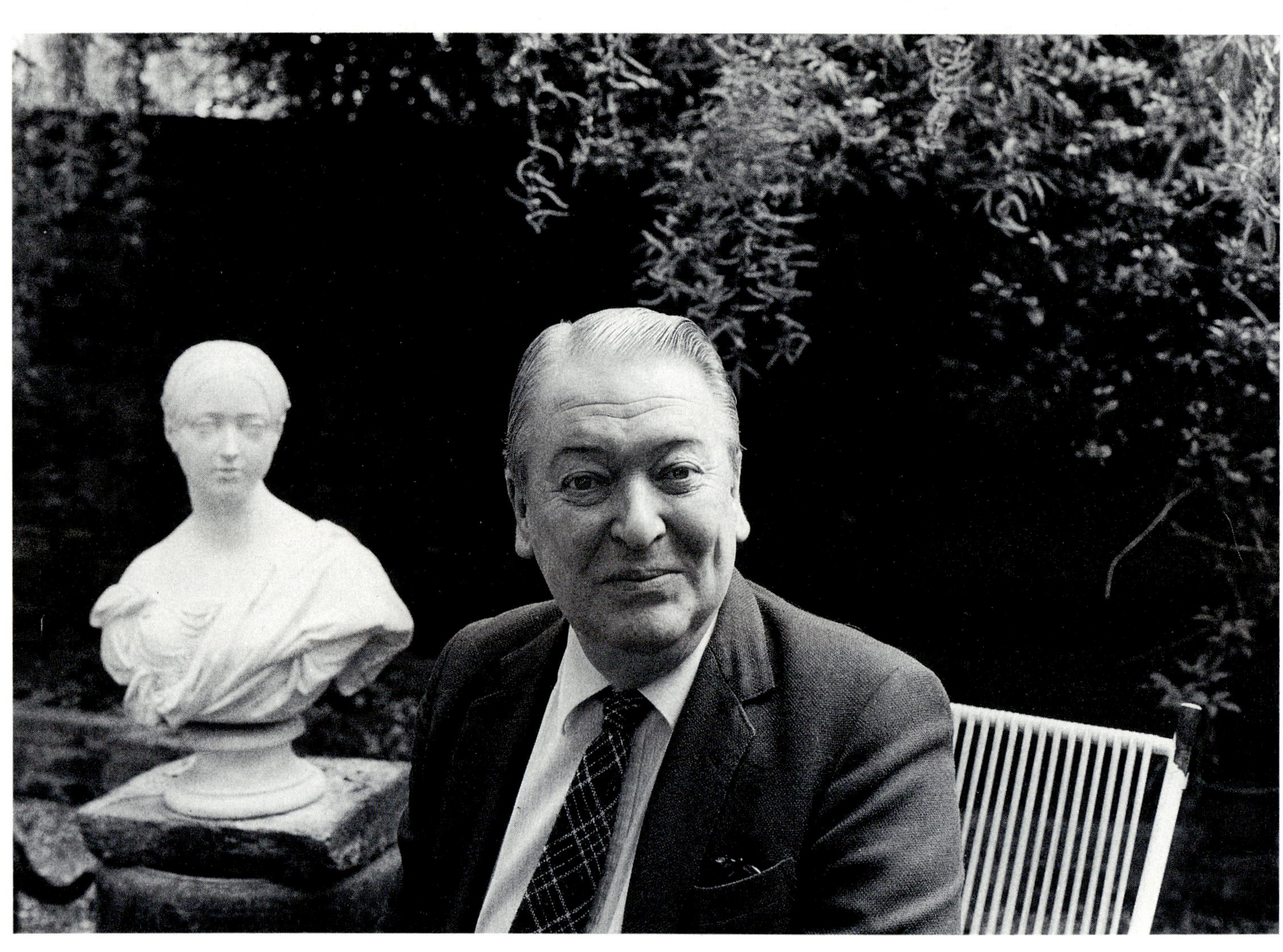

38 – Kingsley Amis, 1984

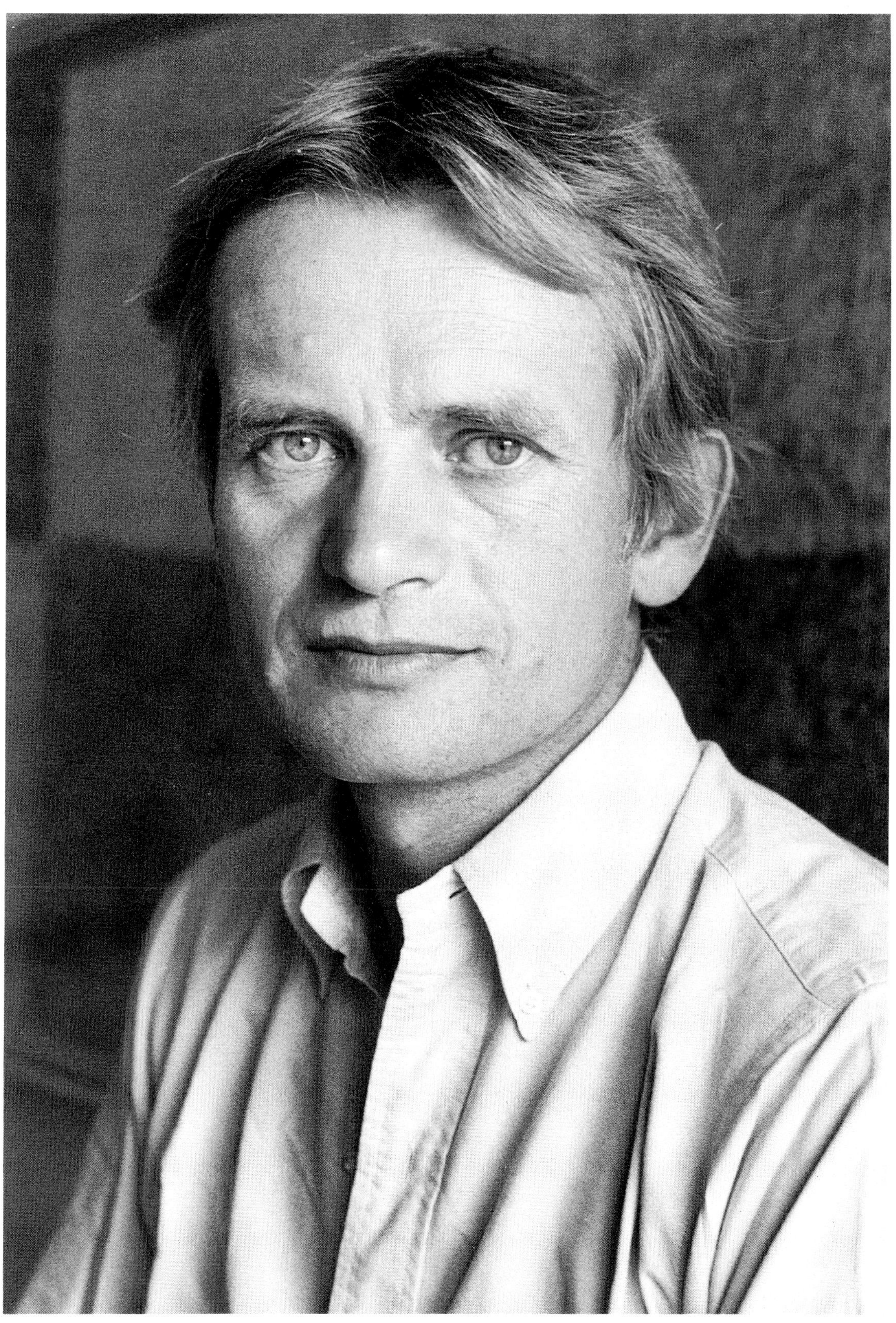

39 – Bruce Chatwin, 1982

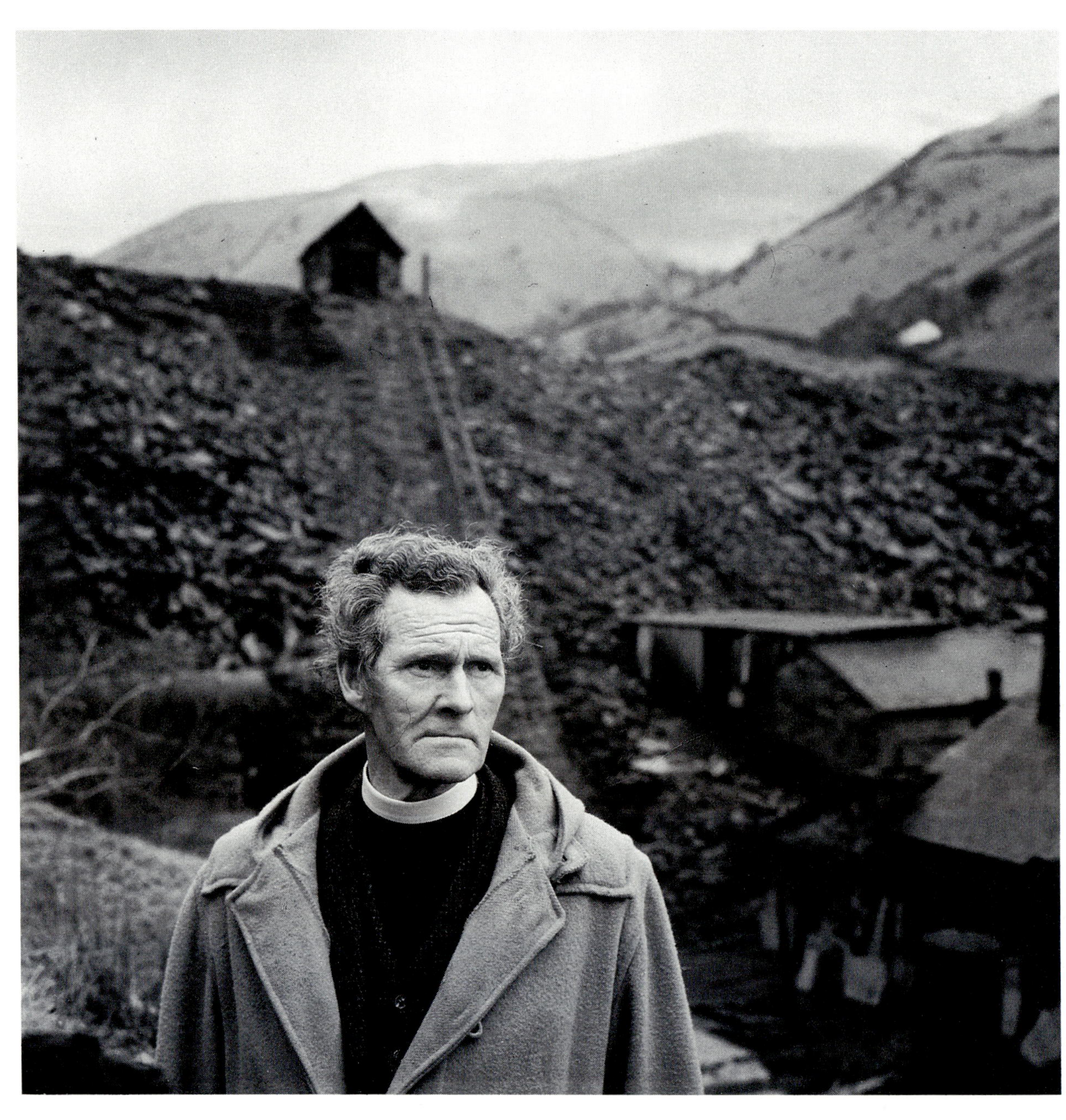

40 – R. S. Thomas, 1964

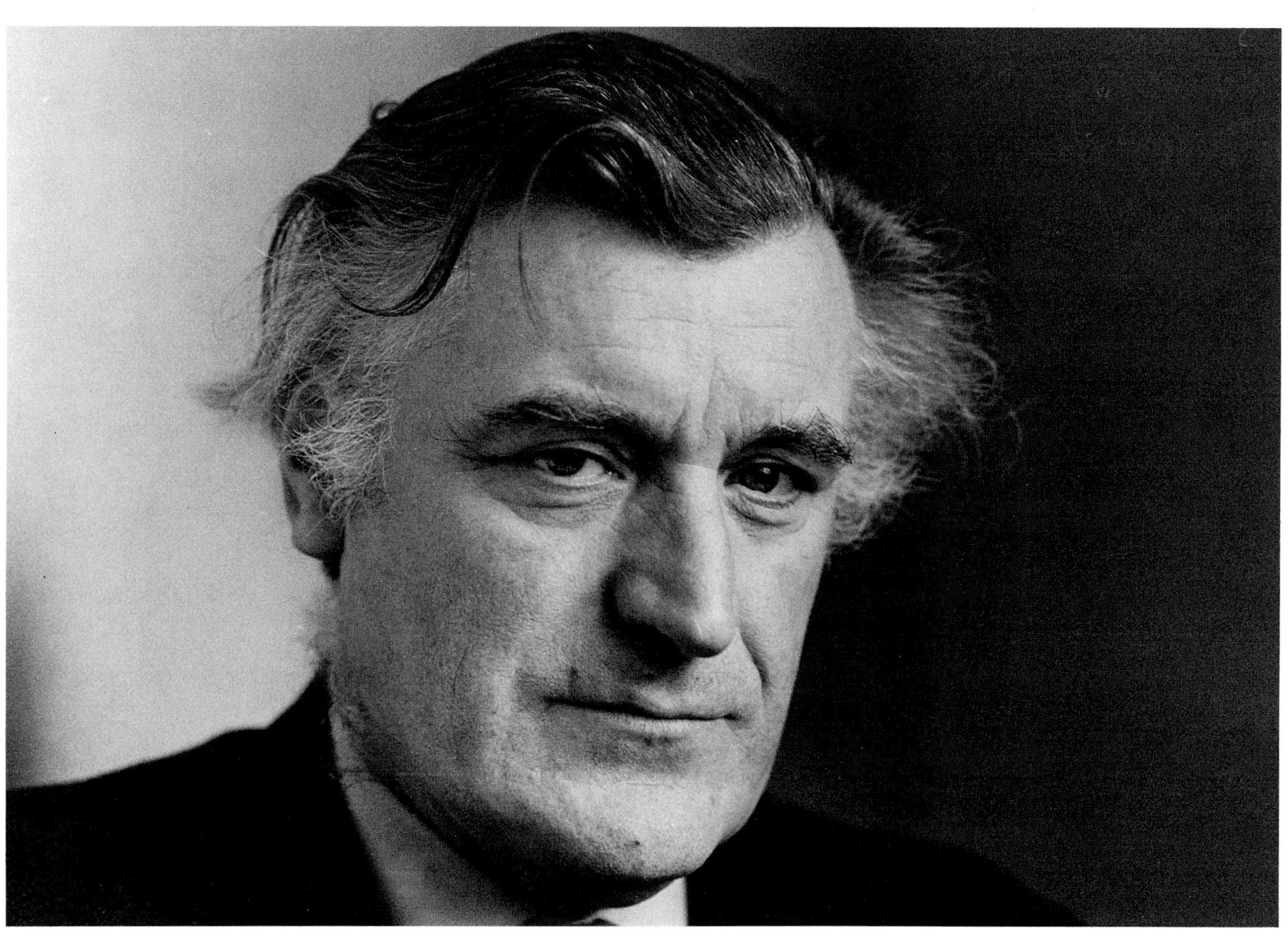

41 – Ted Hughes, 1987

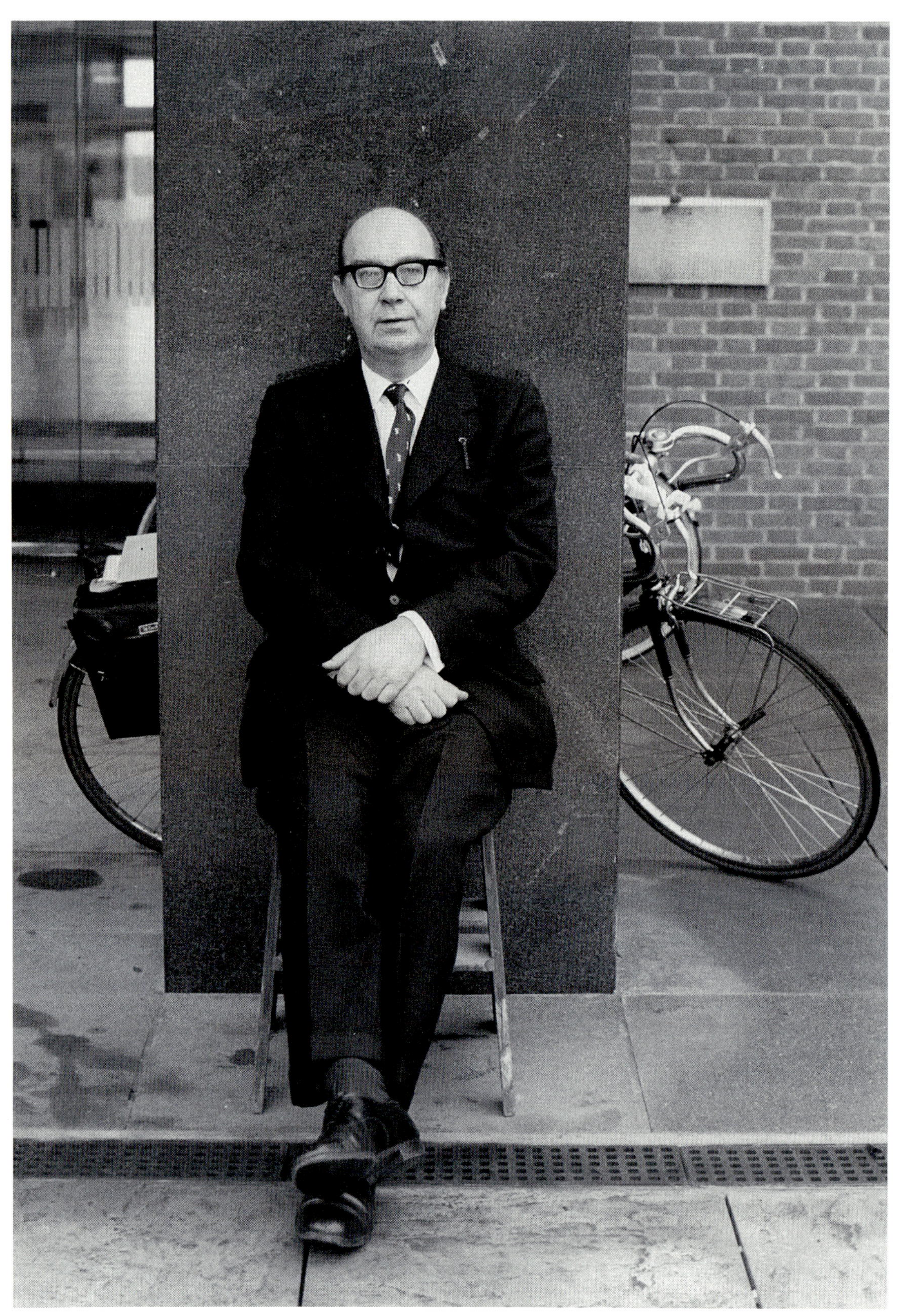

42 – Philip Larkin, 1979

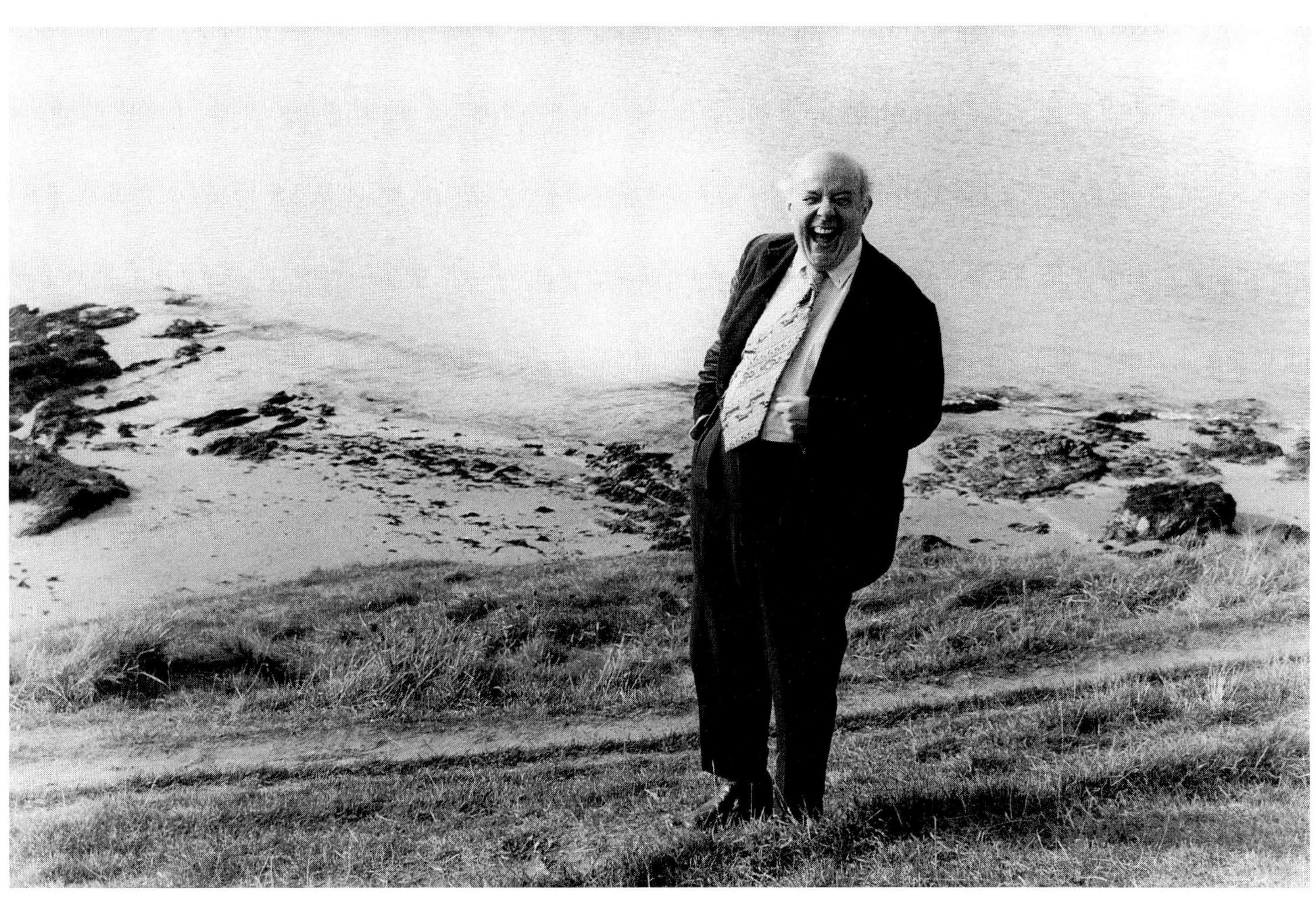

43 – Sir John Betjeman, 1972

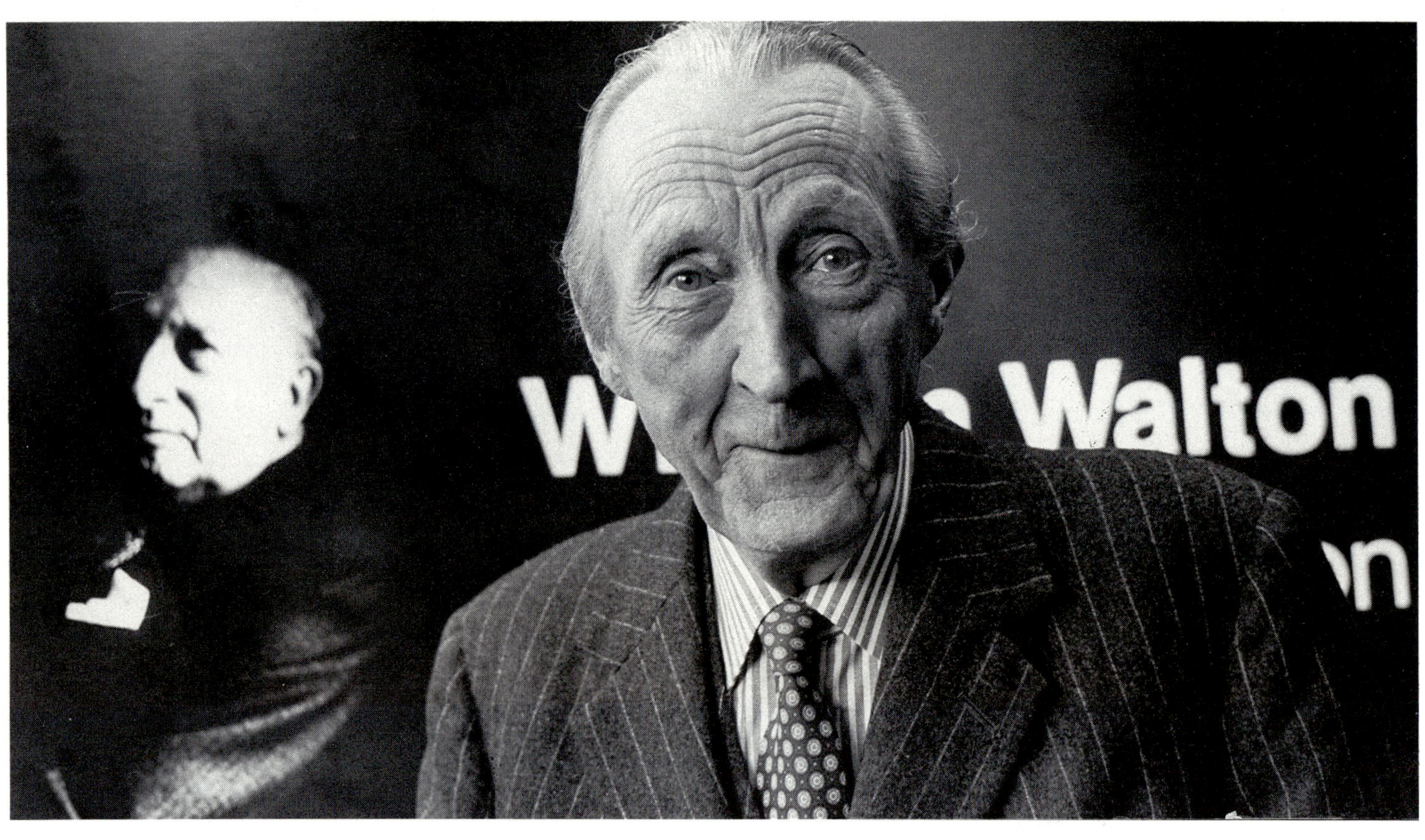

44 – Sir Sacheverell Sitwell, 1982

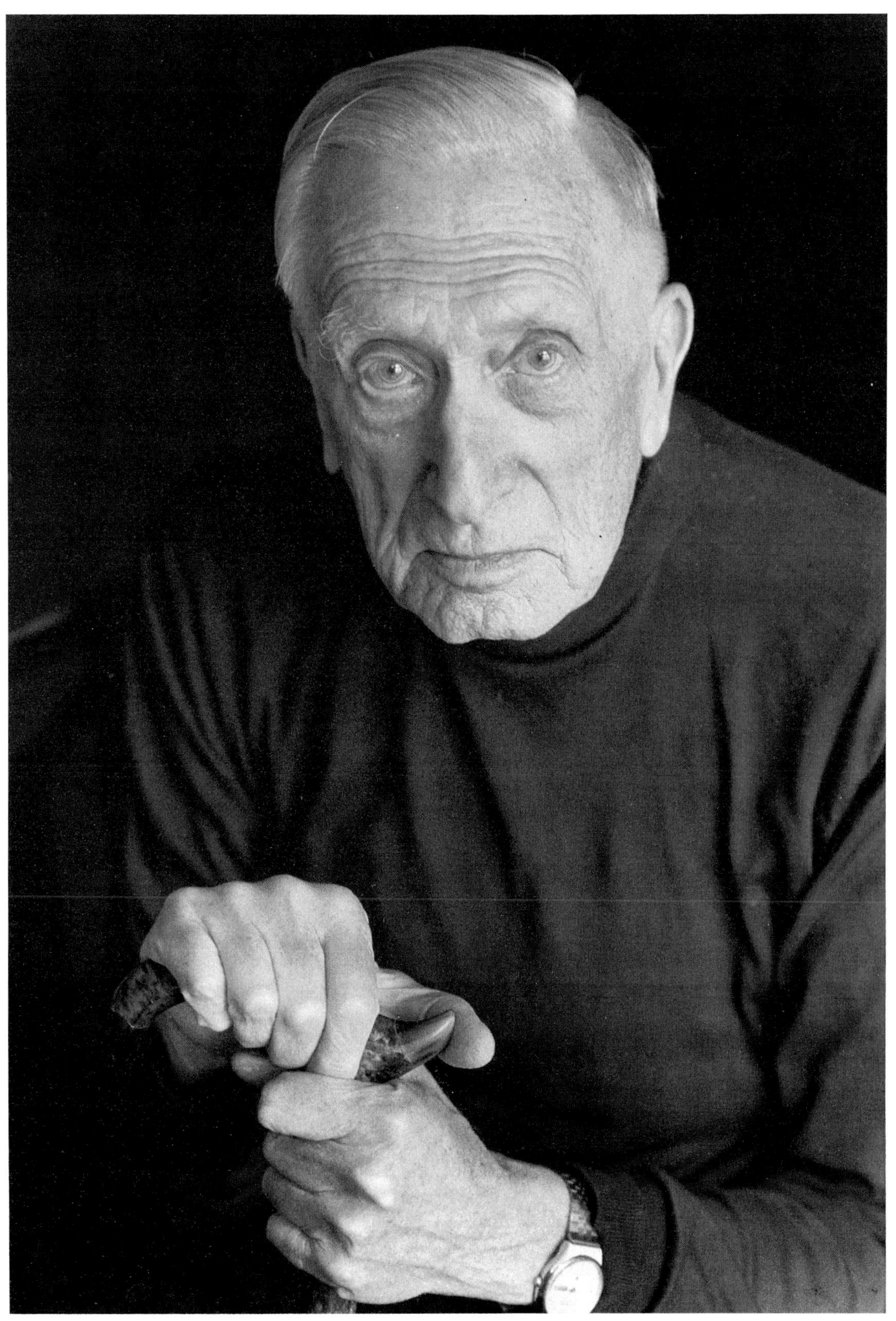

45 – Sir William Walton, 1982

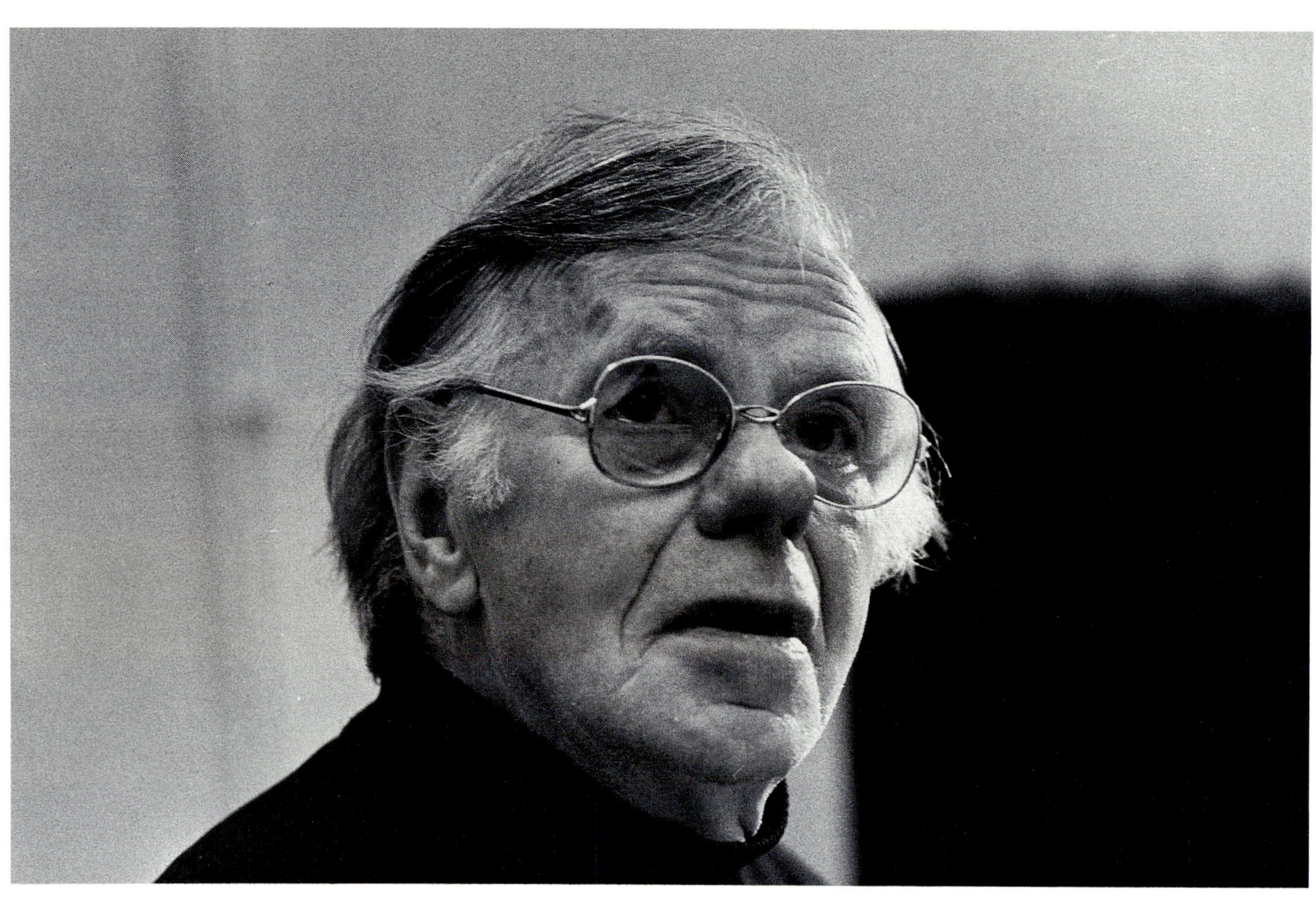

46 – Sir Reginald Goodall, 1982

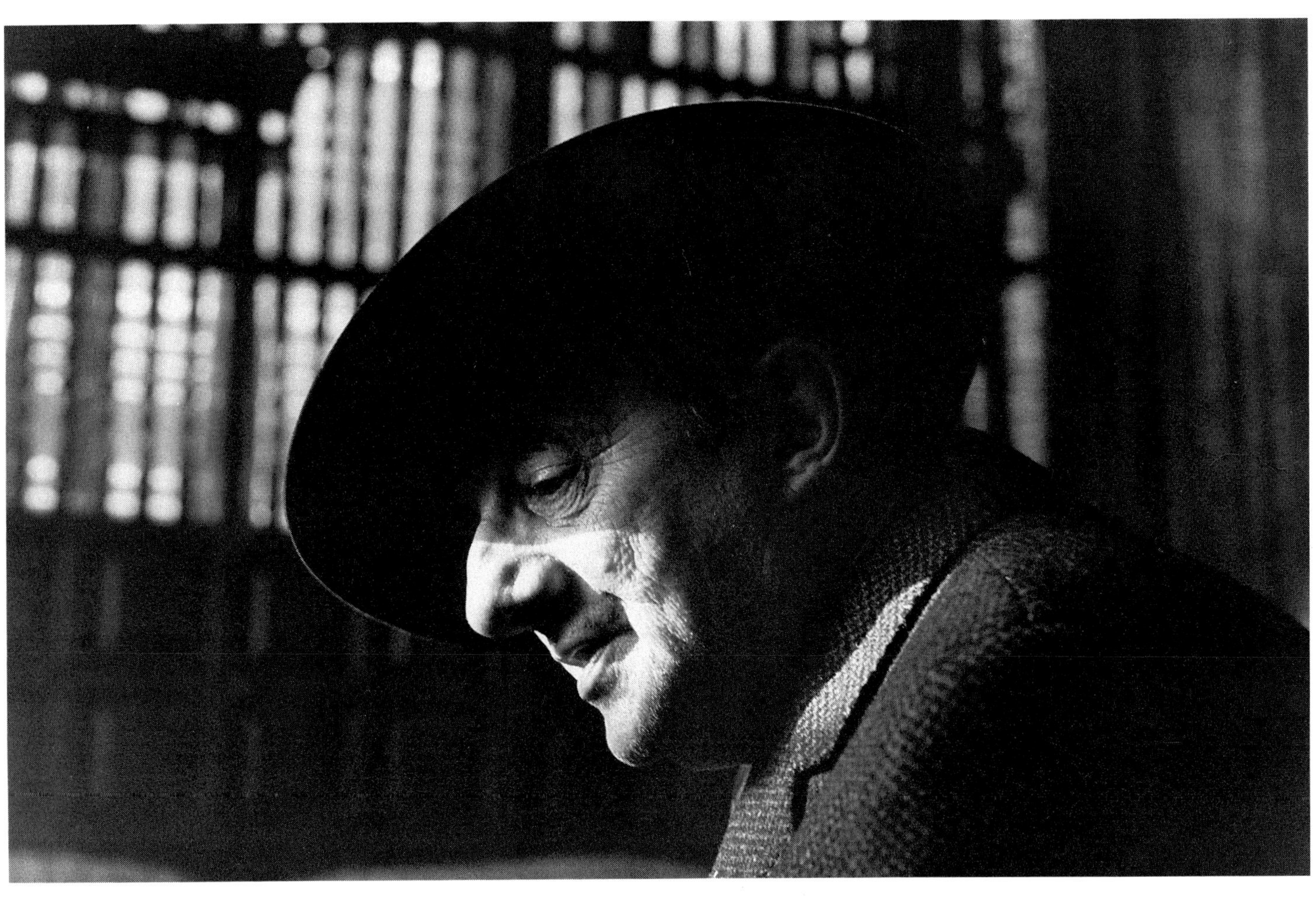

47 – Sir John Barbirolli, 1969

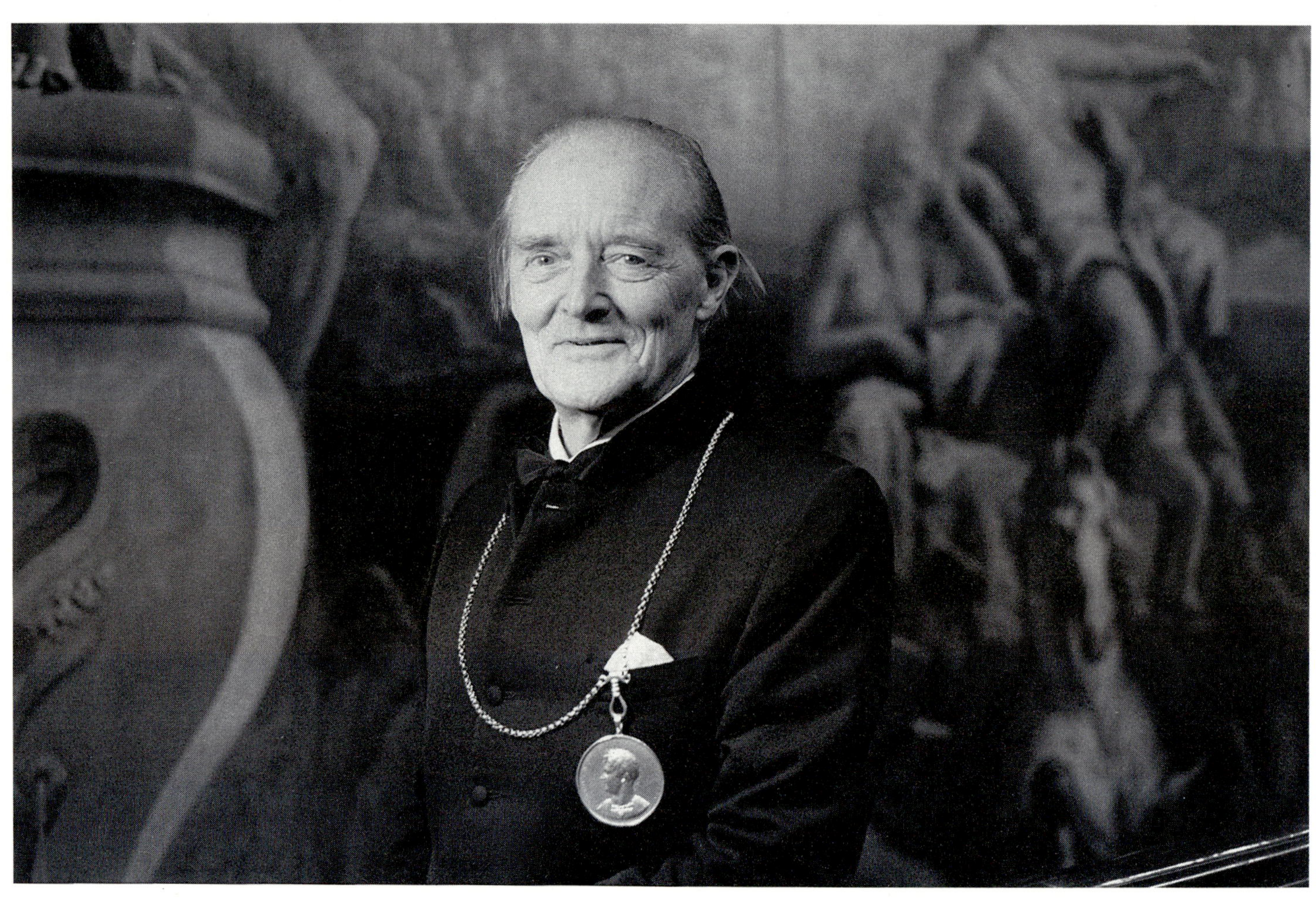

48 – Sir Hugh Casson, 1984

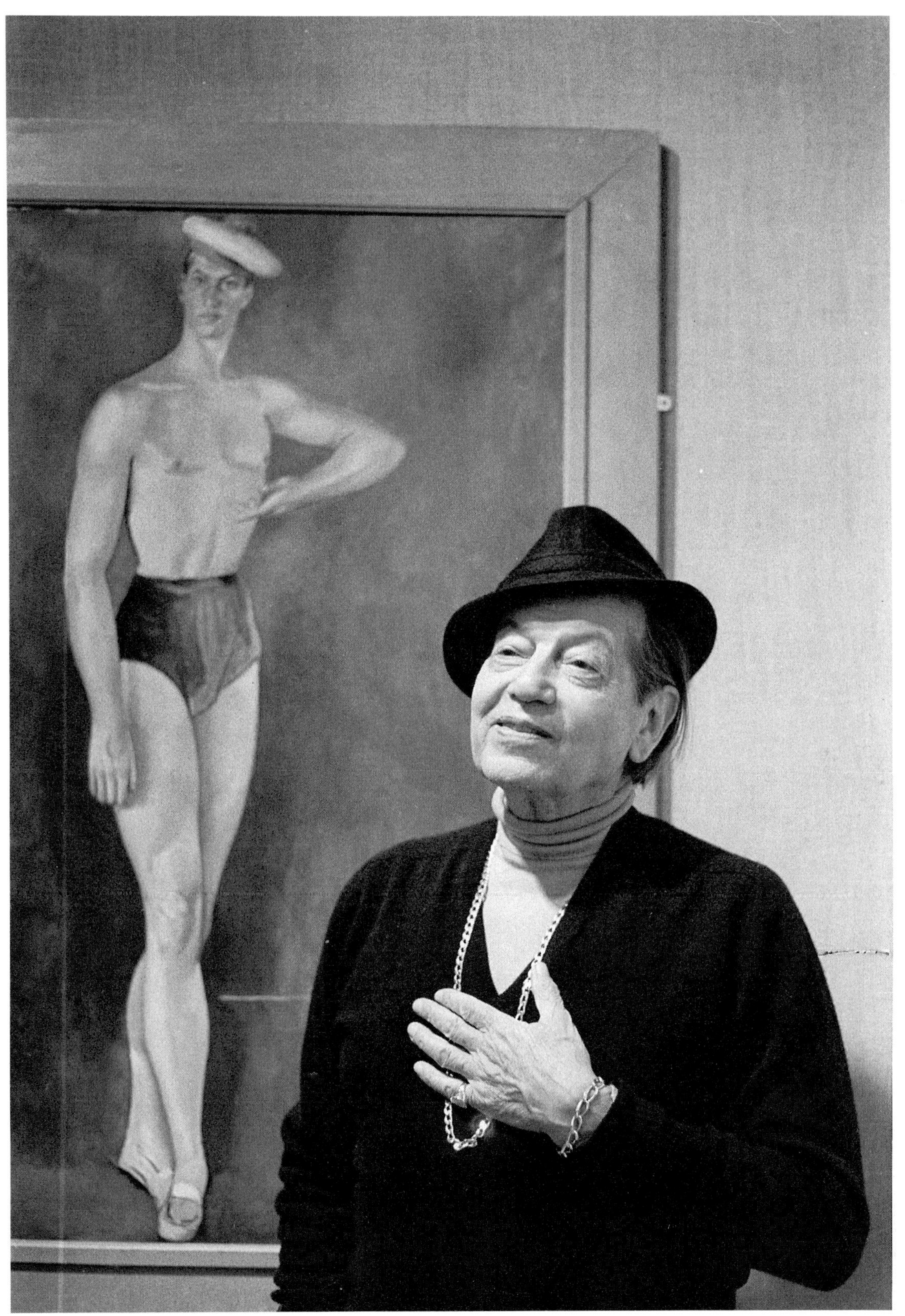

49 – Serge Lifar, 1984

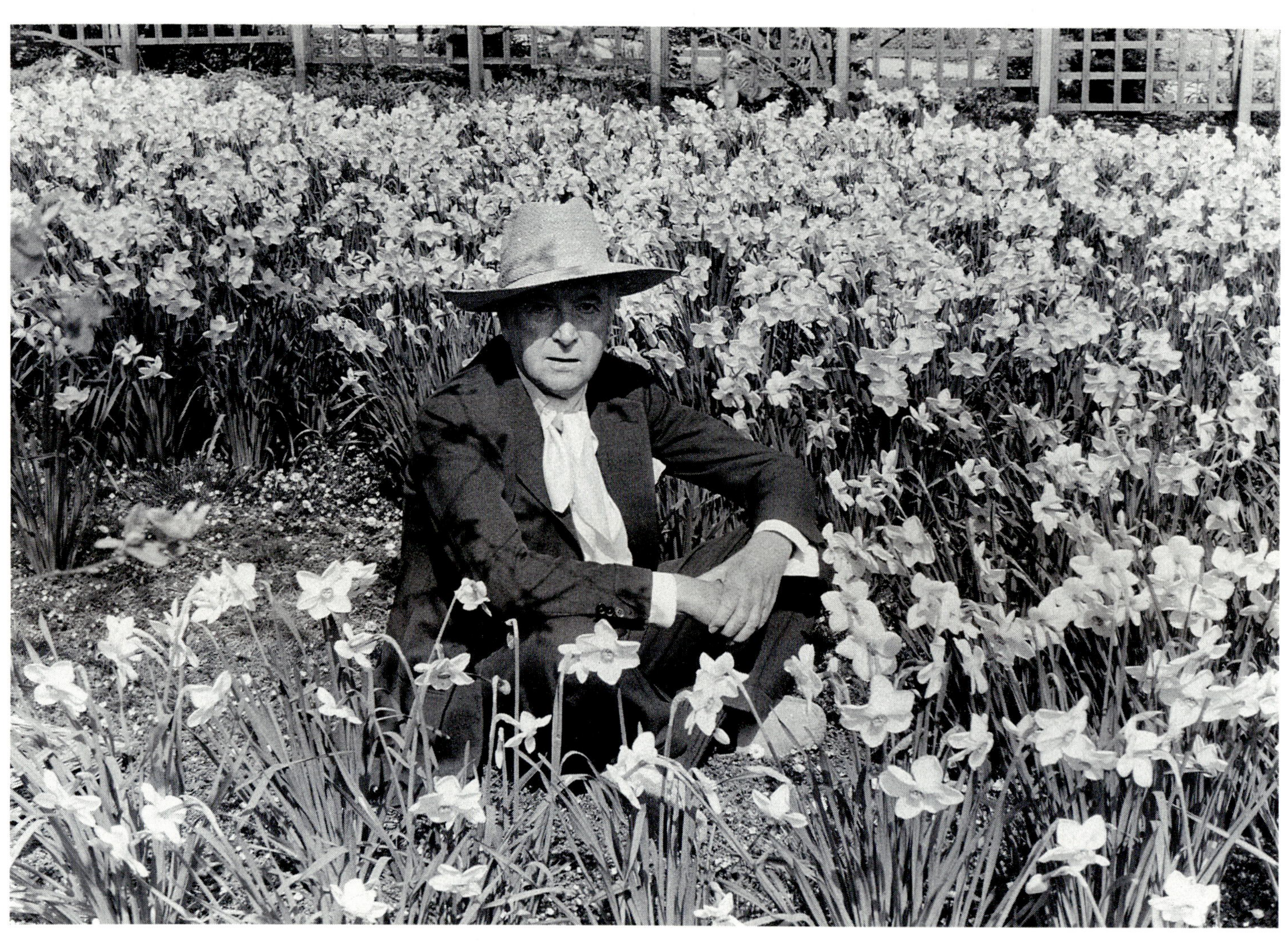

50 – Sir Cecil Beaton, 1974

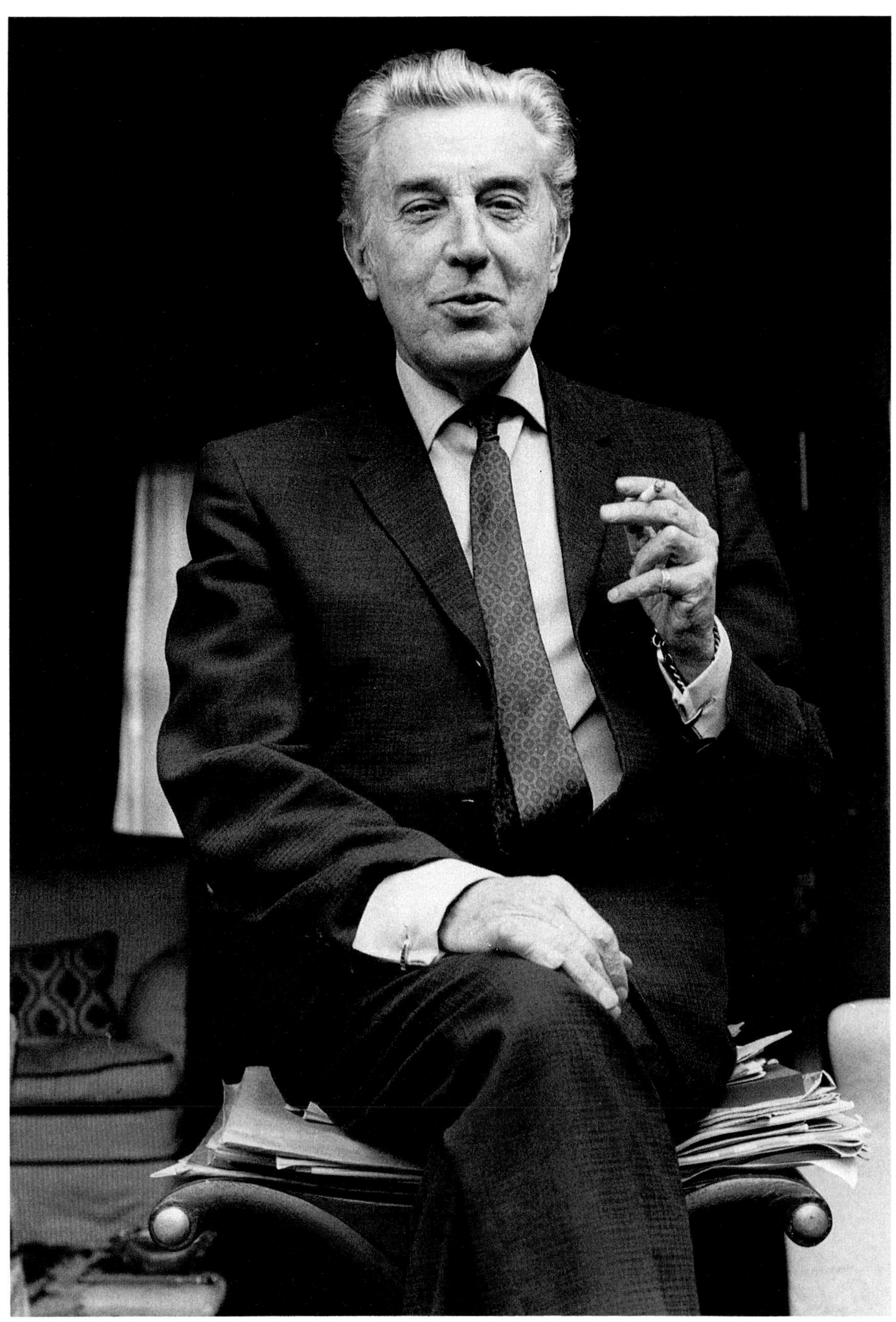

51 – Sir Frederick Ashton, 1970

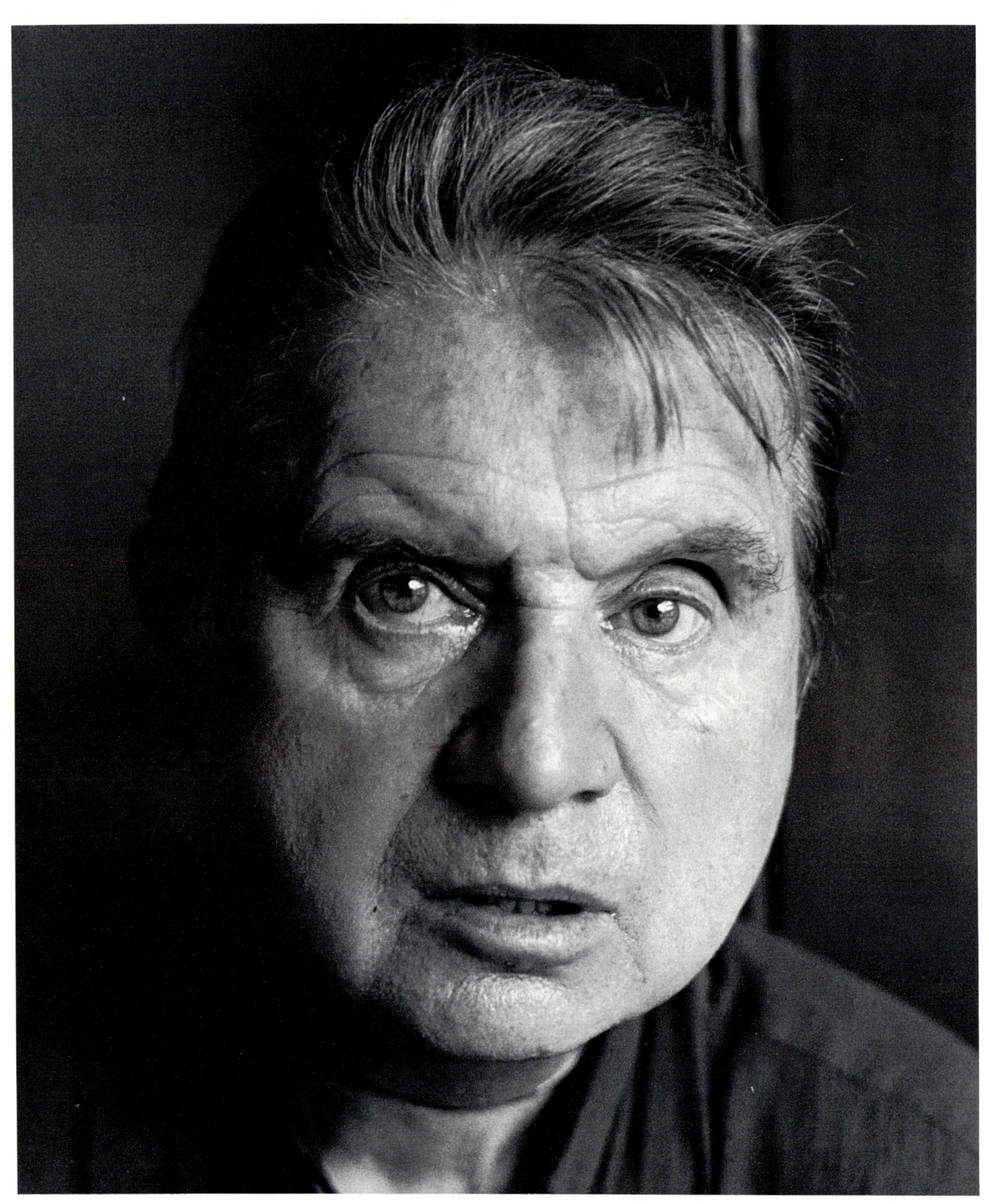

52 – Francis Bacon, 1985

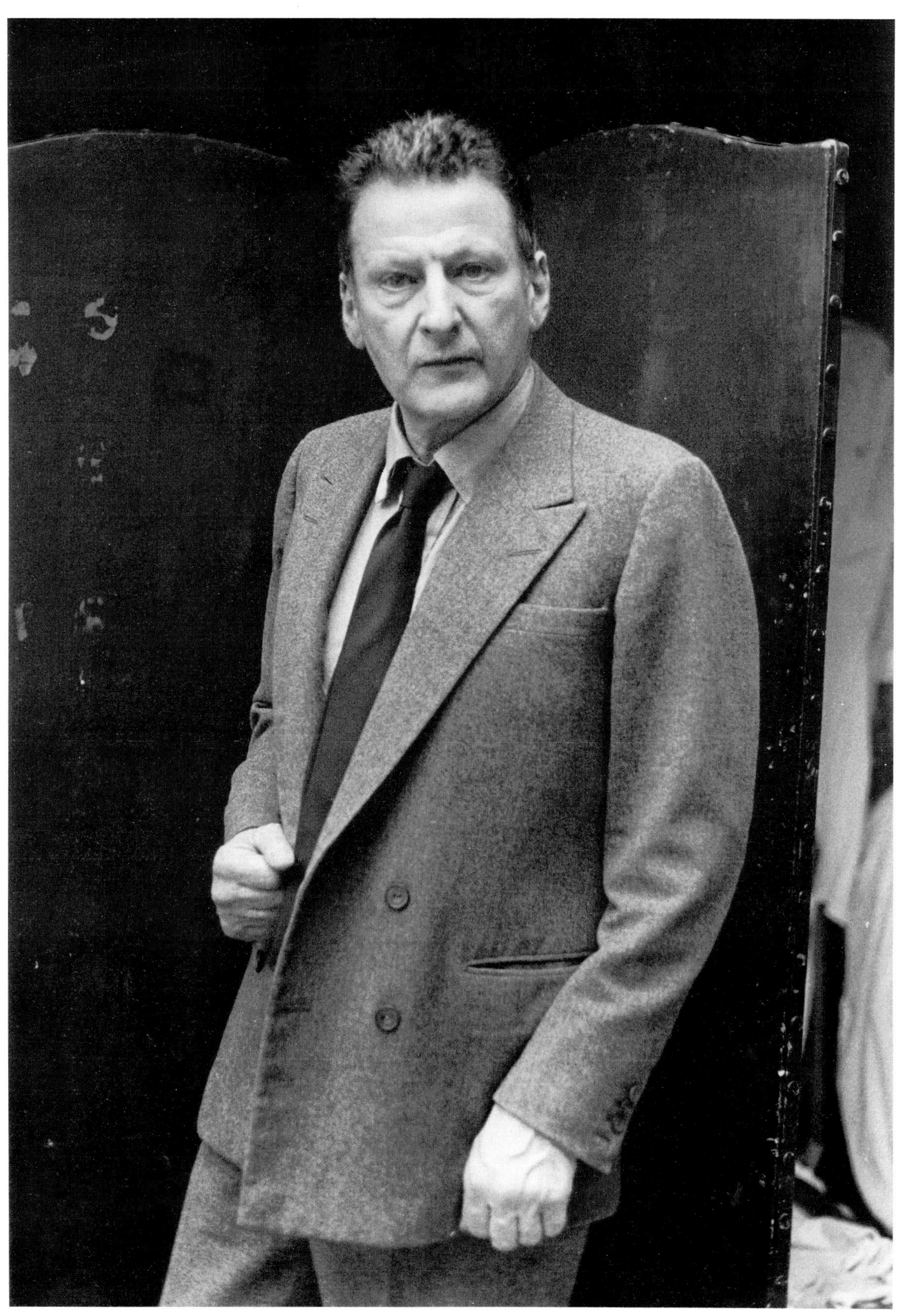

53 – Lucien Freud, 1983

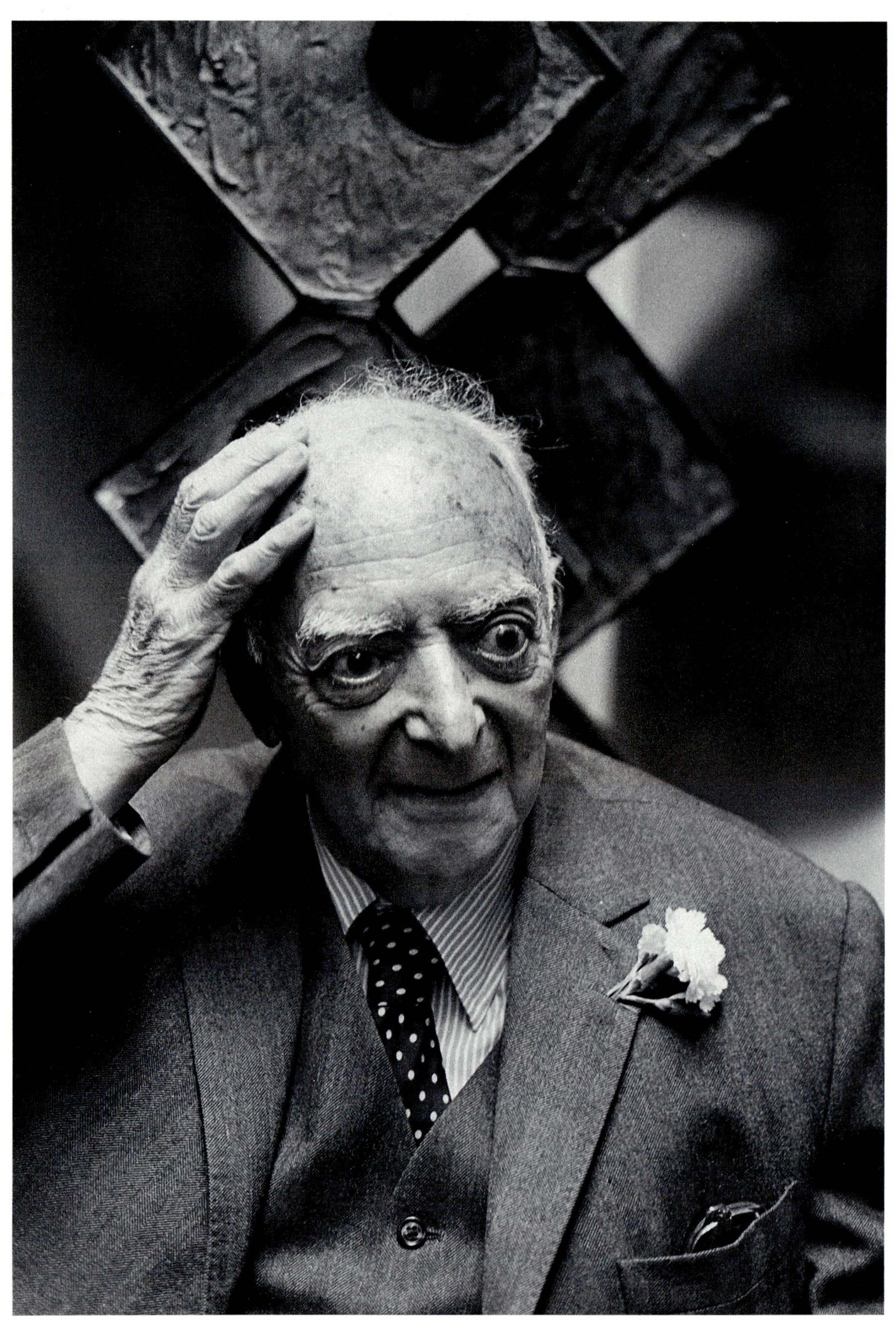

54 – Brassaï, 1982

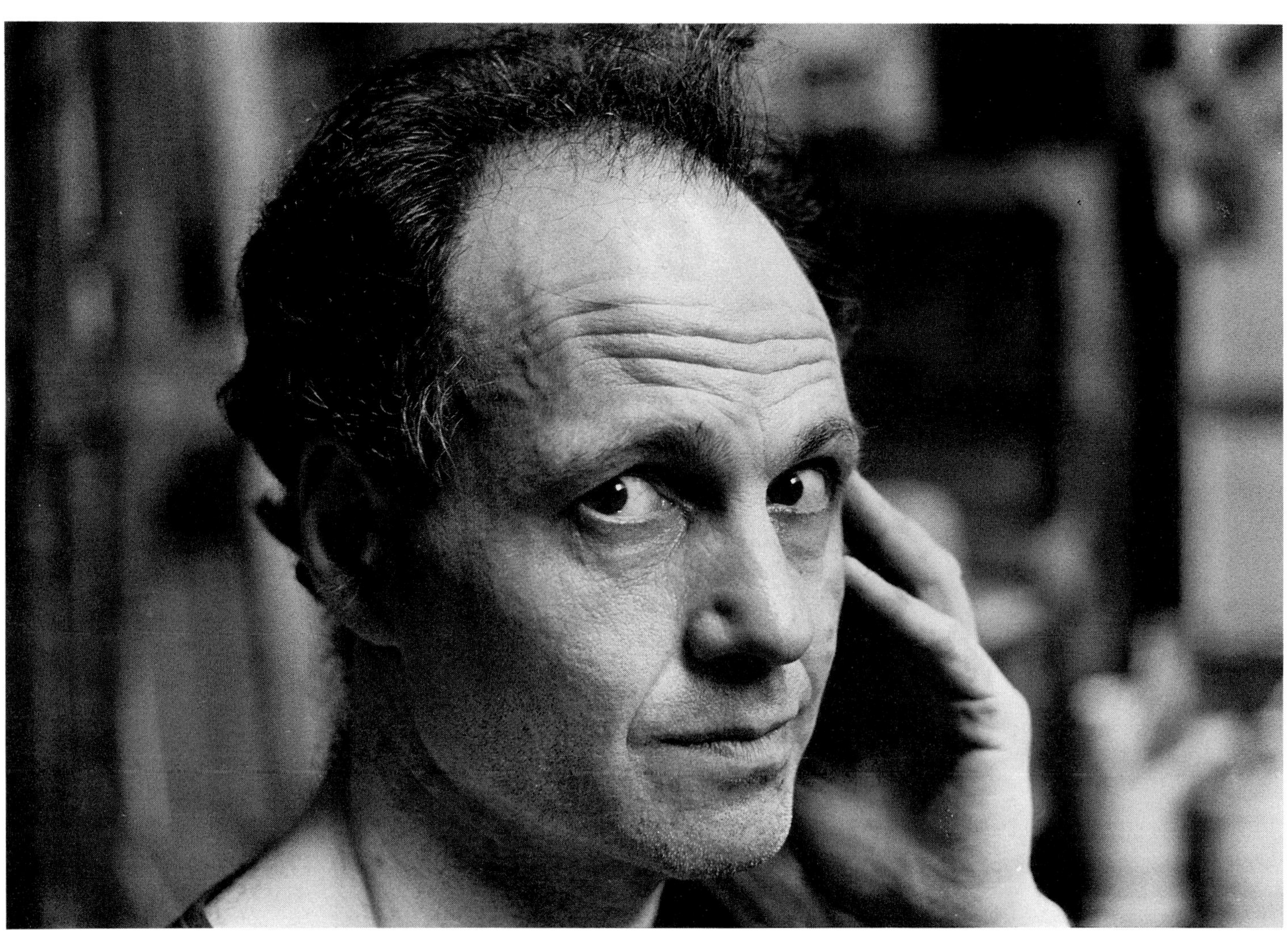

55 – Frank Auerbach, 1986

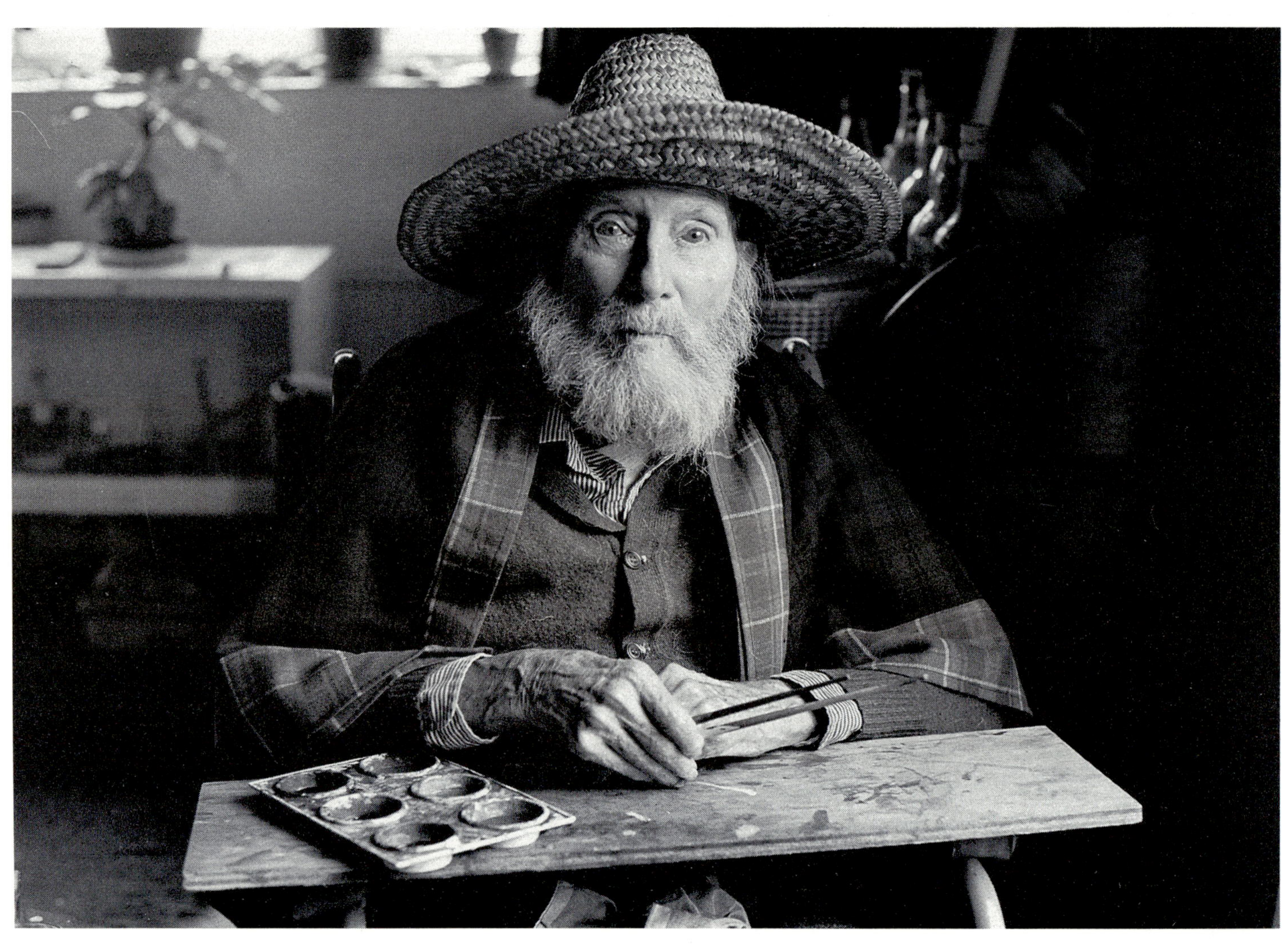

56 – Duncan Grant, 1978

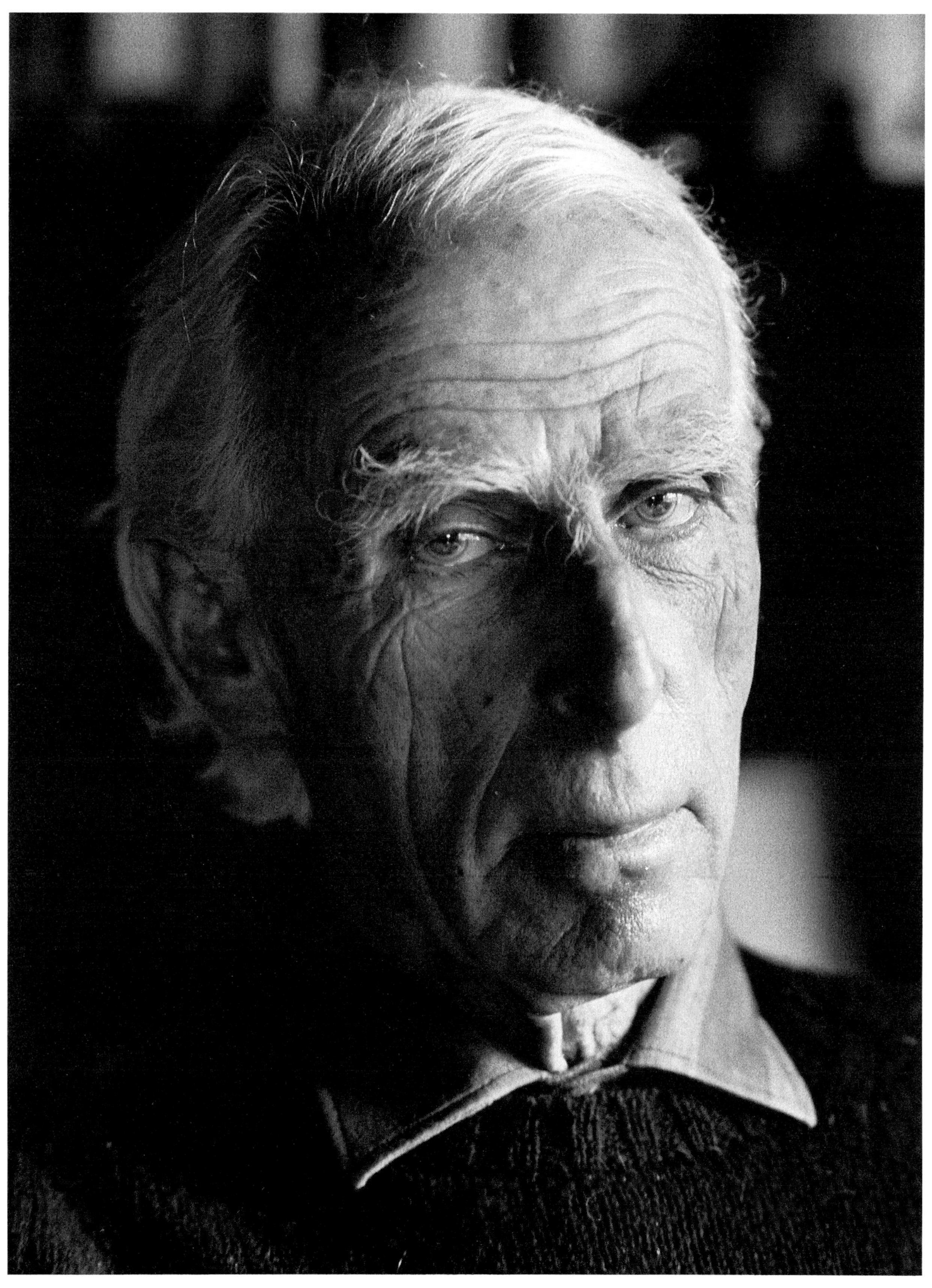

57 – John Piper, 1983

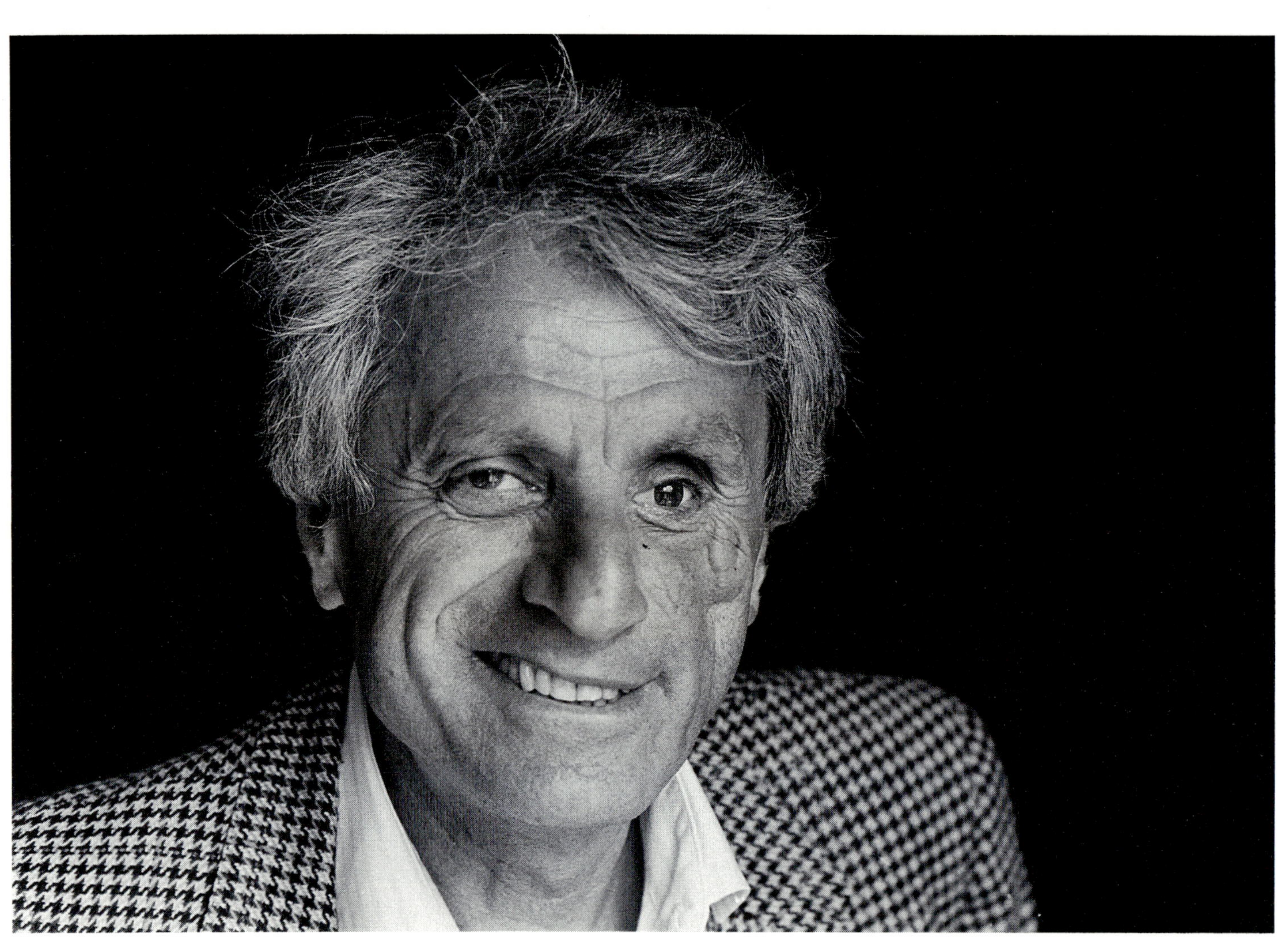

58 – Iannis Xenakis, 1987

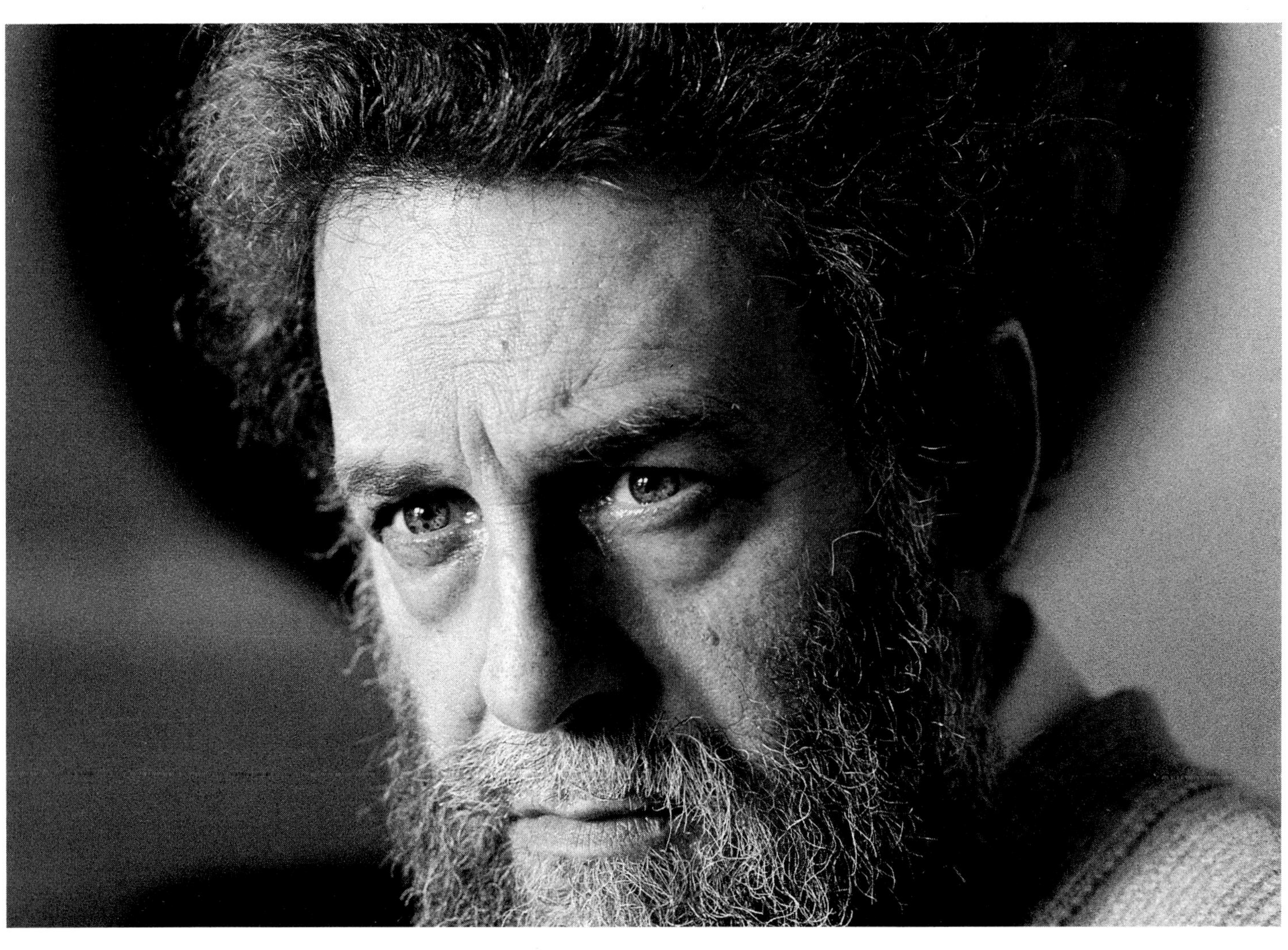

59 – John Barton, 1981

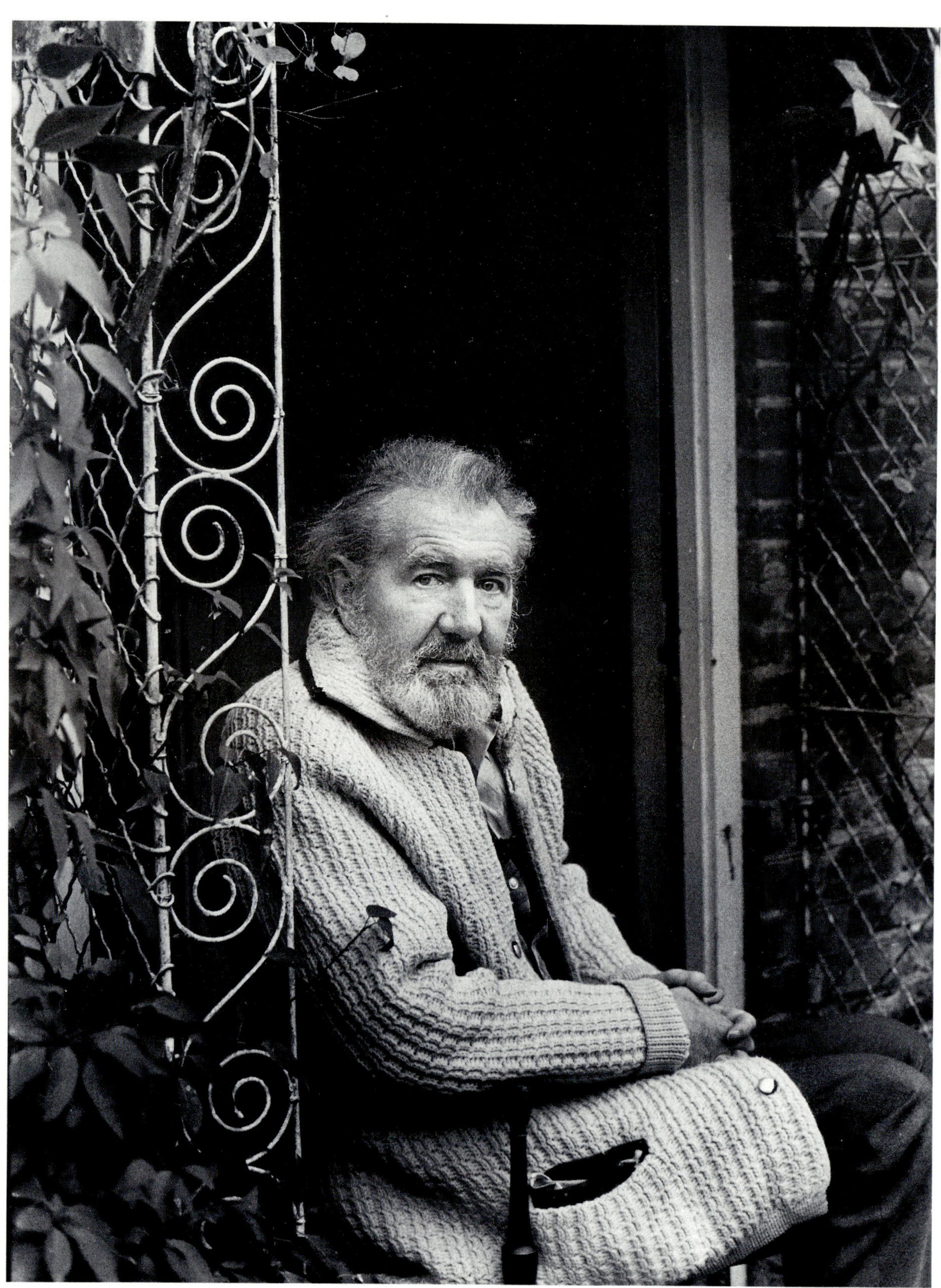

60 – Sir Michael Redgrave, 1983

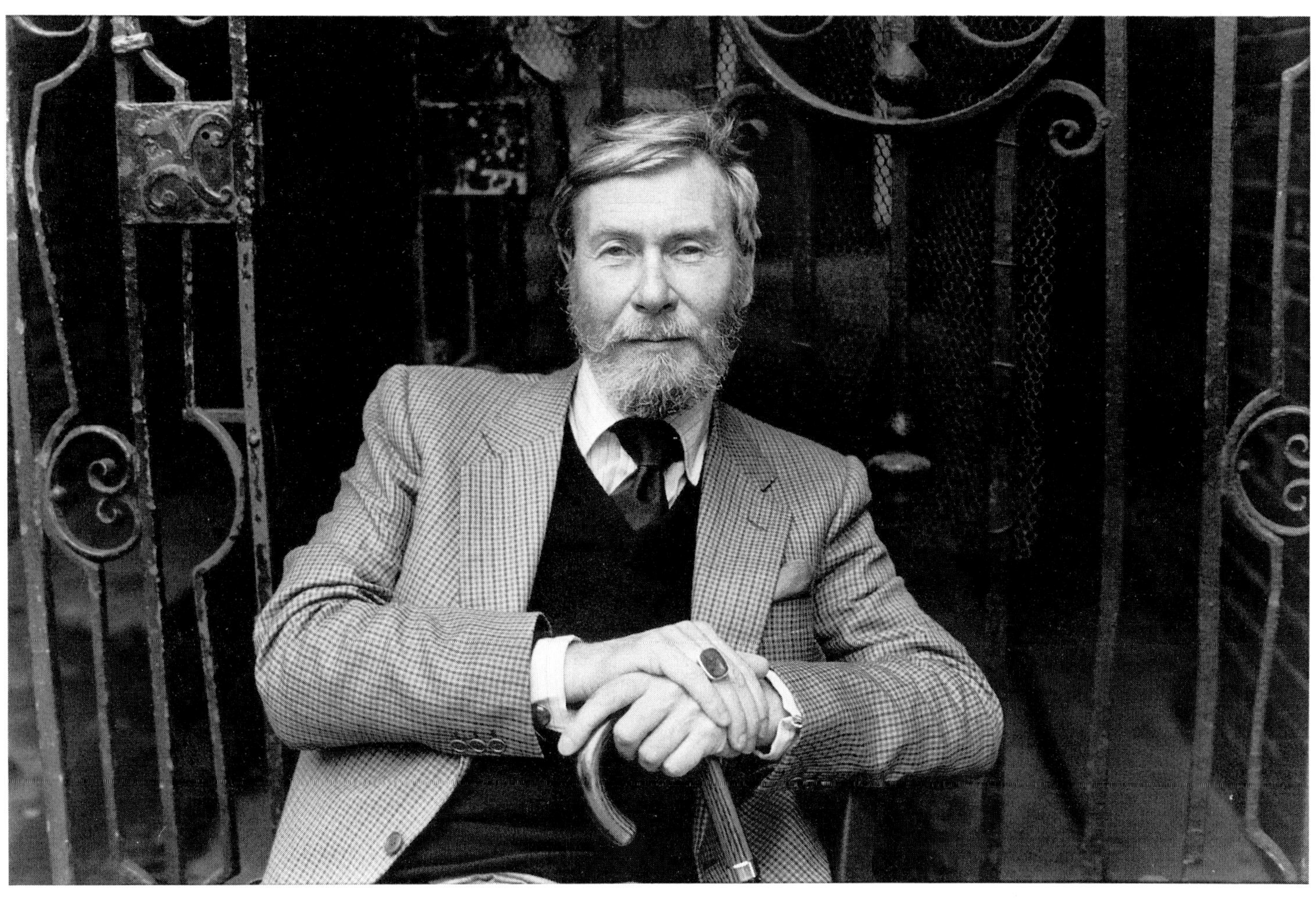

61 – John Osborne, 1986

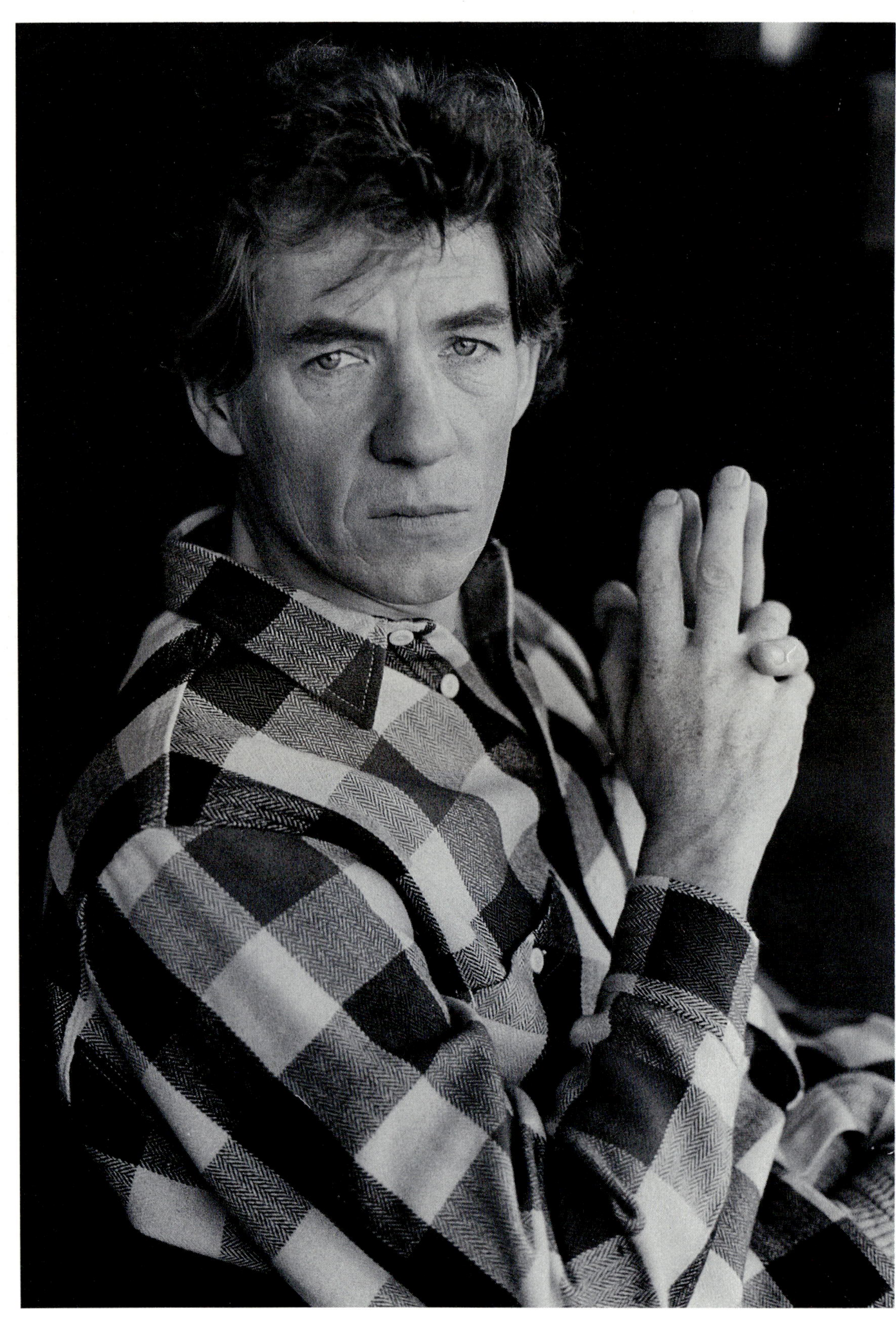

62 – Ian McKellen, 1984

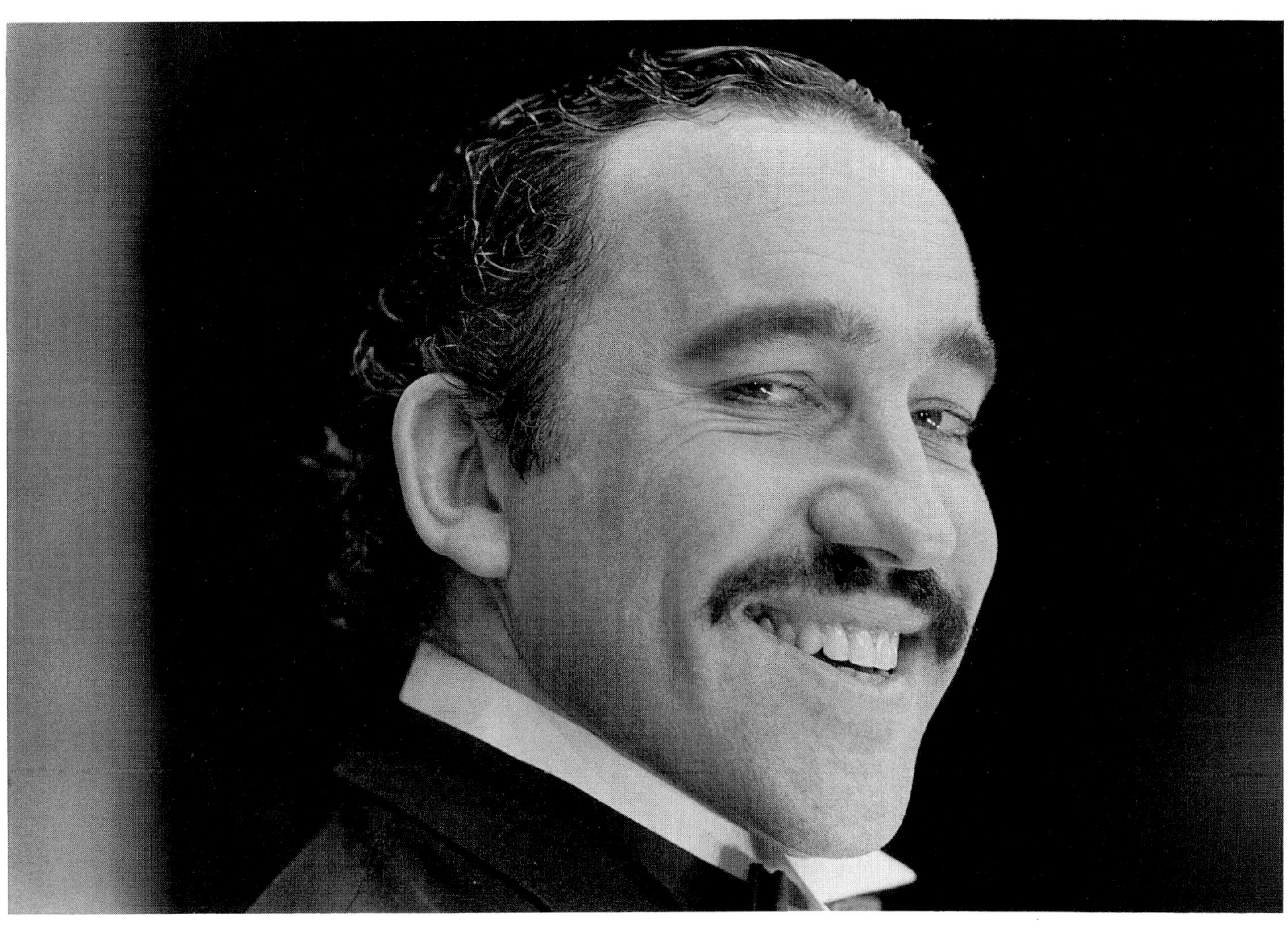

63 – Simon Callow, 1984

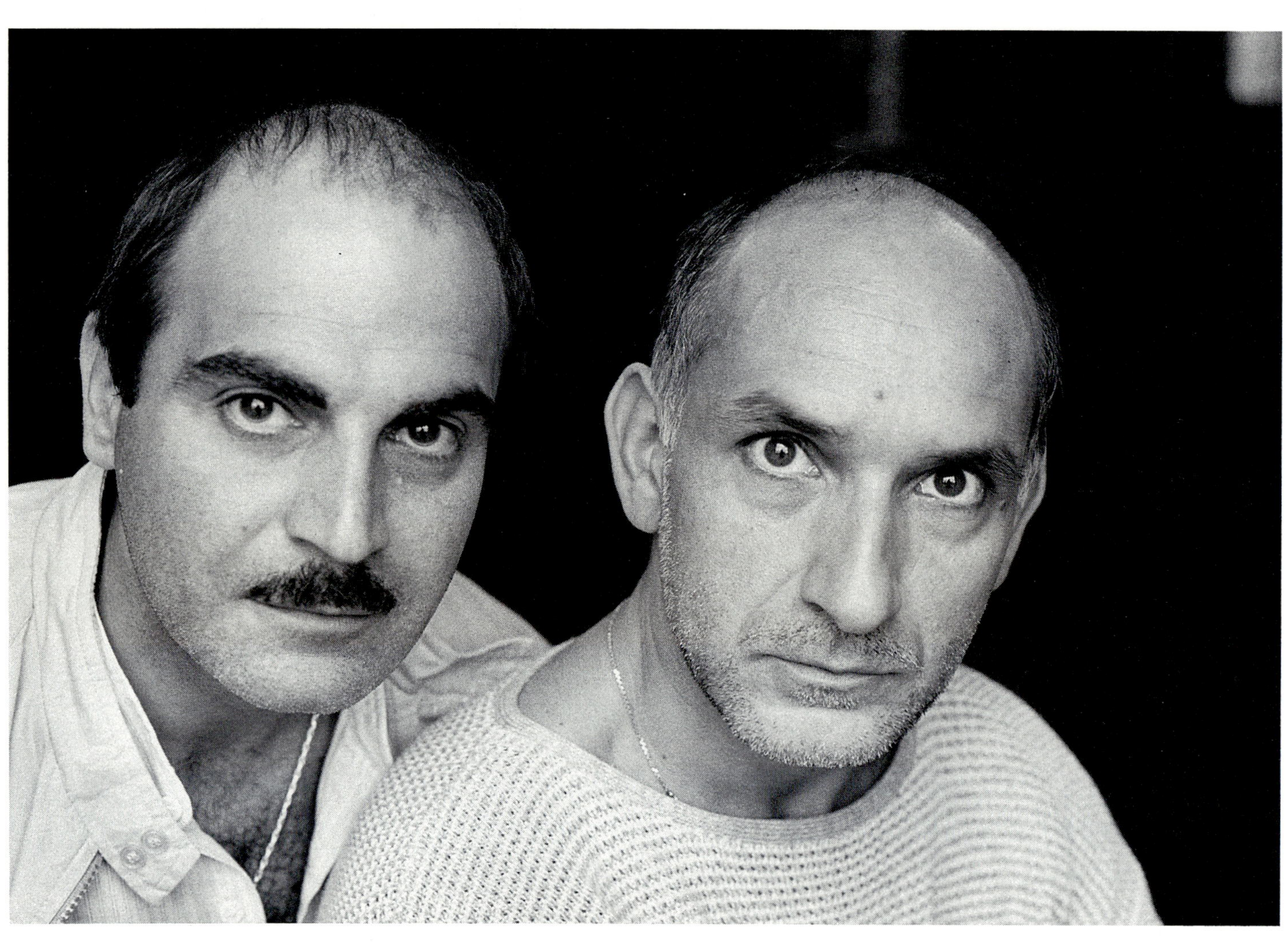

64 – David Suchet and Ben Kingsley, 1985

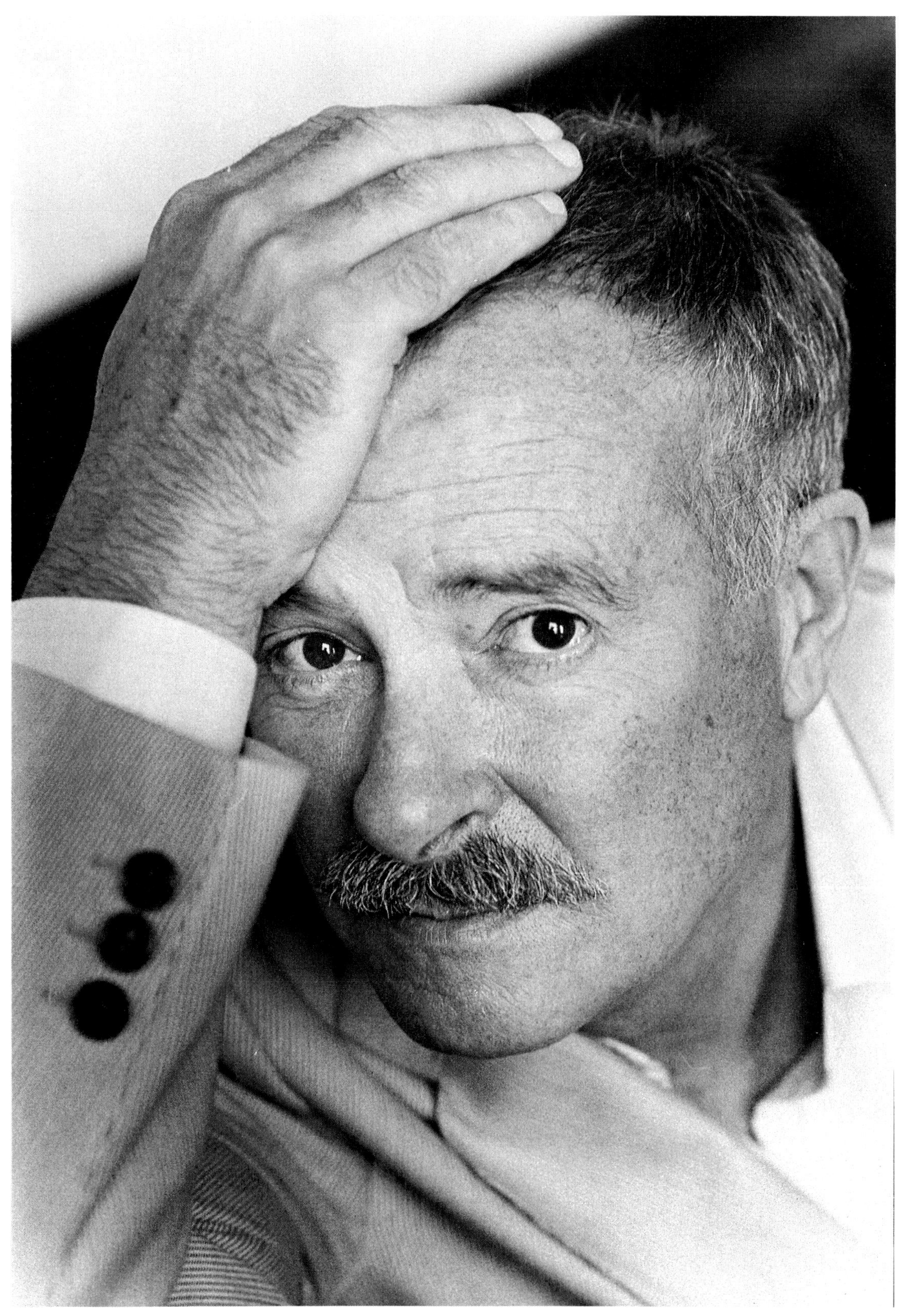

65 – Alec McCowen, 1984

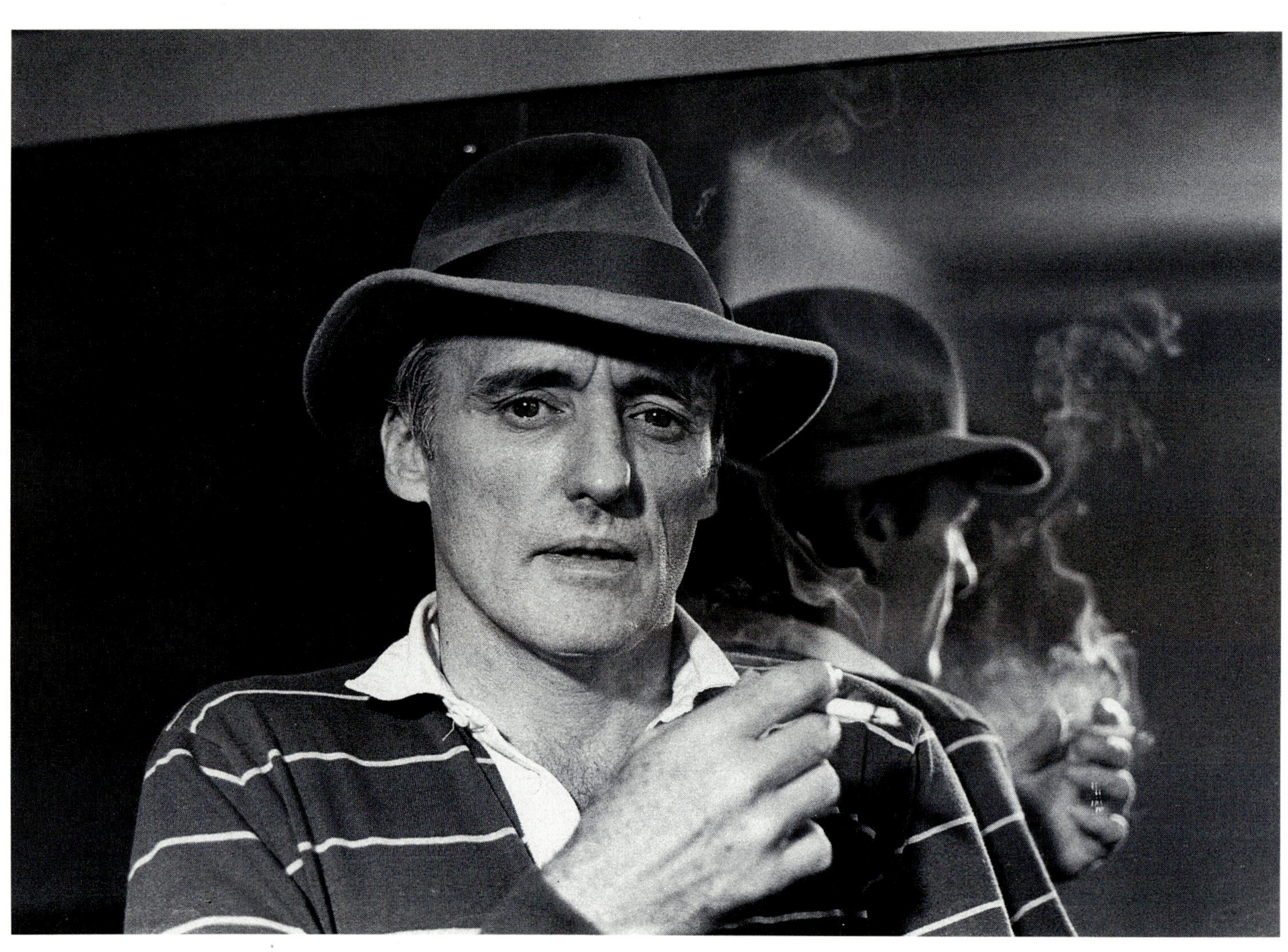

66 – Dennis Hopper, 1982

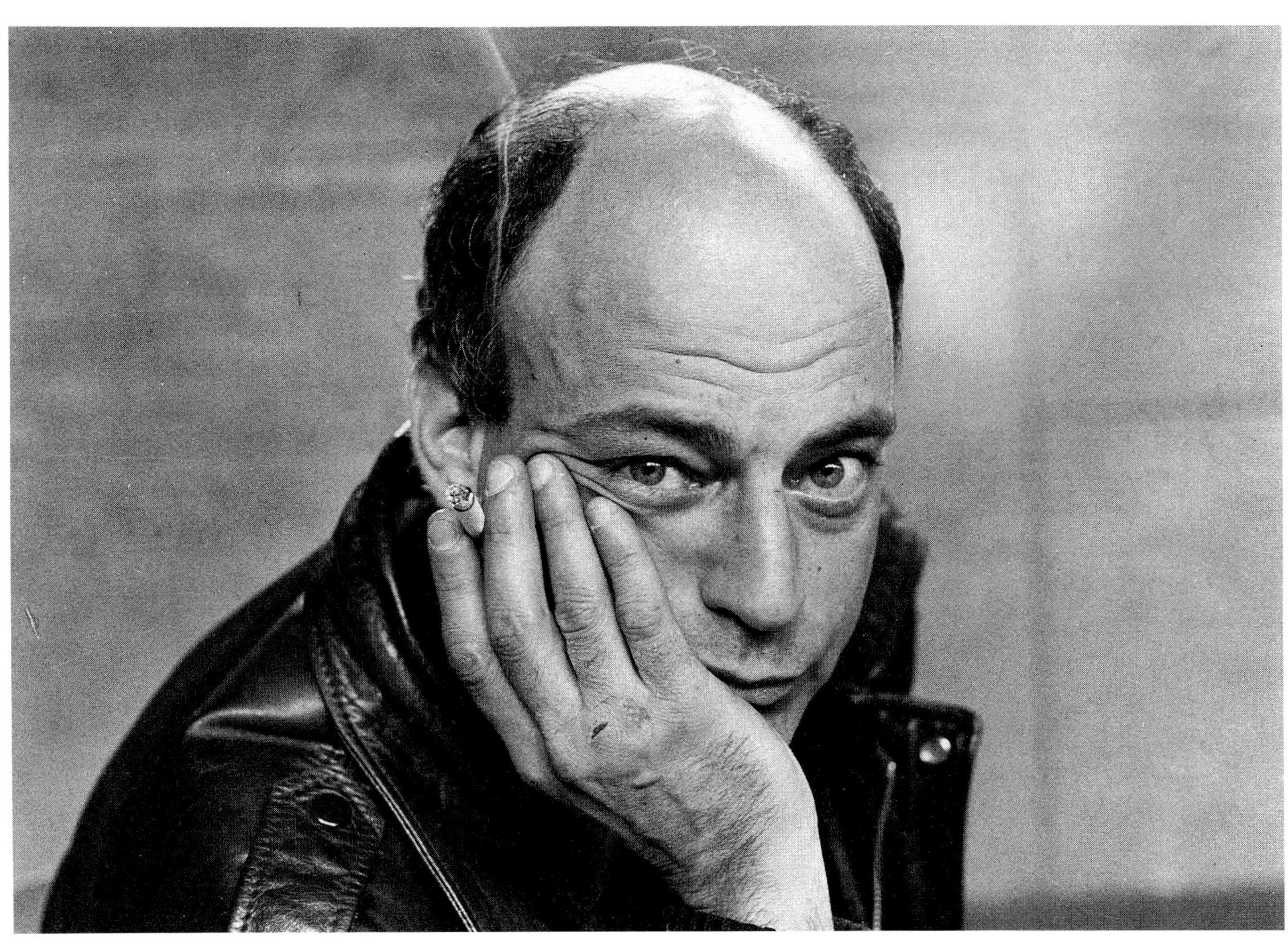

67 – Bernard Pomerance, 1980

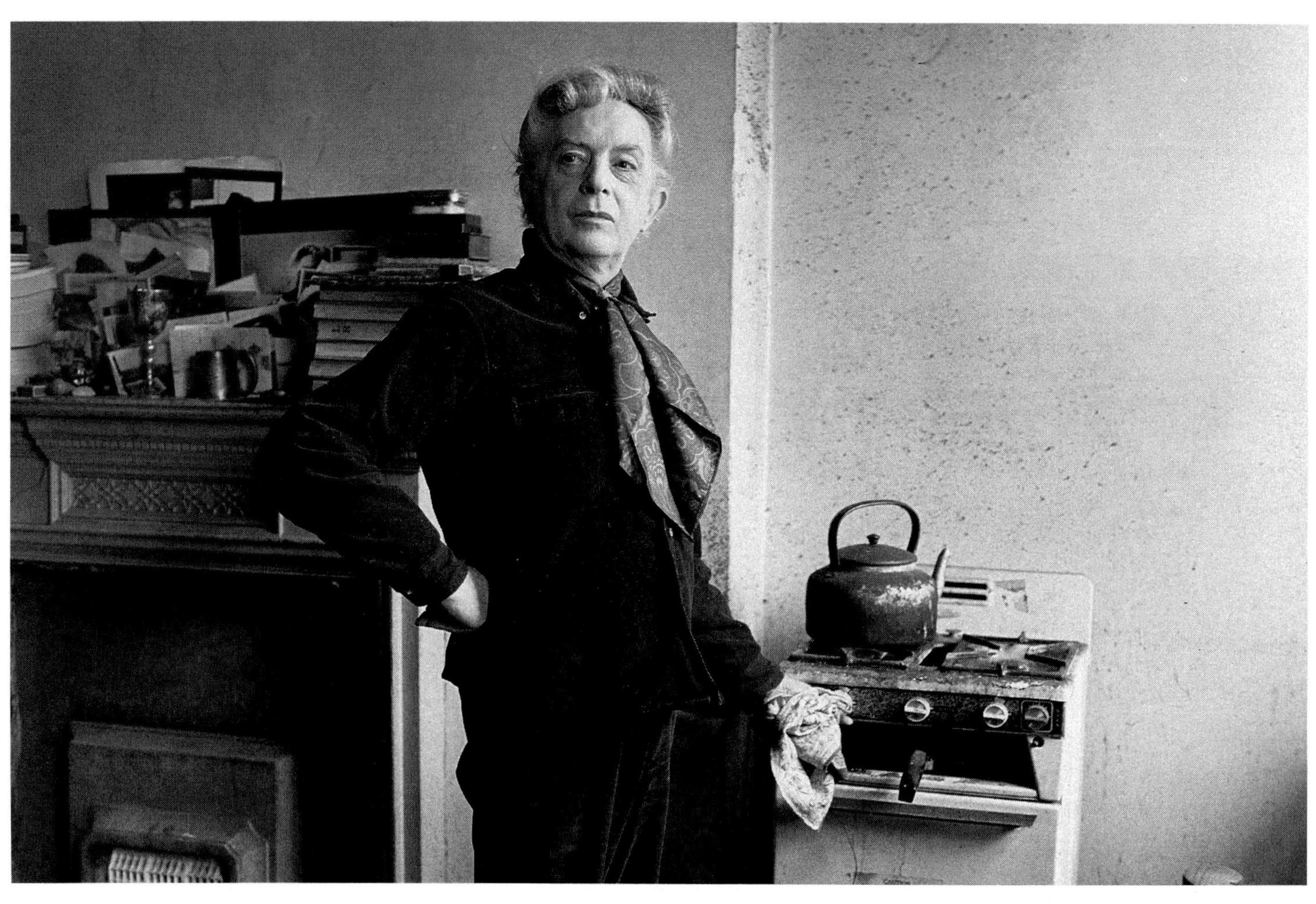

68 – Quentin Crisp, 1978

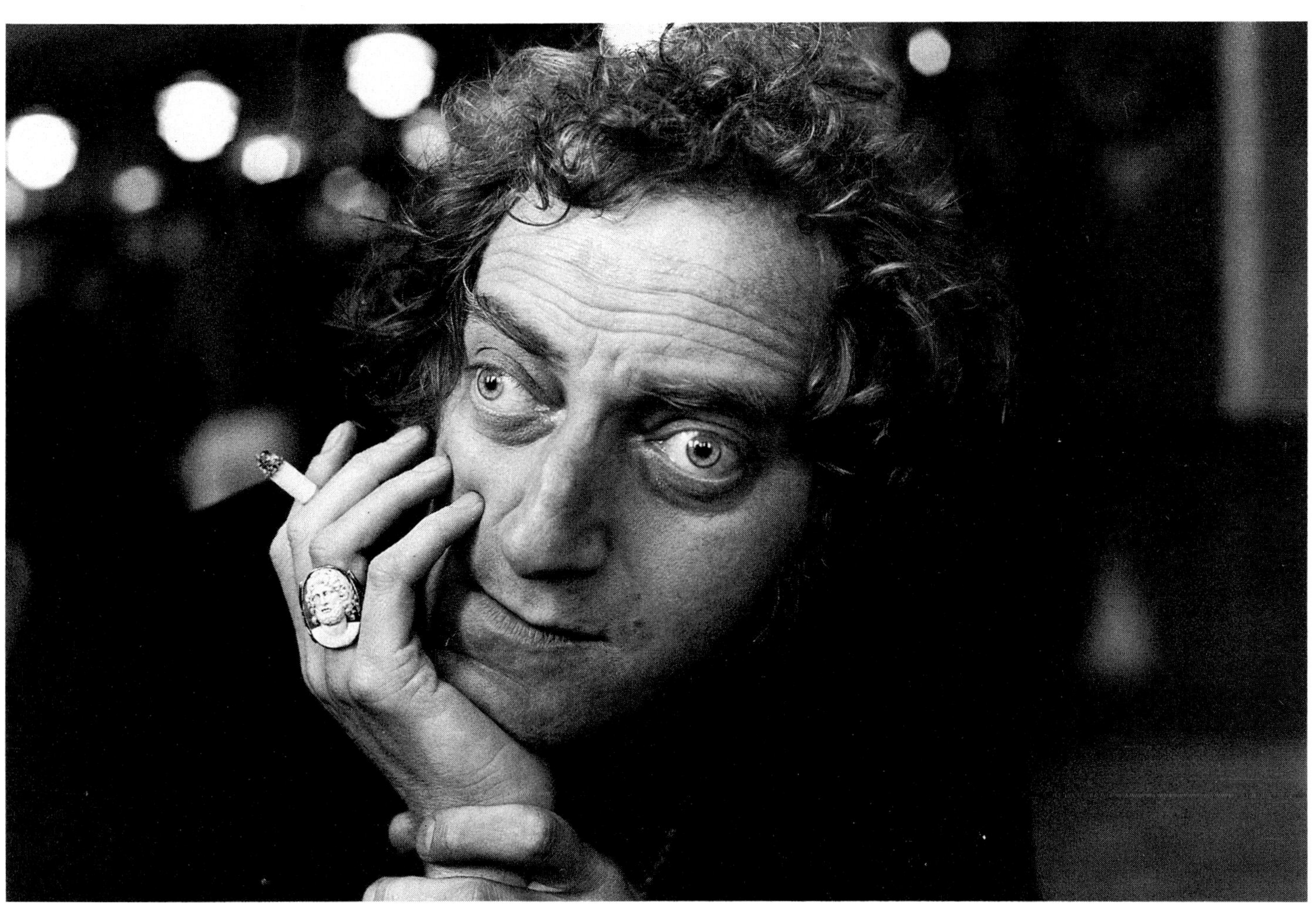

69 – Marty Feldman, 1969

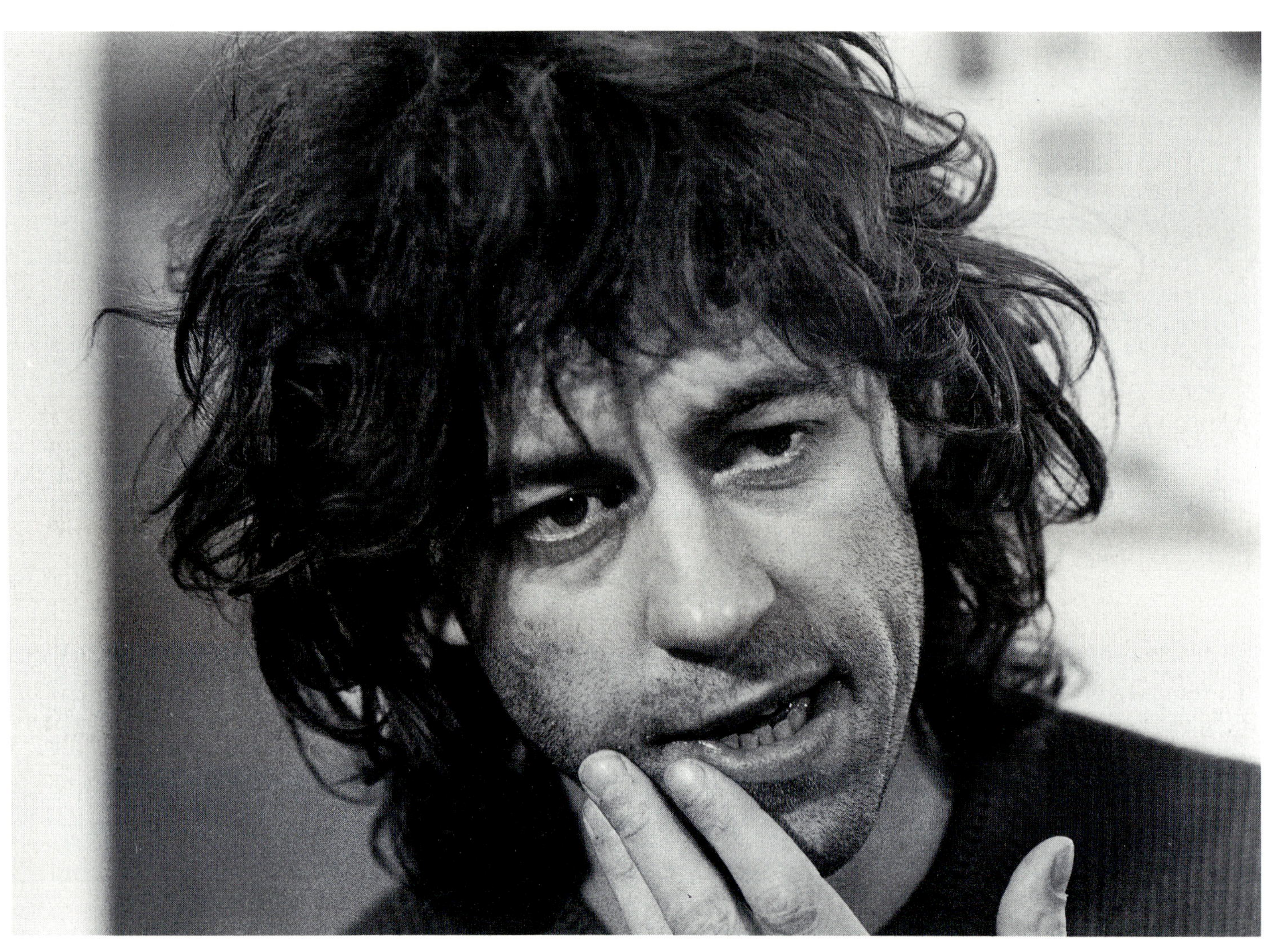

70 – Bob Geldof, 1987

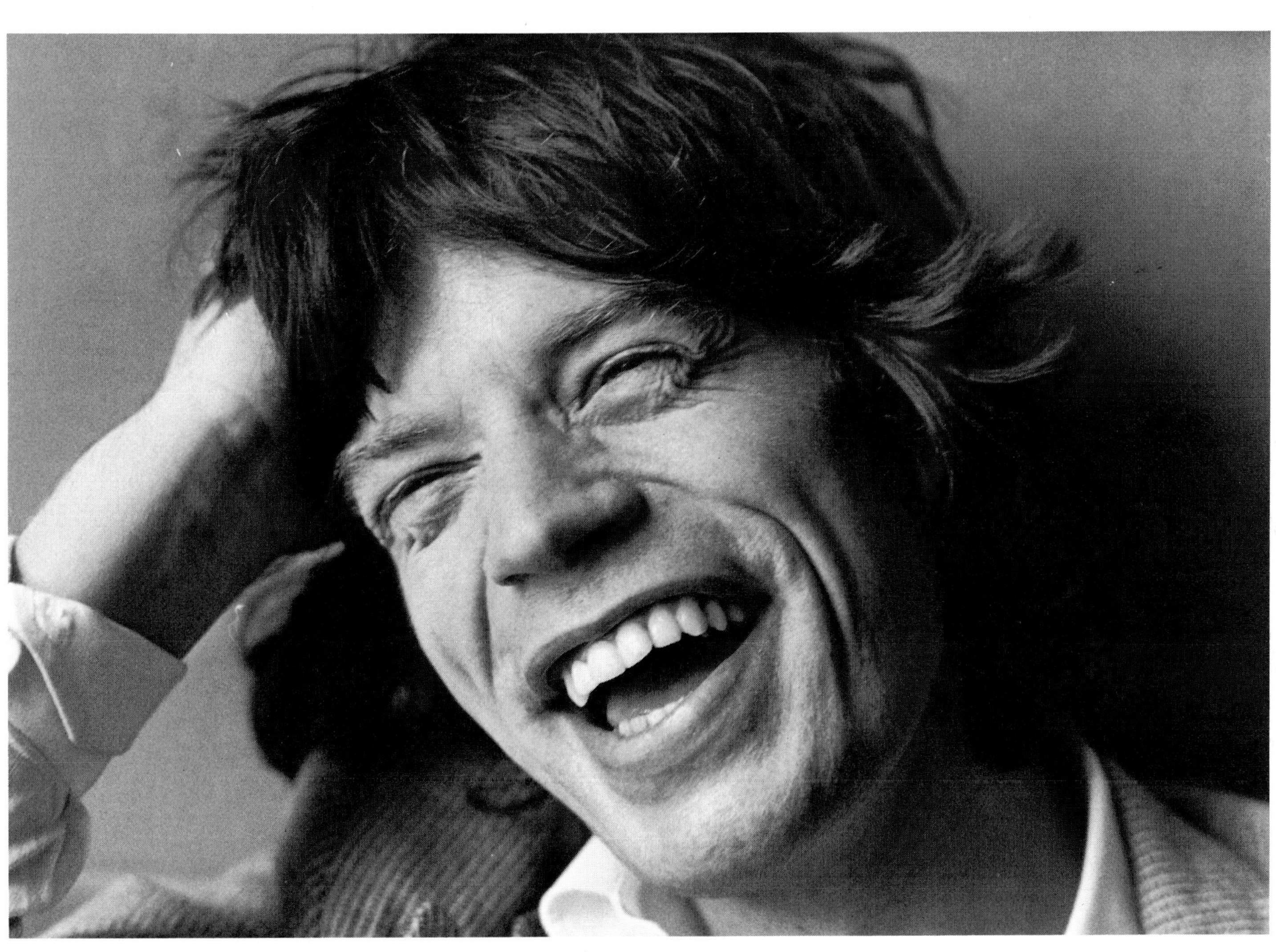

71 – Mick Jagger, 1973

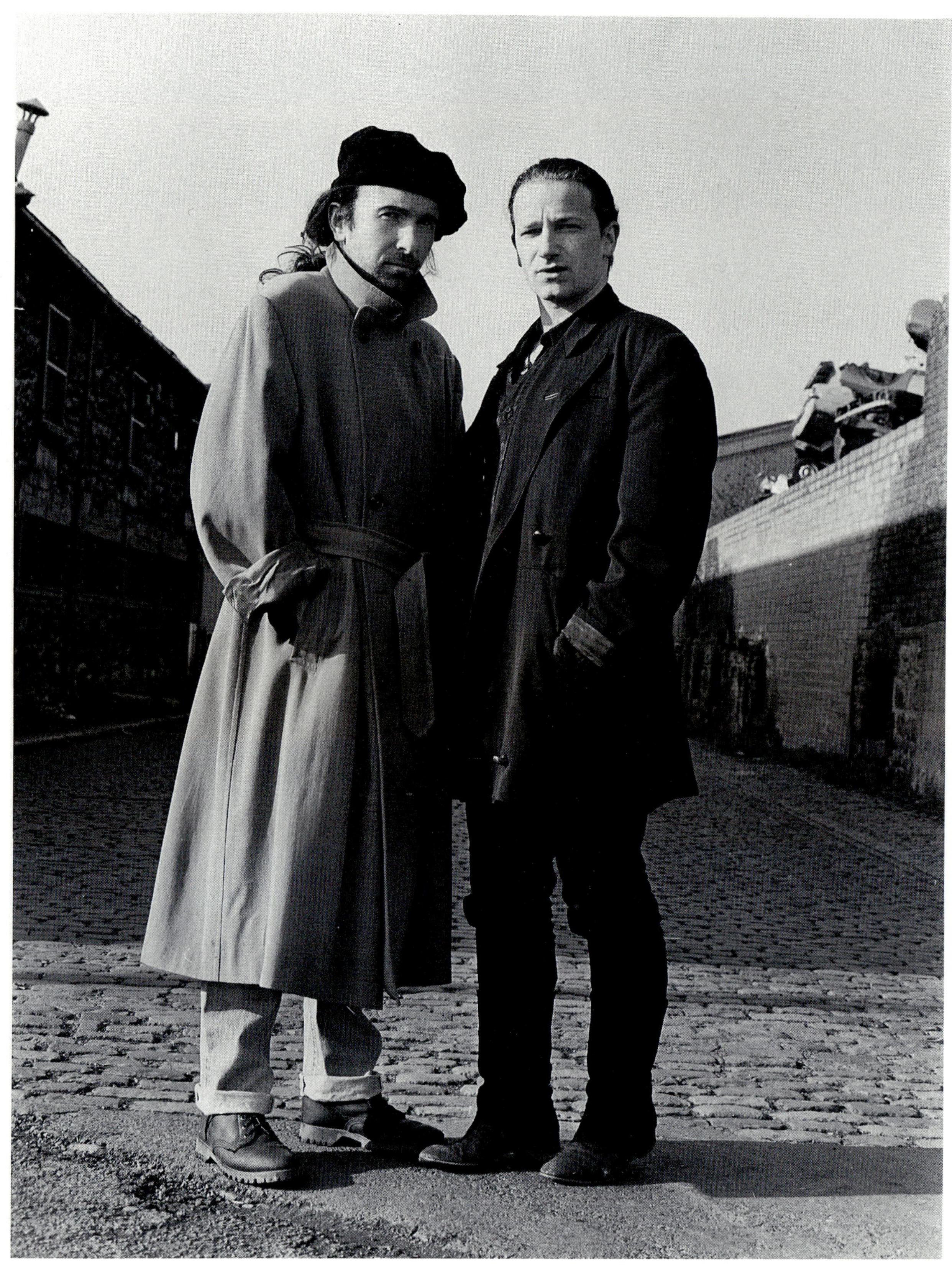

72 – Bono and The Edge, 1987

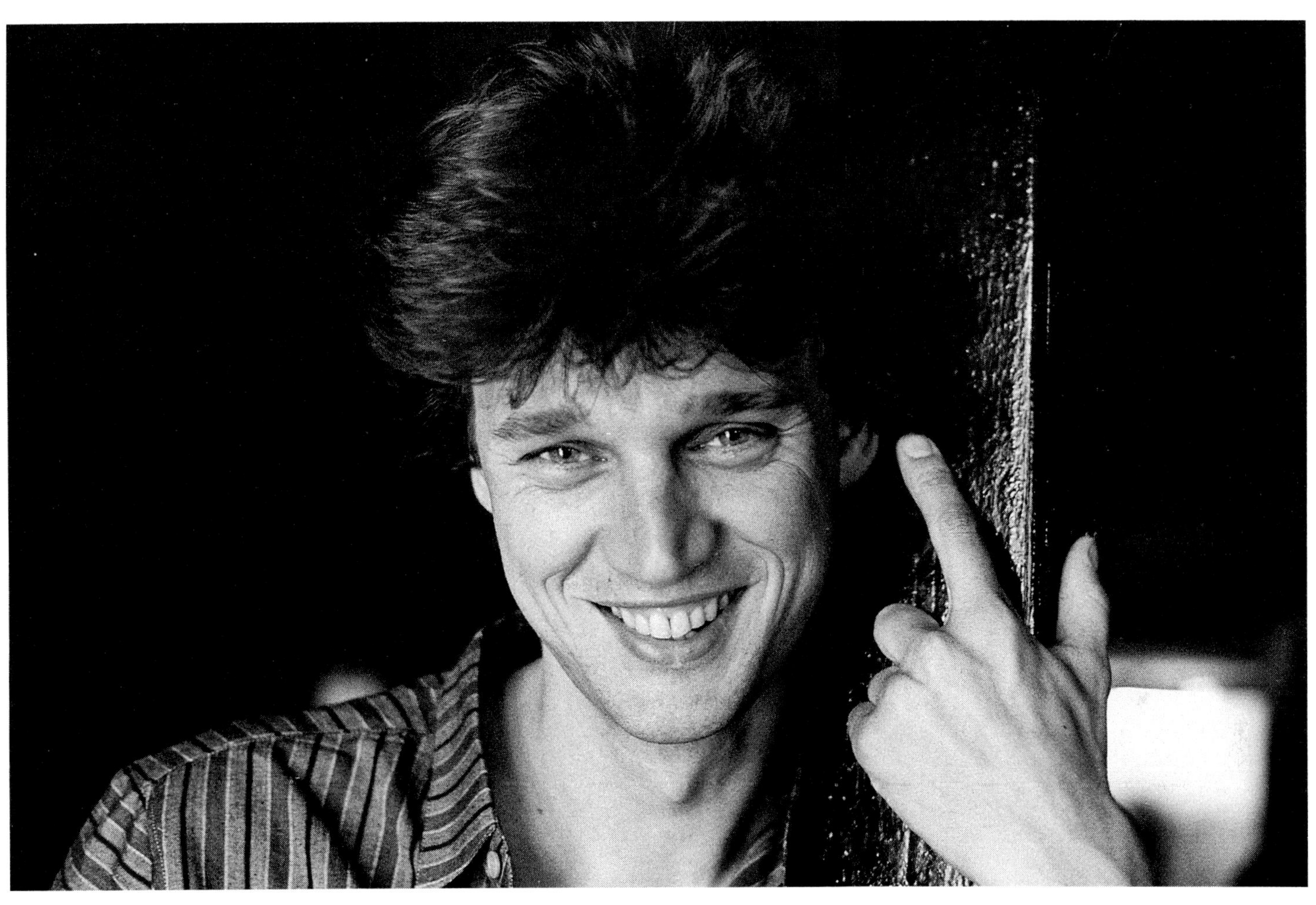

73 – David Knopfler, 1984

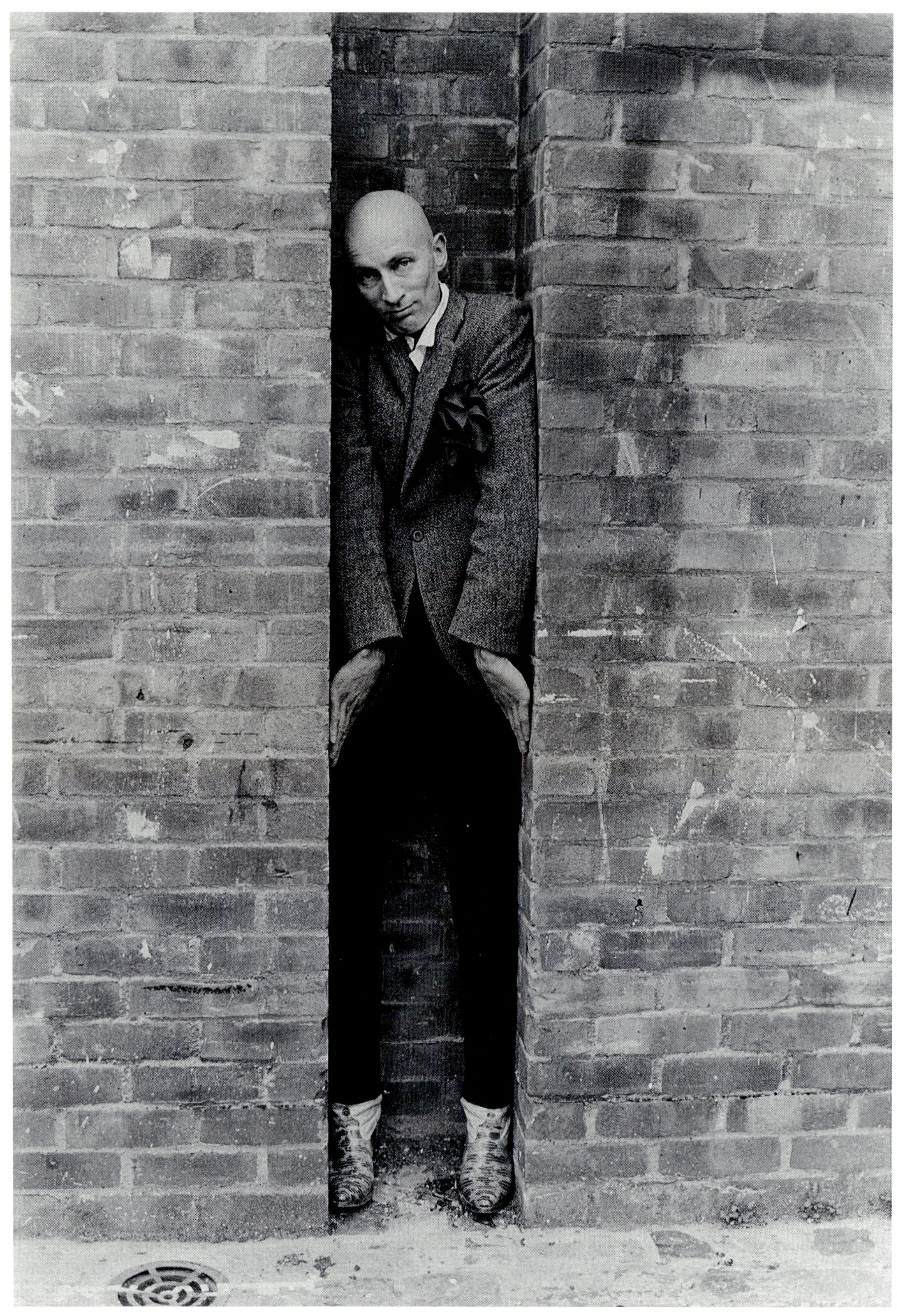

74 – Richard O'Brien, 1984

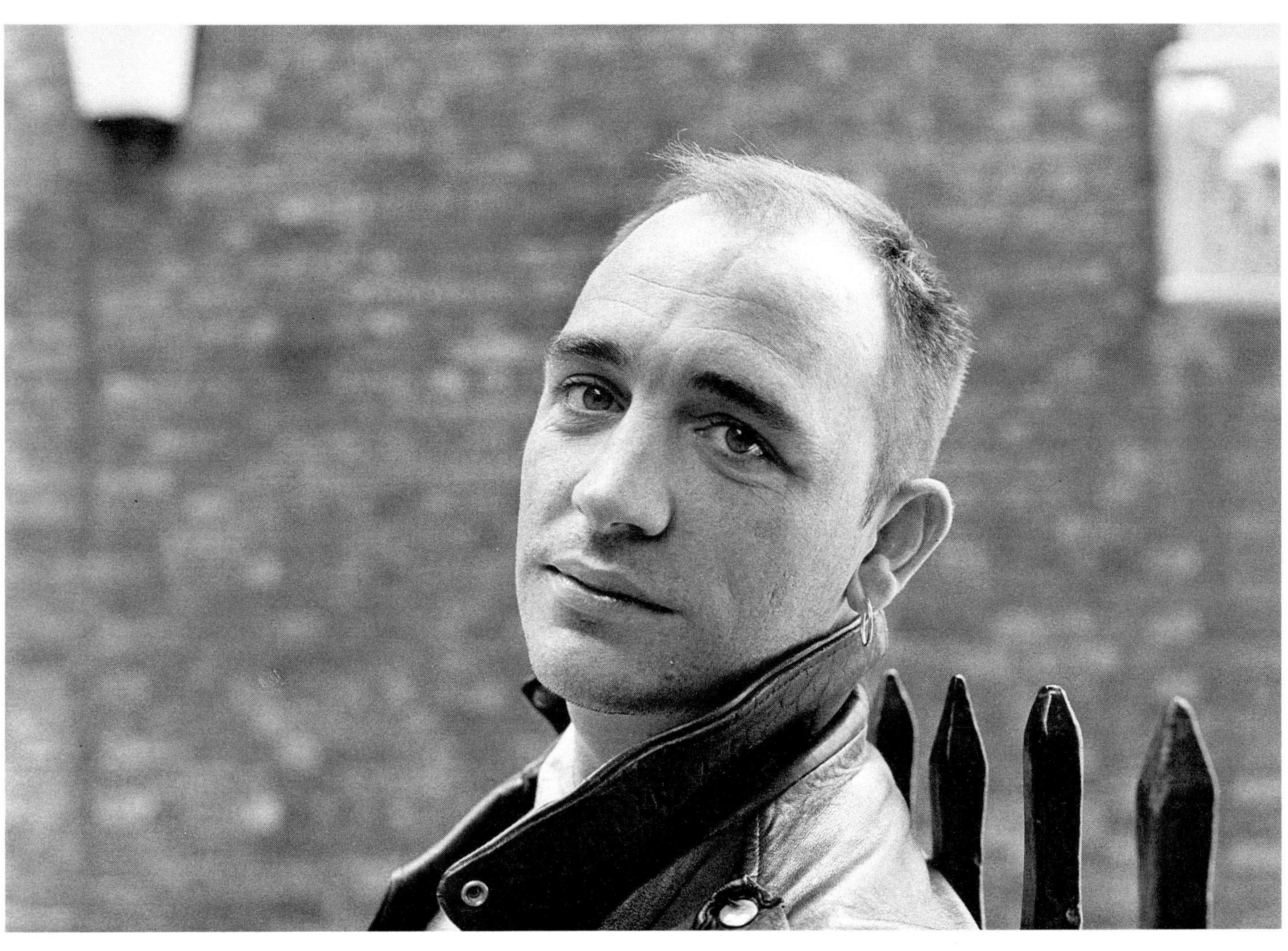

75 – Frank Clark, 1985

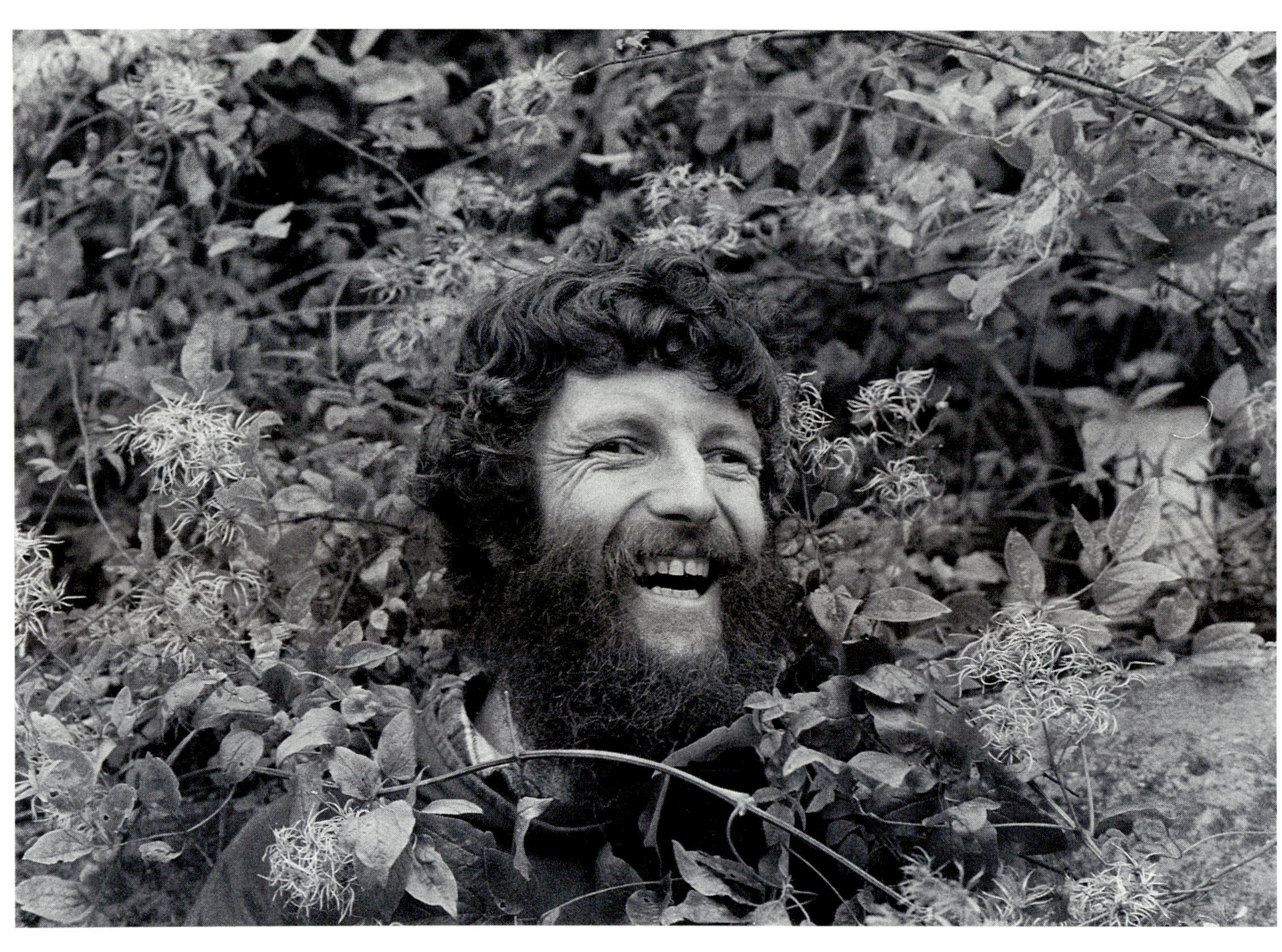

76 – Kit Williams, 1981

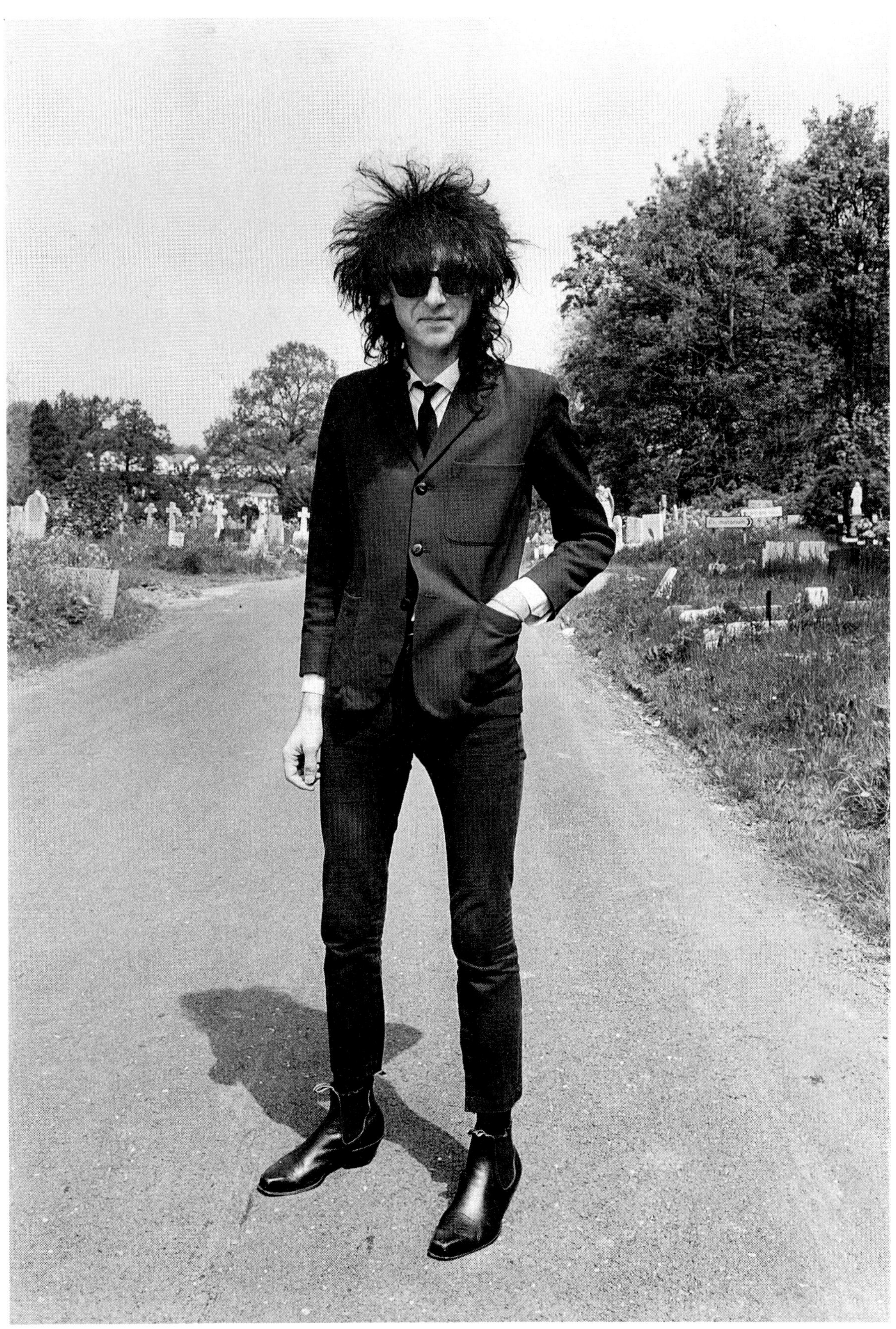

77 – John Cooper Clark, 1985

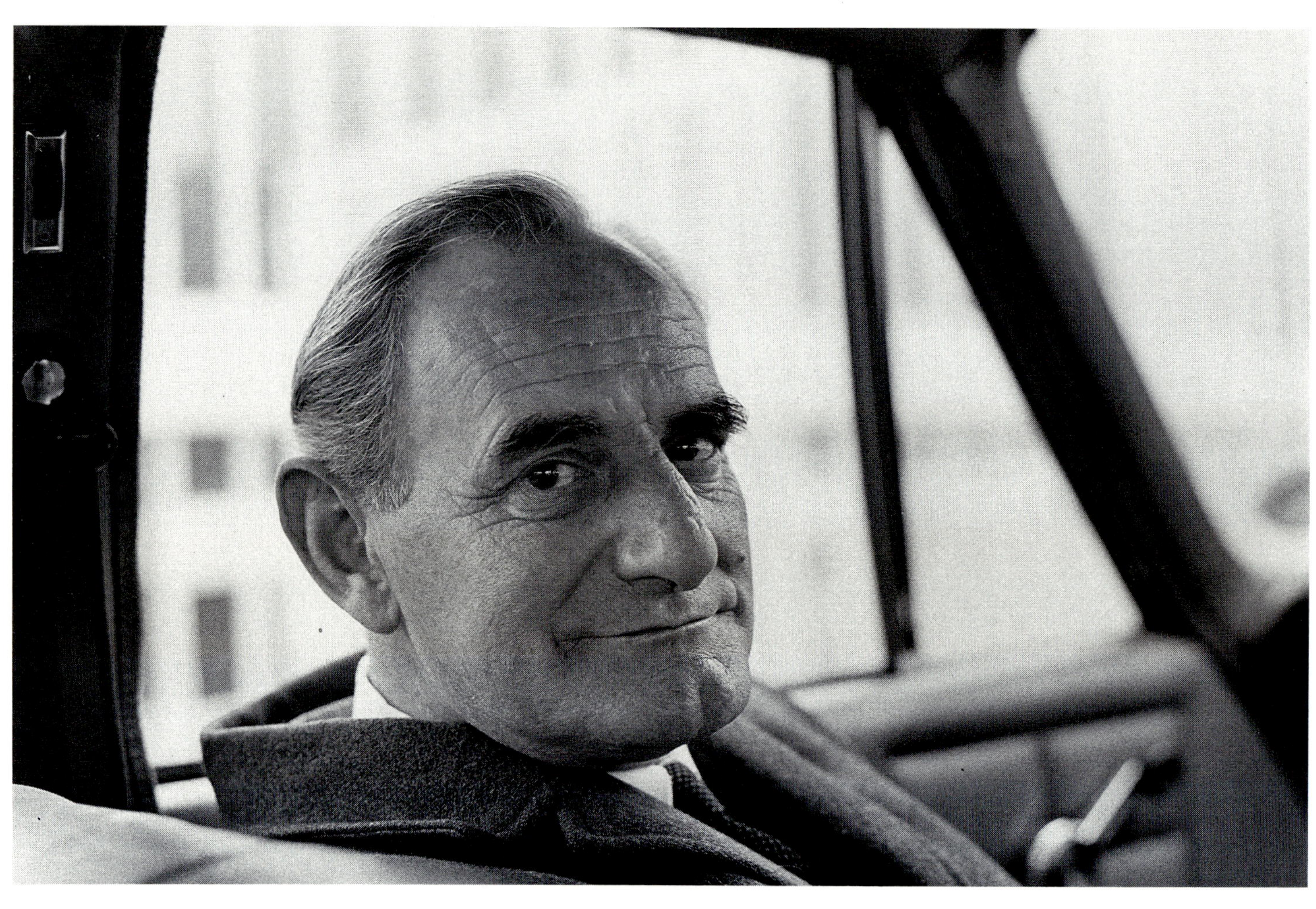

78 – Huw Wheldon, 1972

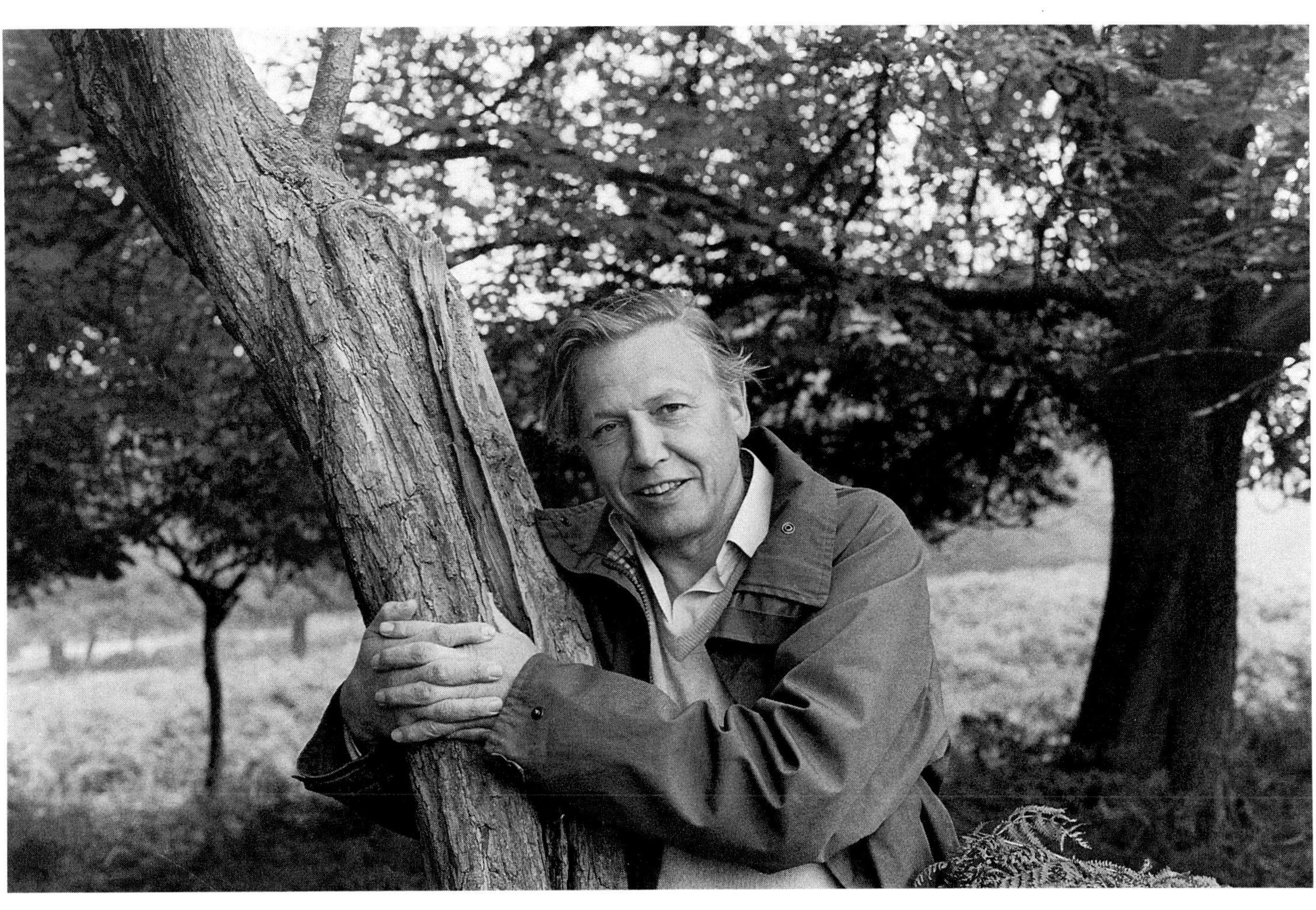

79 – Sir David Attenborough, 1985

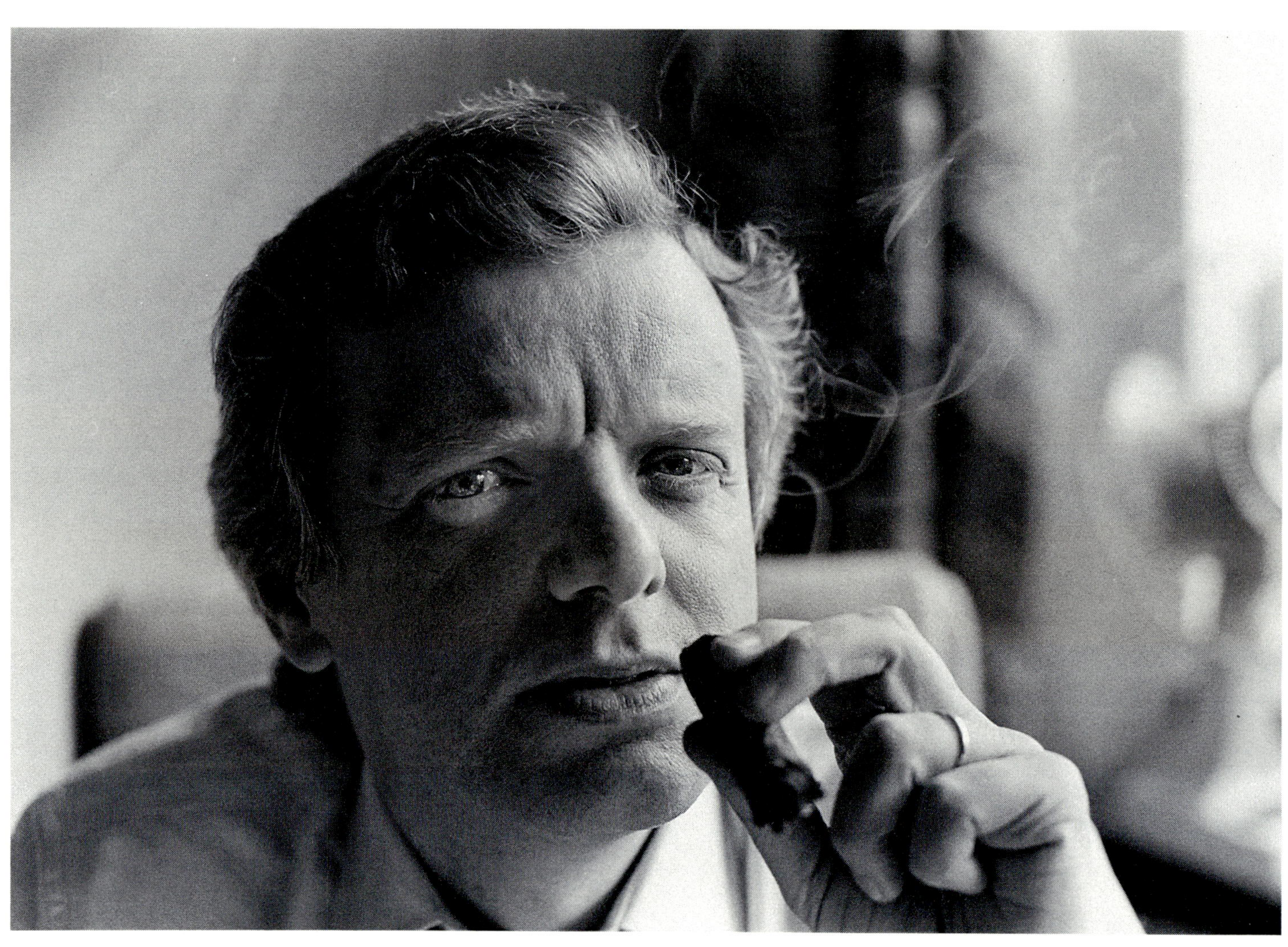

80 – Michael Grade, 1986

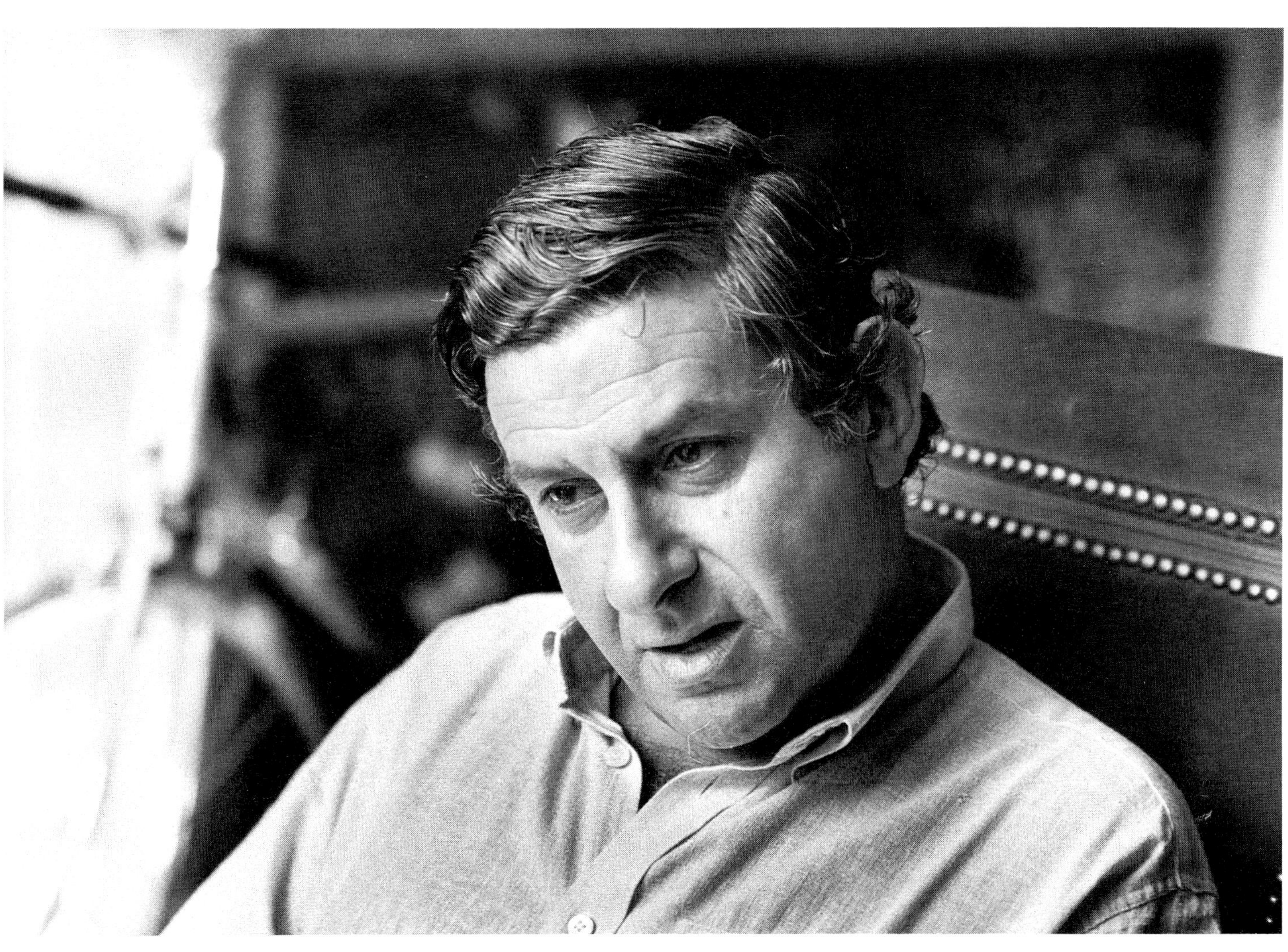

81 – Jeremy Isaacs, 1980

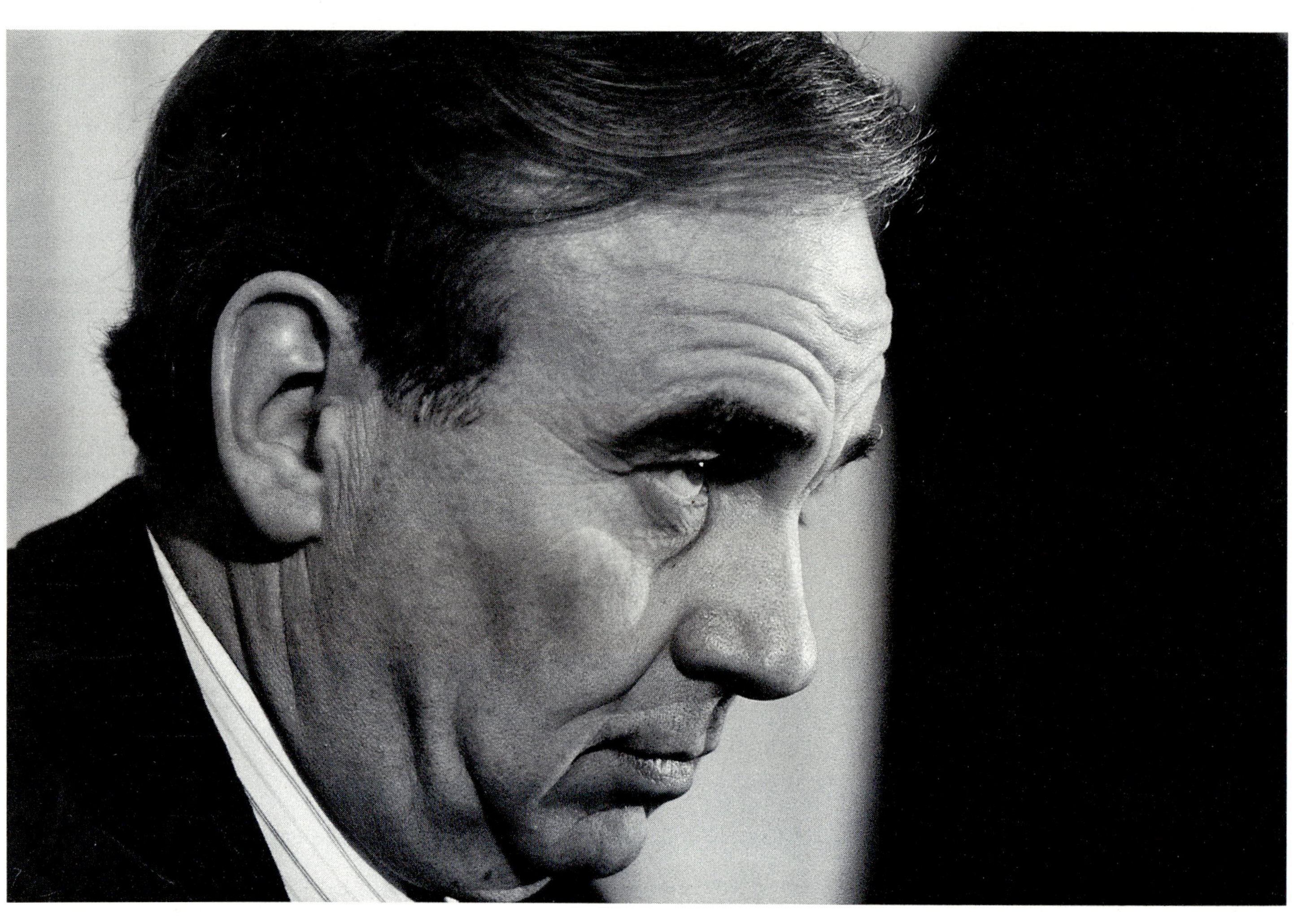

82 – Rupert Murdoch, 1981

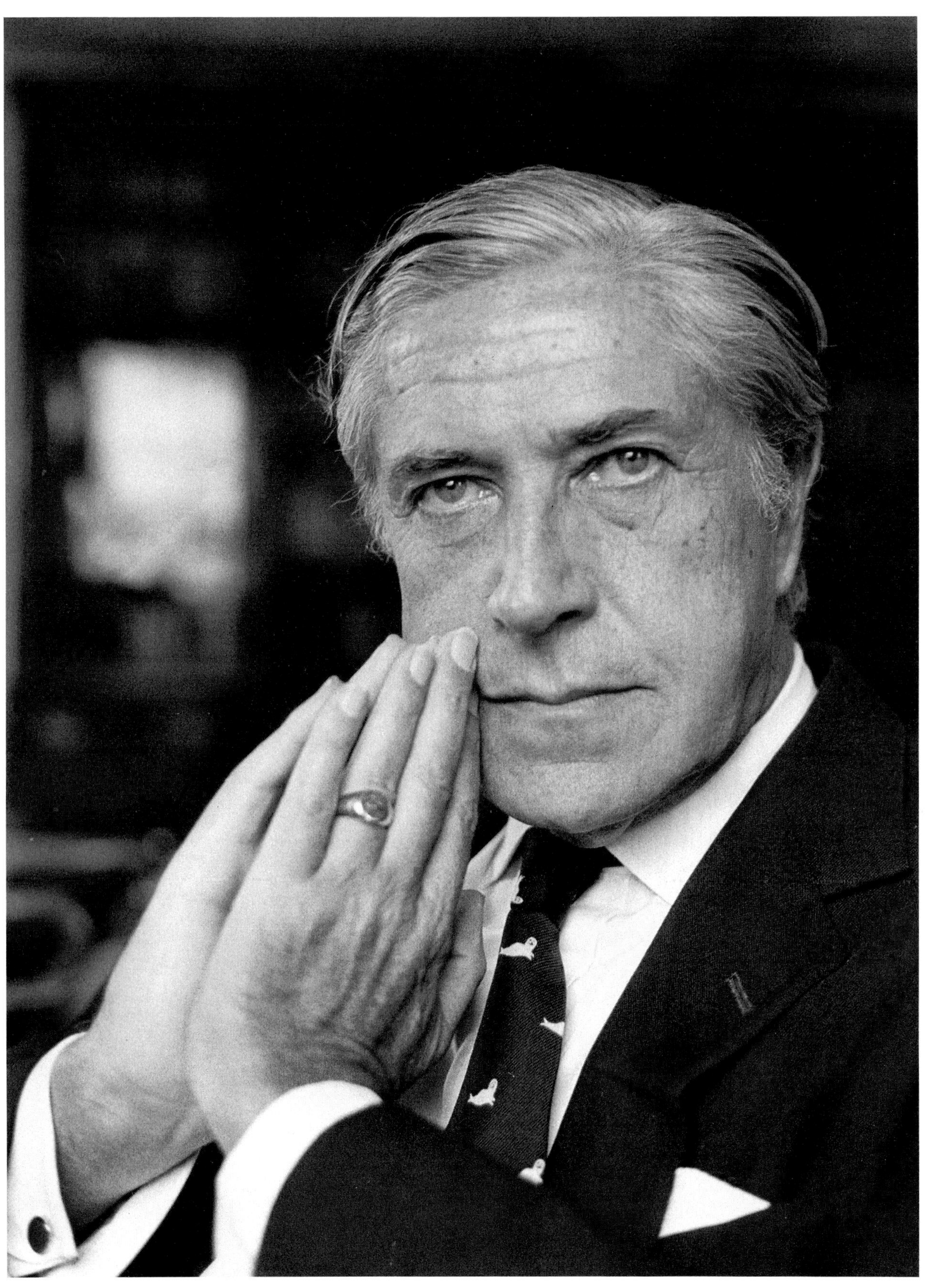

83 – Tiny Rowland, 1981

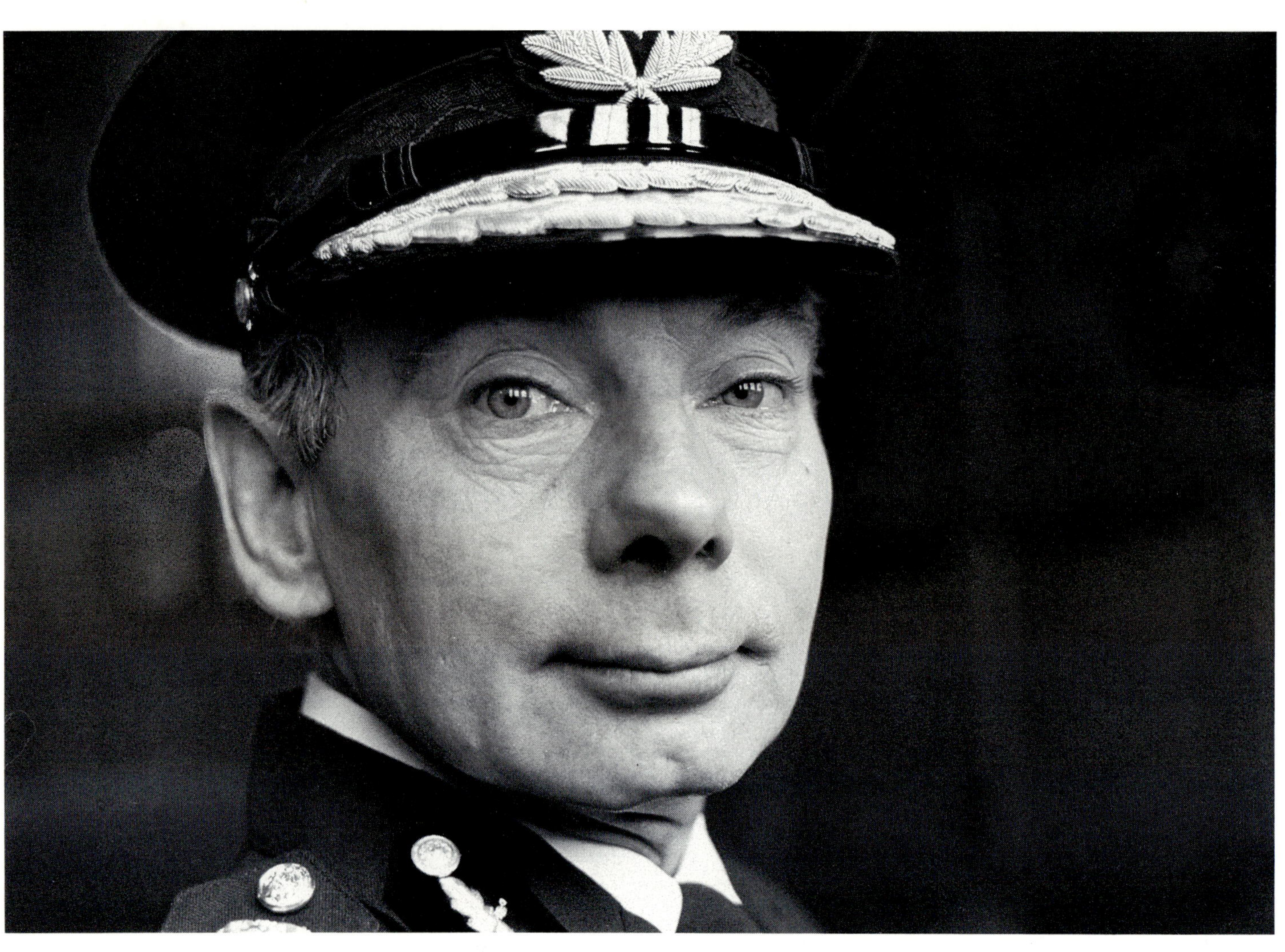

84 – Chief Superintendent Newman, 1982

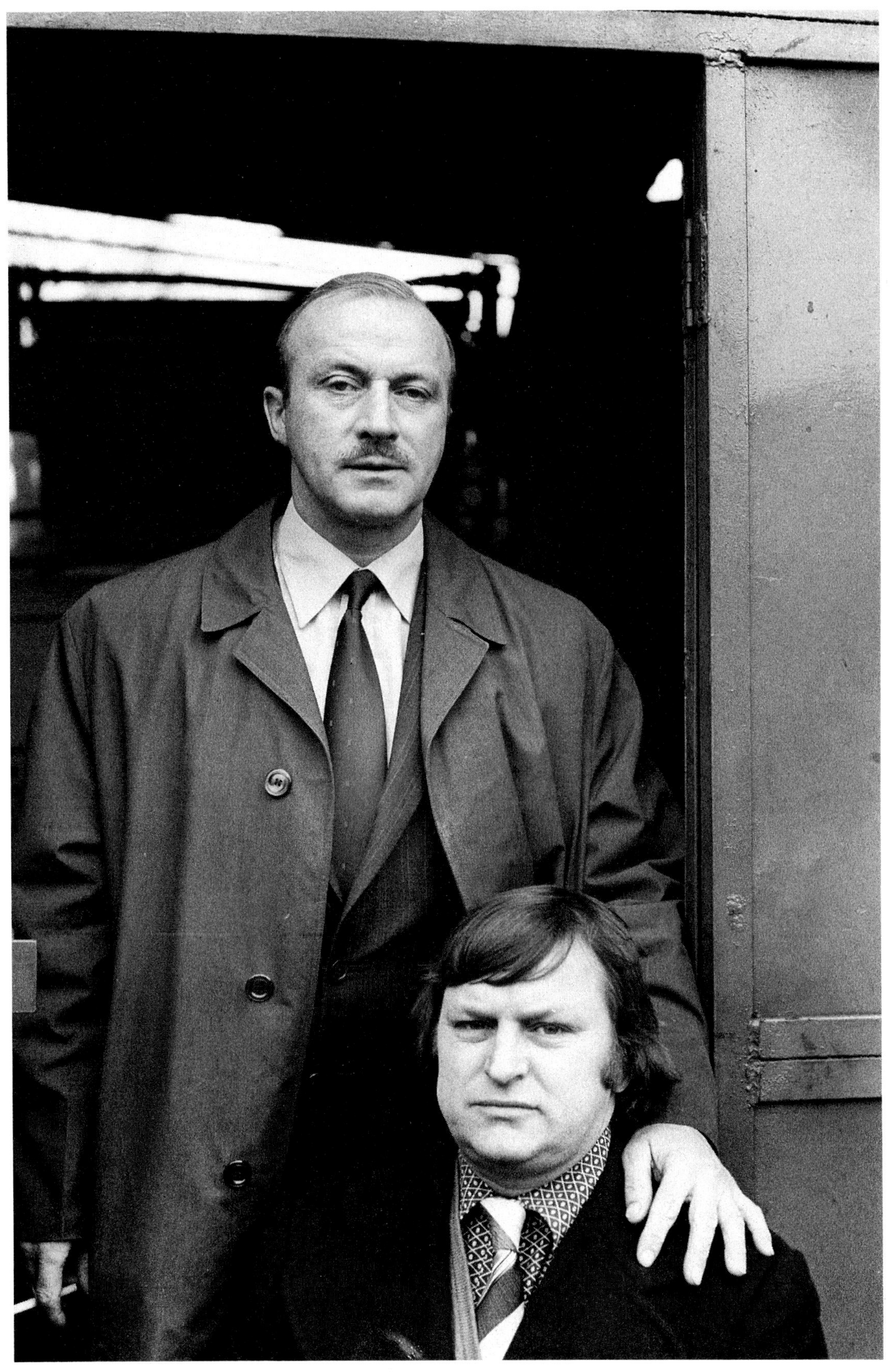

85 – Charles Richardson and 'minder', 1981

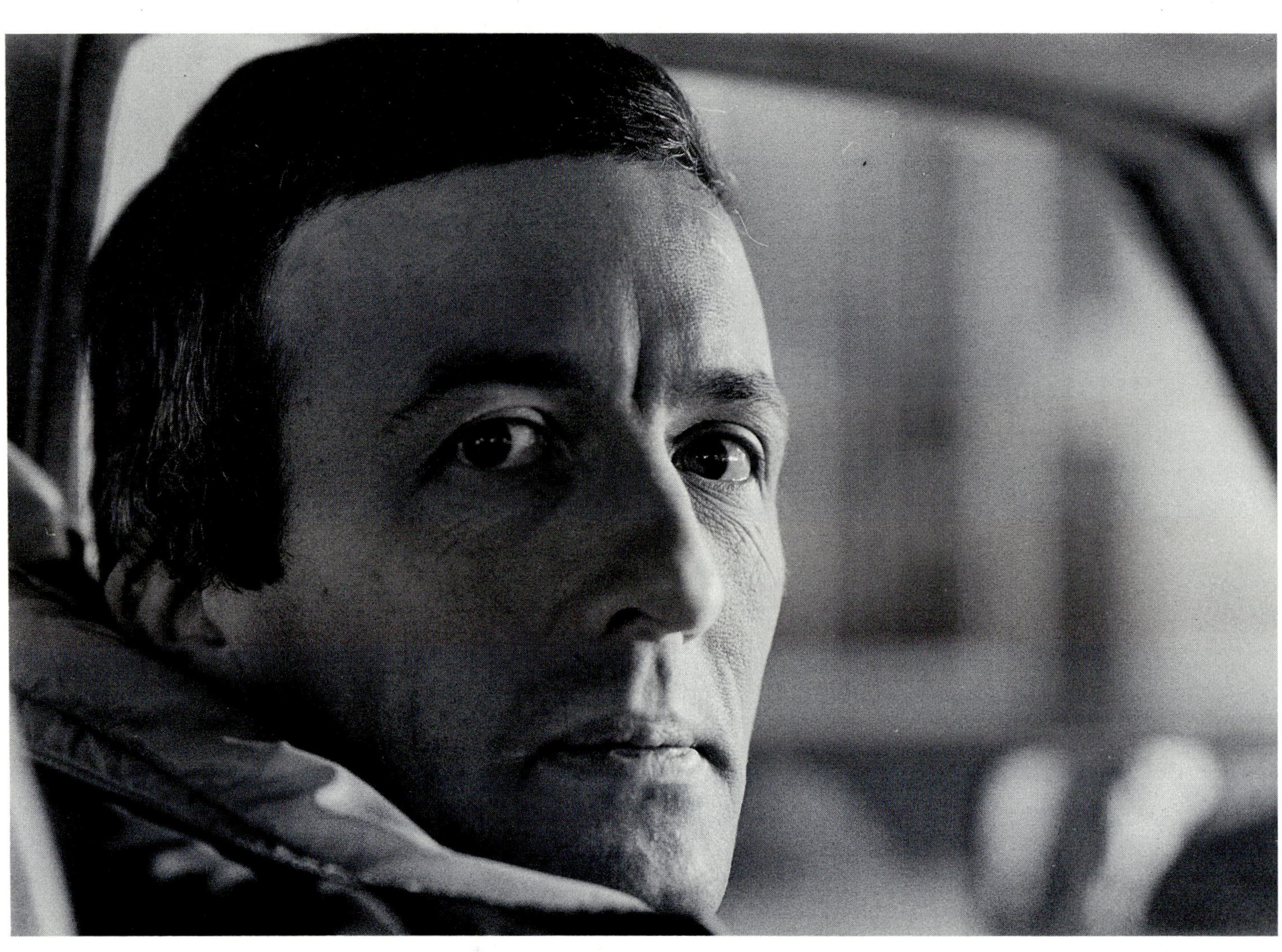

86 – Clive Ponting, 1985

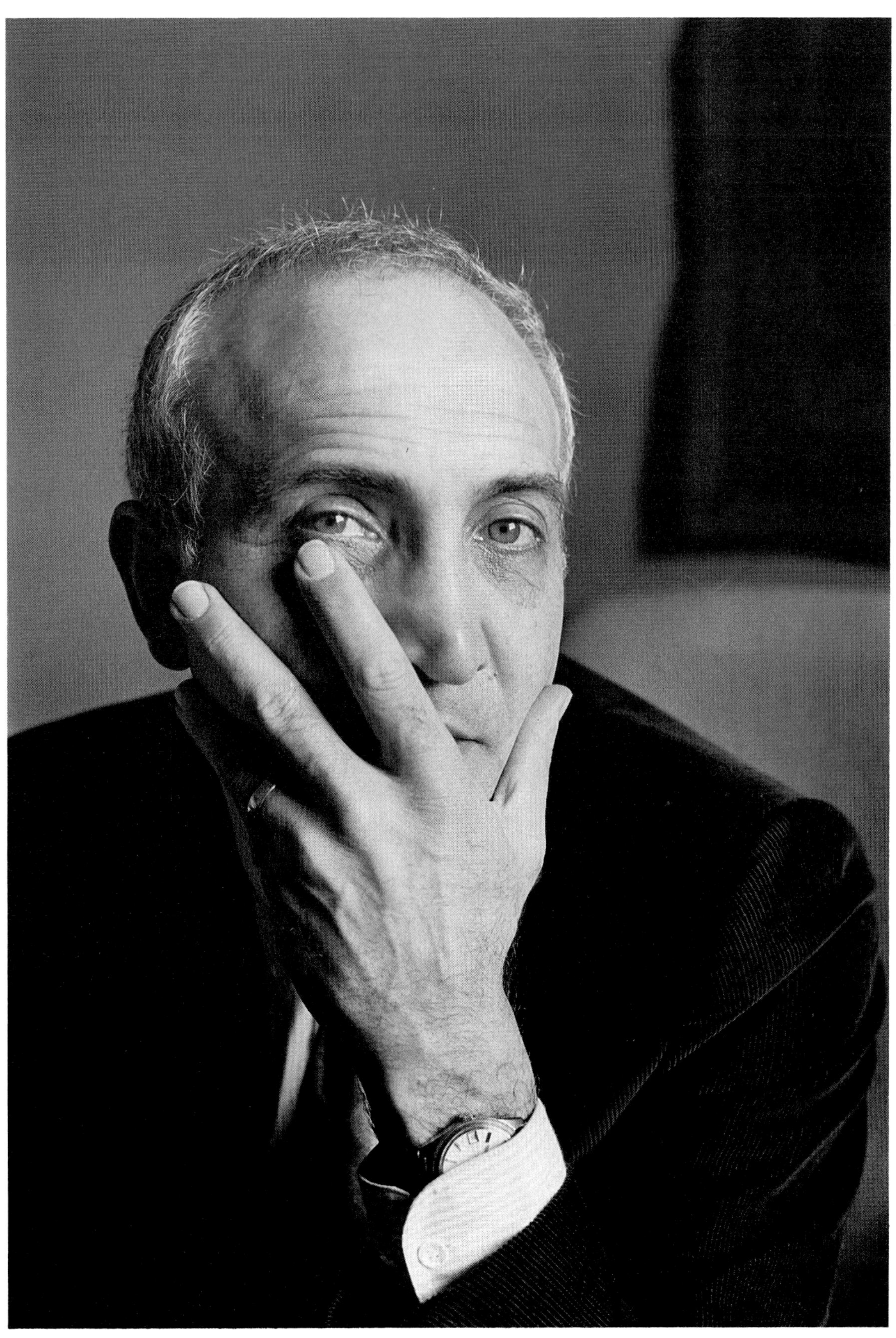

87 – Dr Masud Hoghughi, 1985

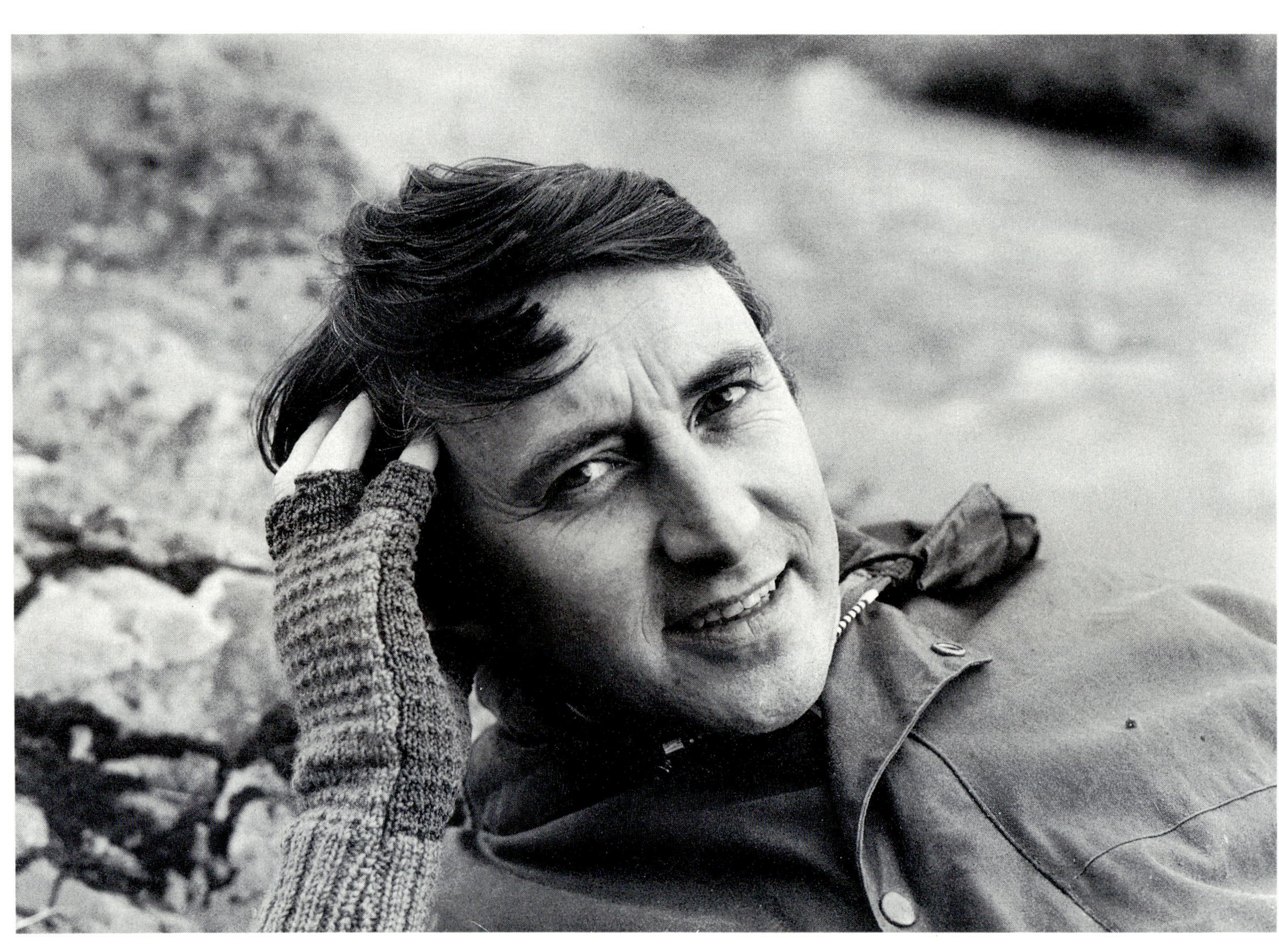

88 – David Steel, 1985

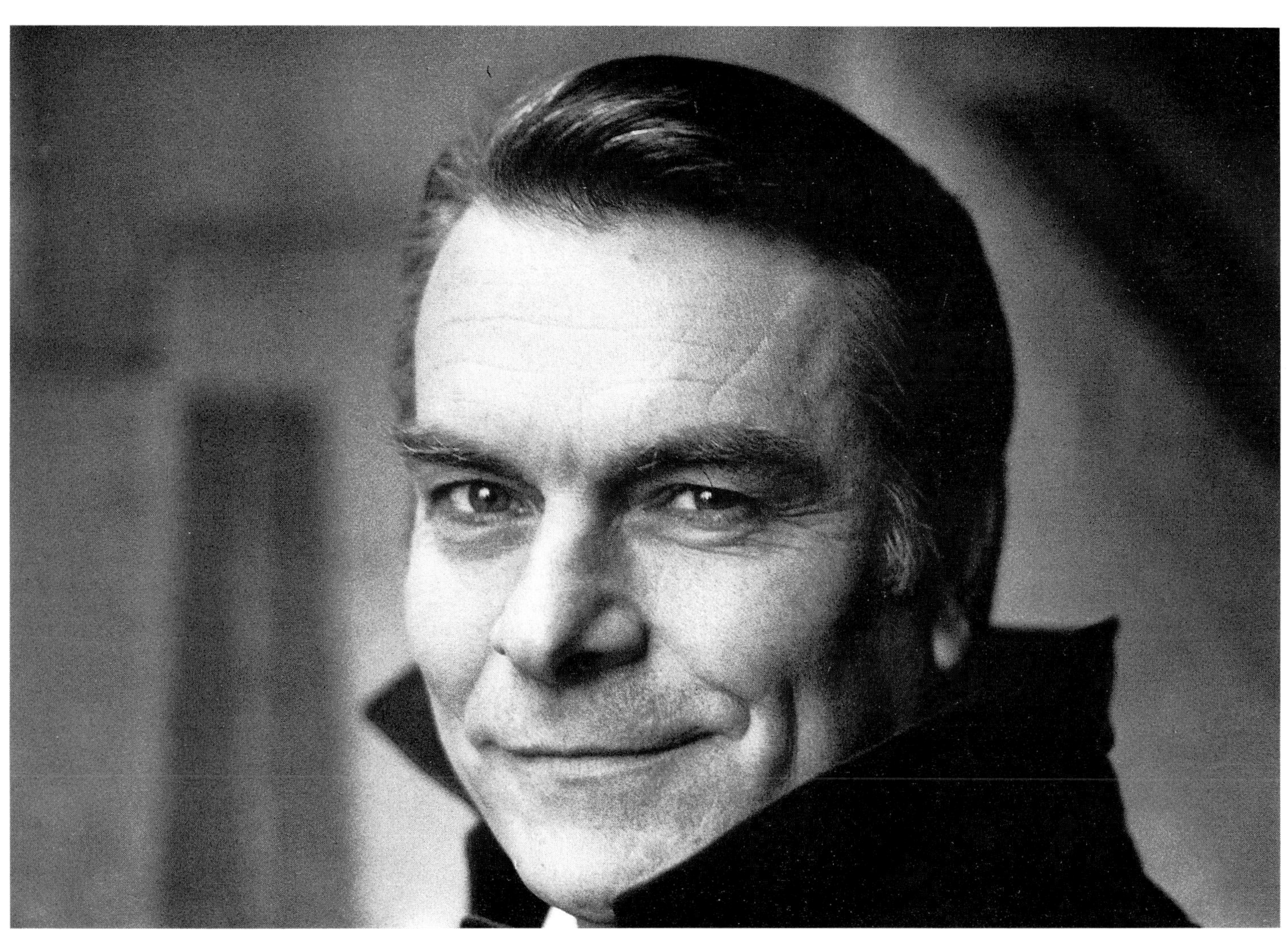

89 – Dr David Owen, 1985

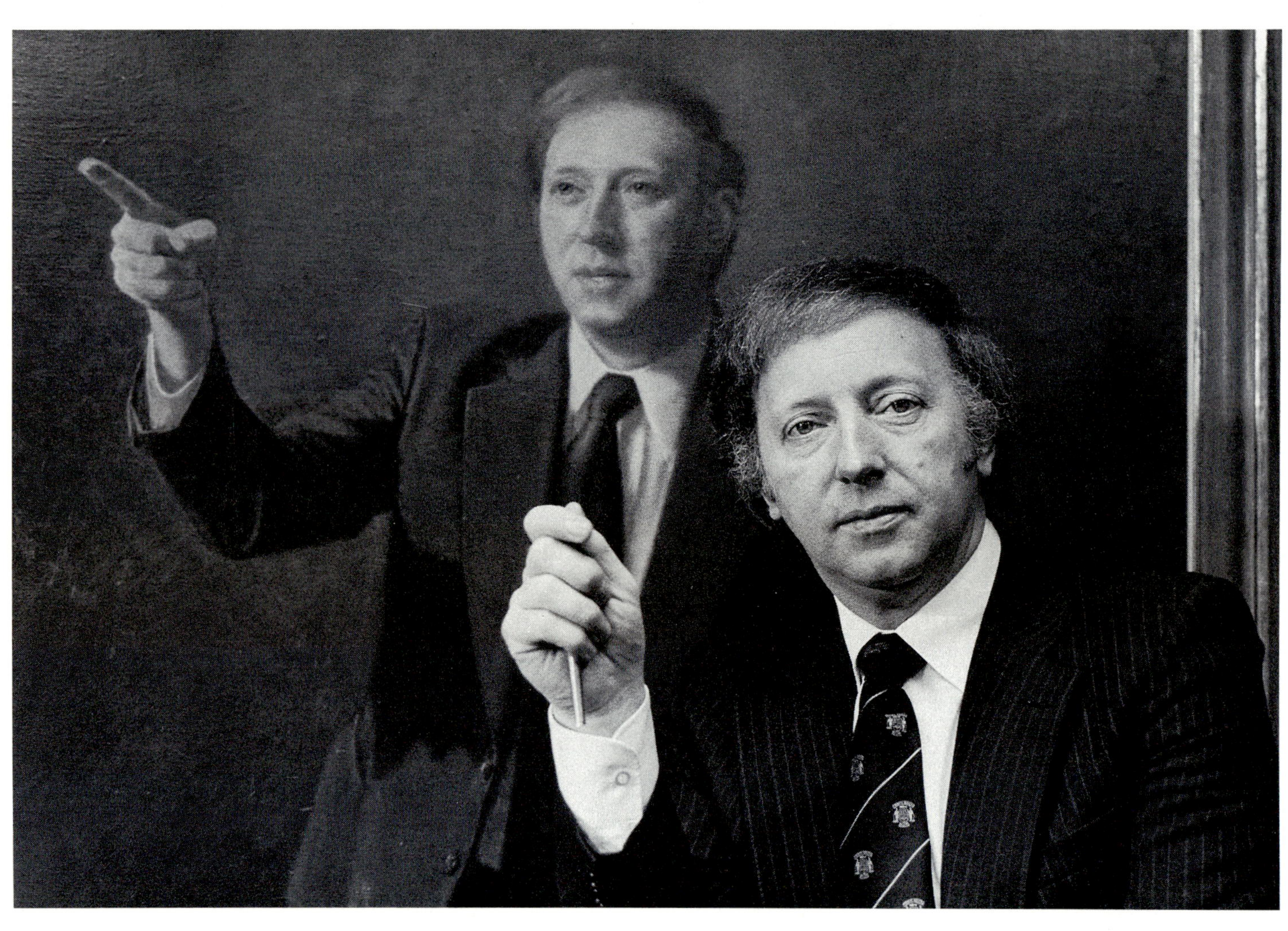

90 – Arthur Scargill, 1981

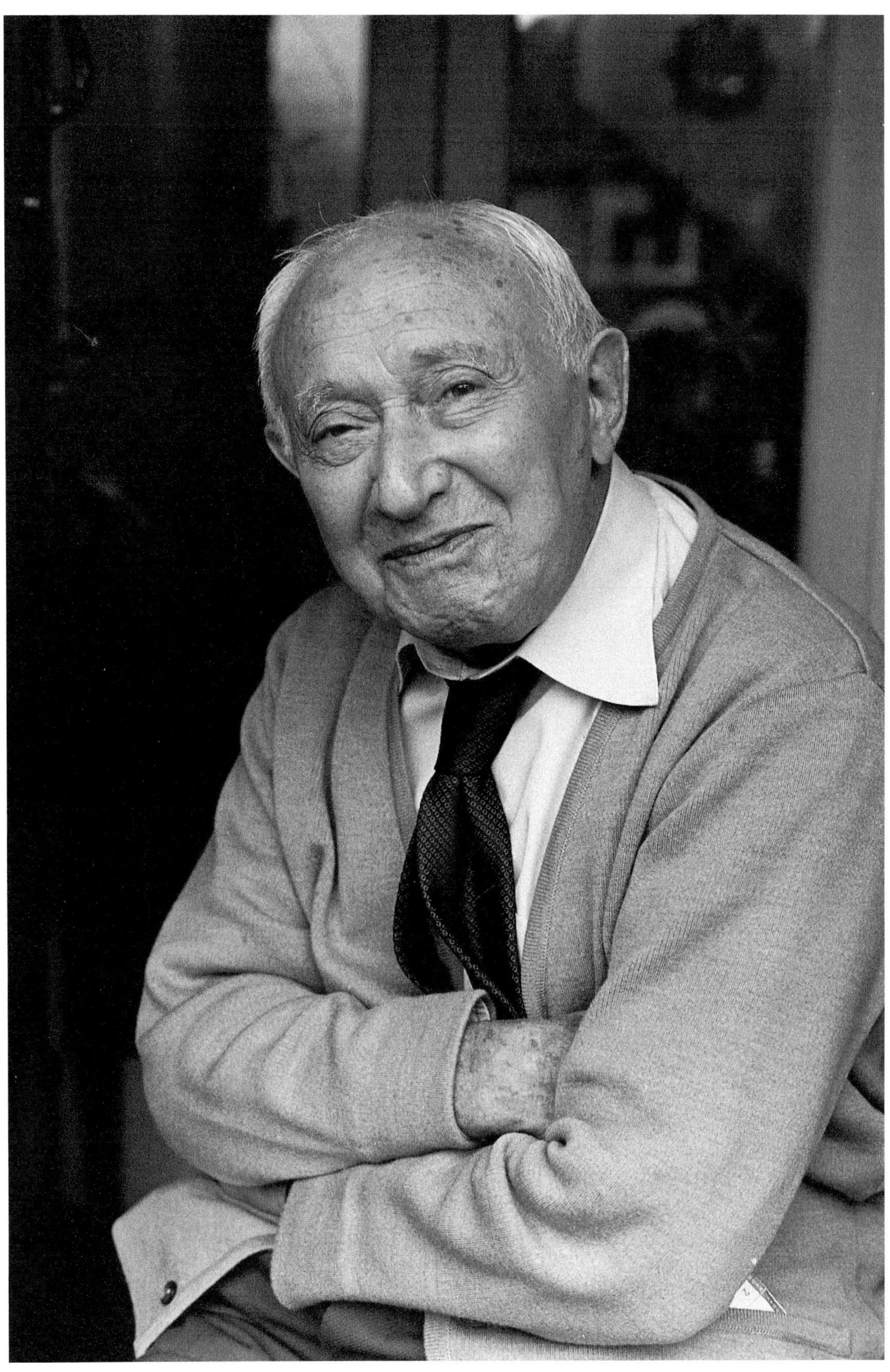

91 – Manny Shinwell, 1981

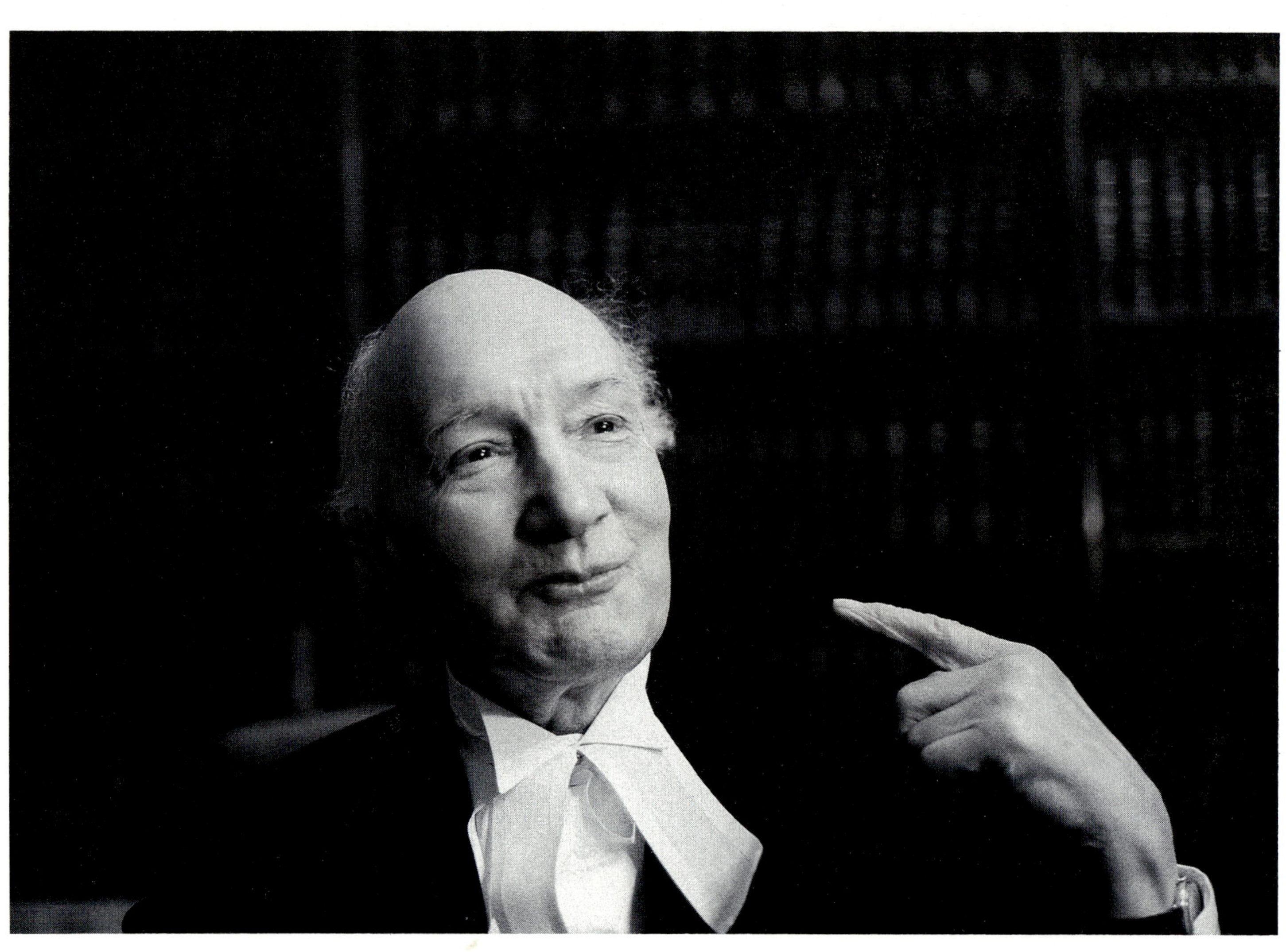

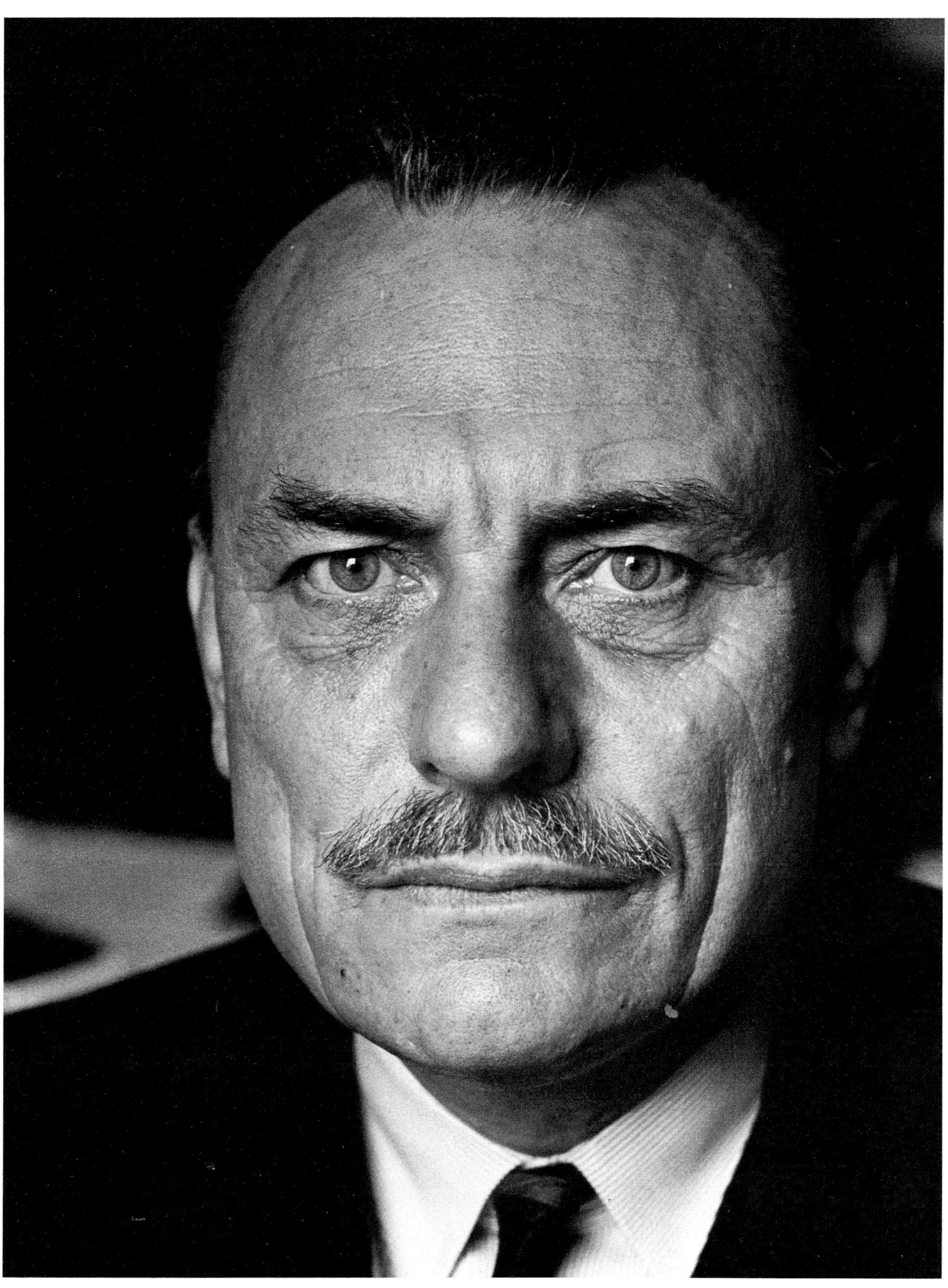

93 – Enoch Powell, 1968

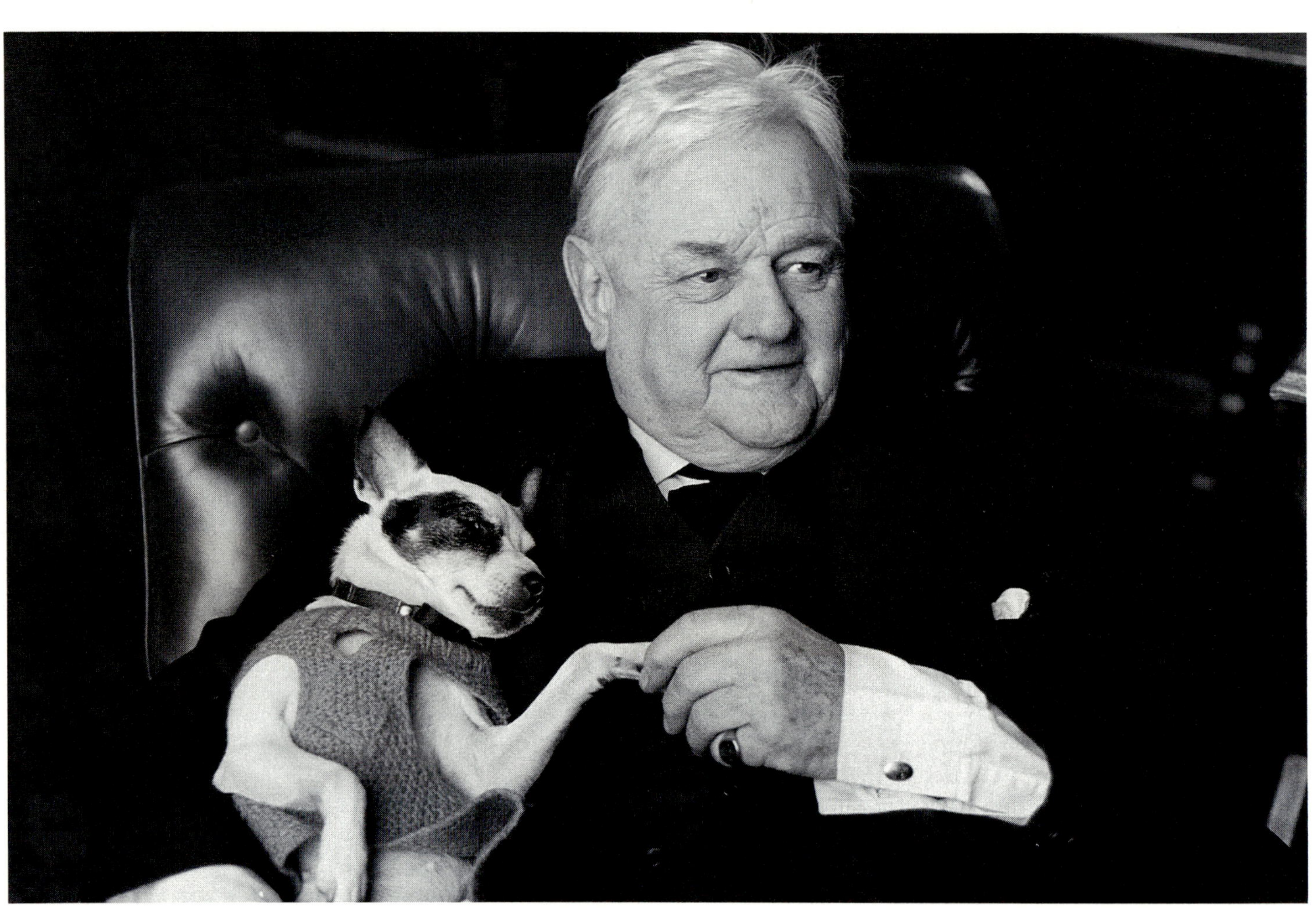

94 – Lord Hailsham, 1981

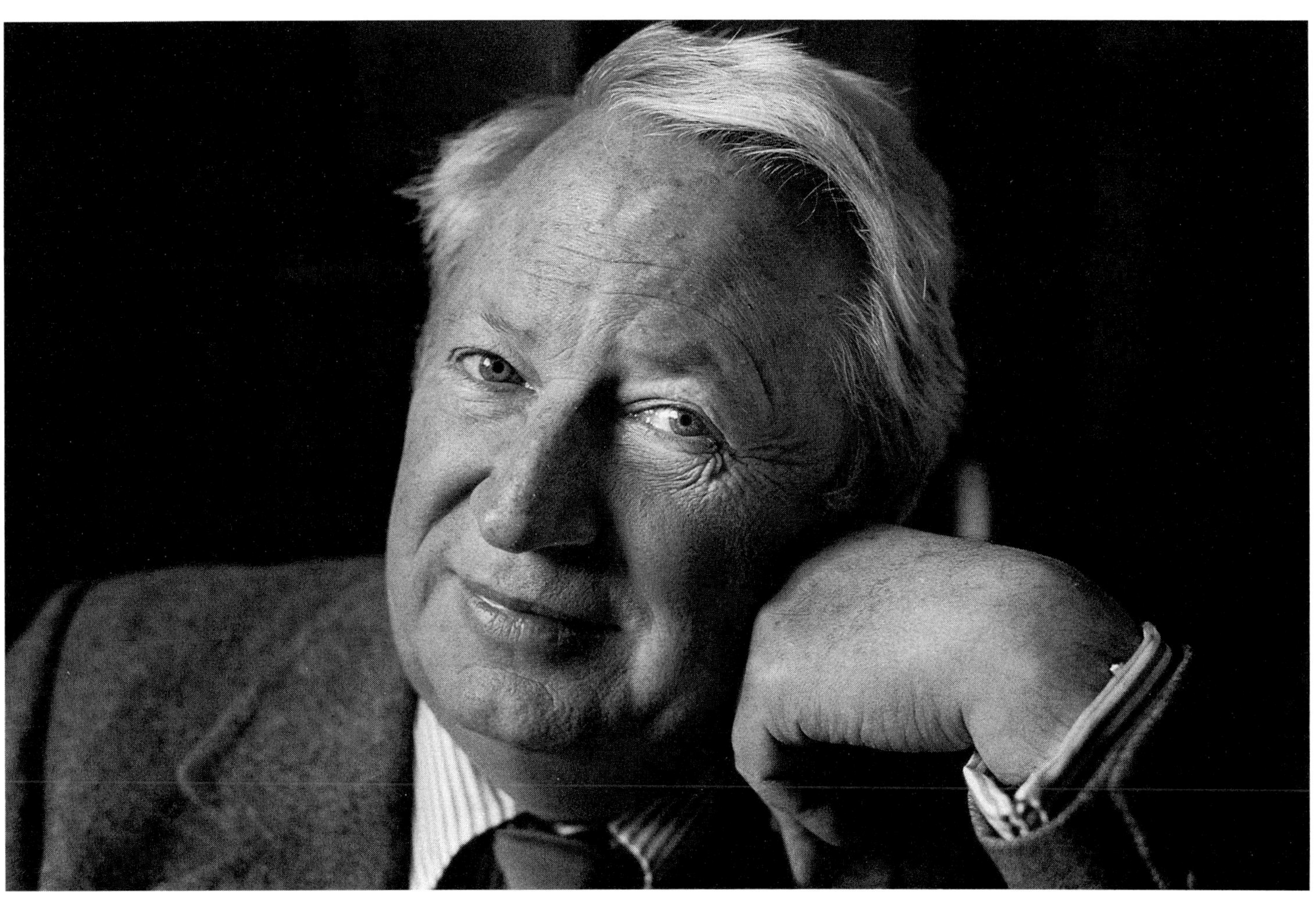

95 – Edward Heath, 1978

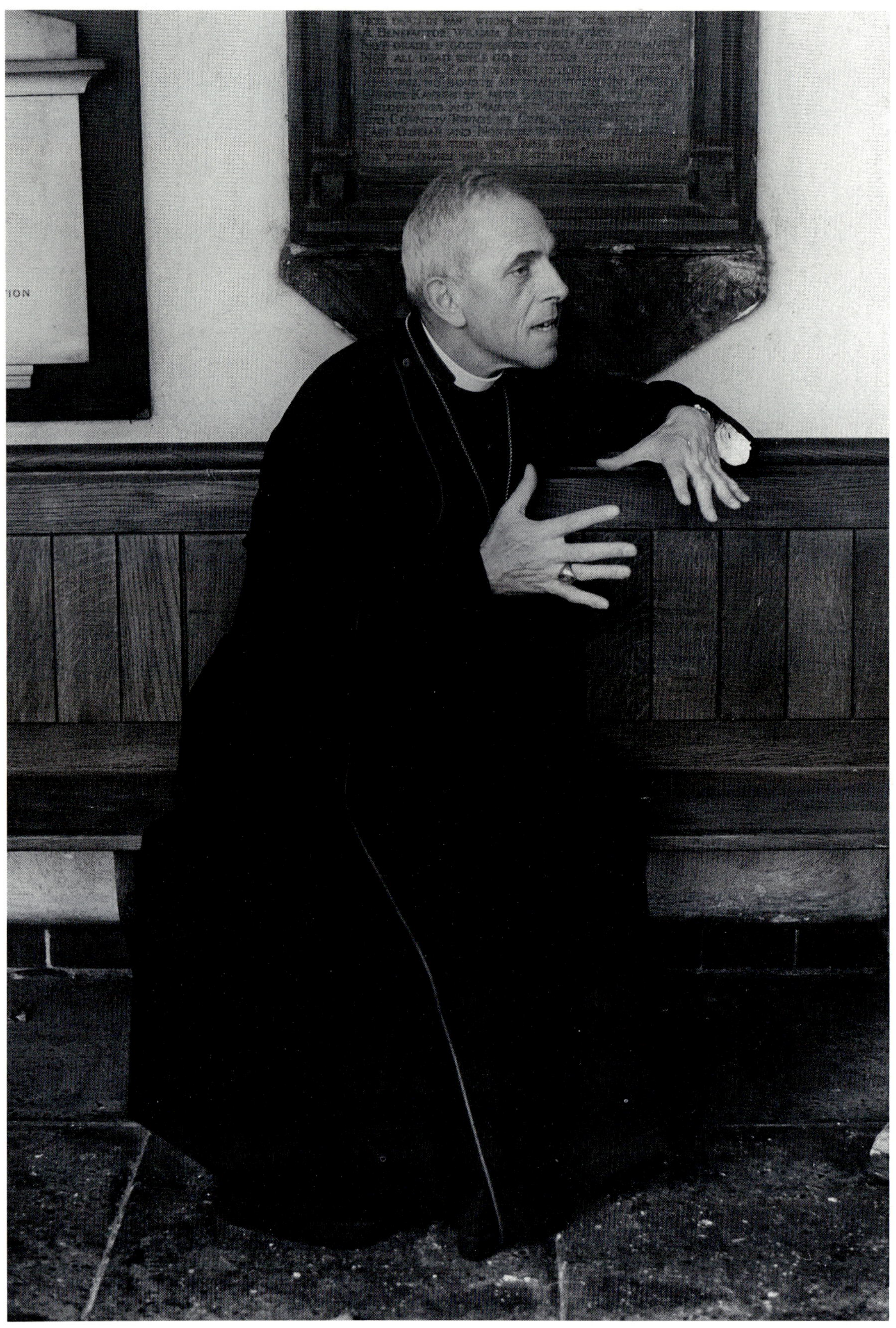

96 – Bishop Trevor Huddleston, 1968

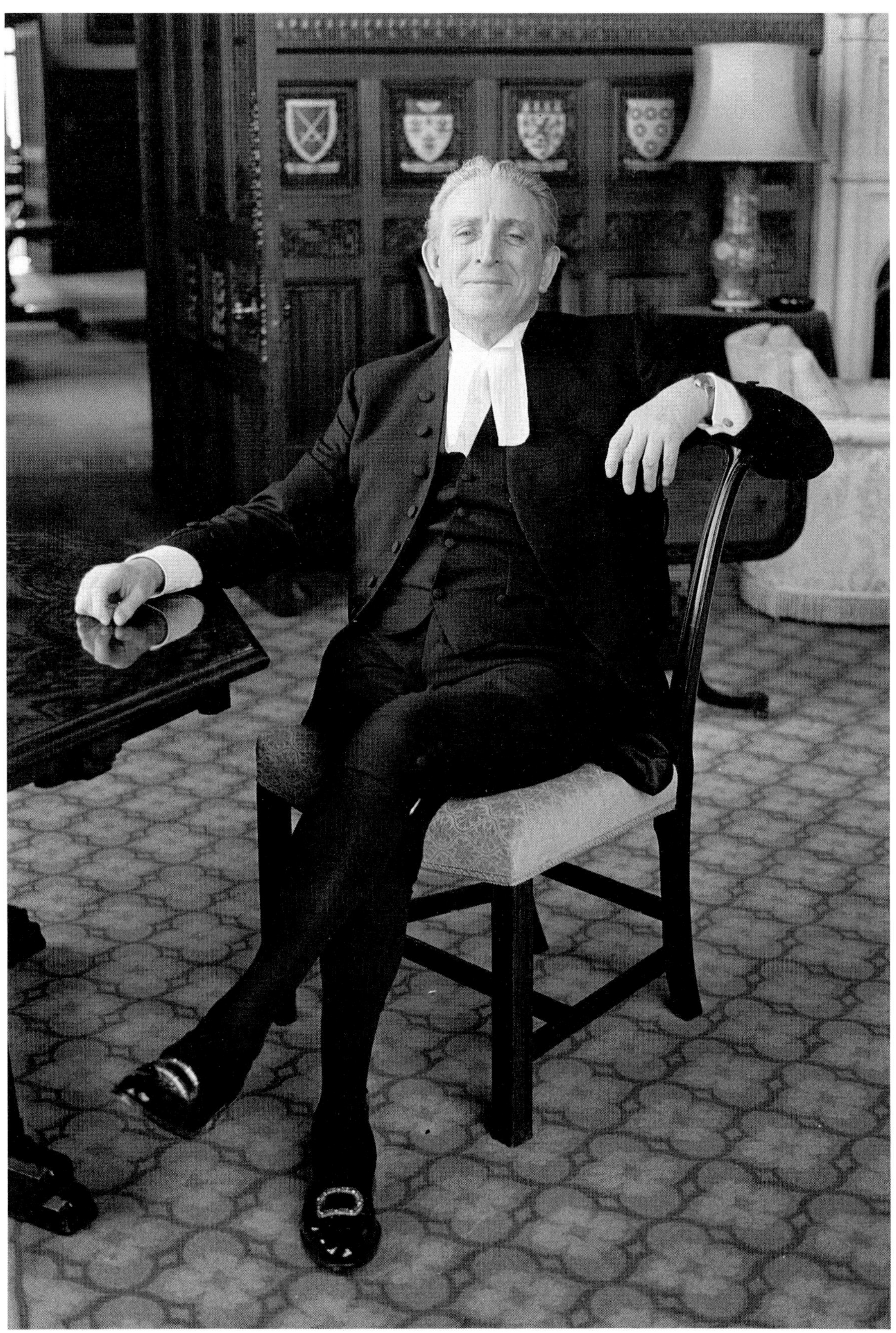

97 – George Thomas, 1982

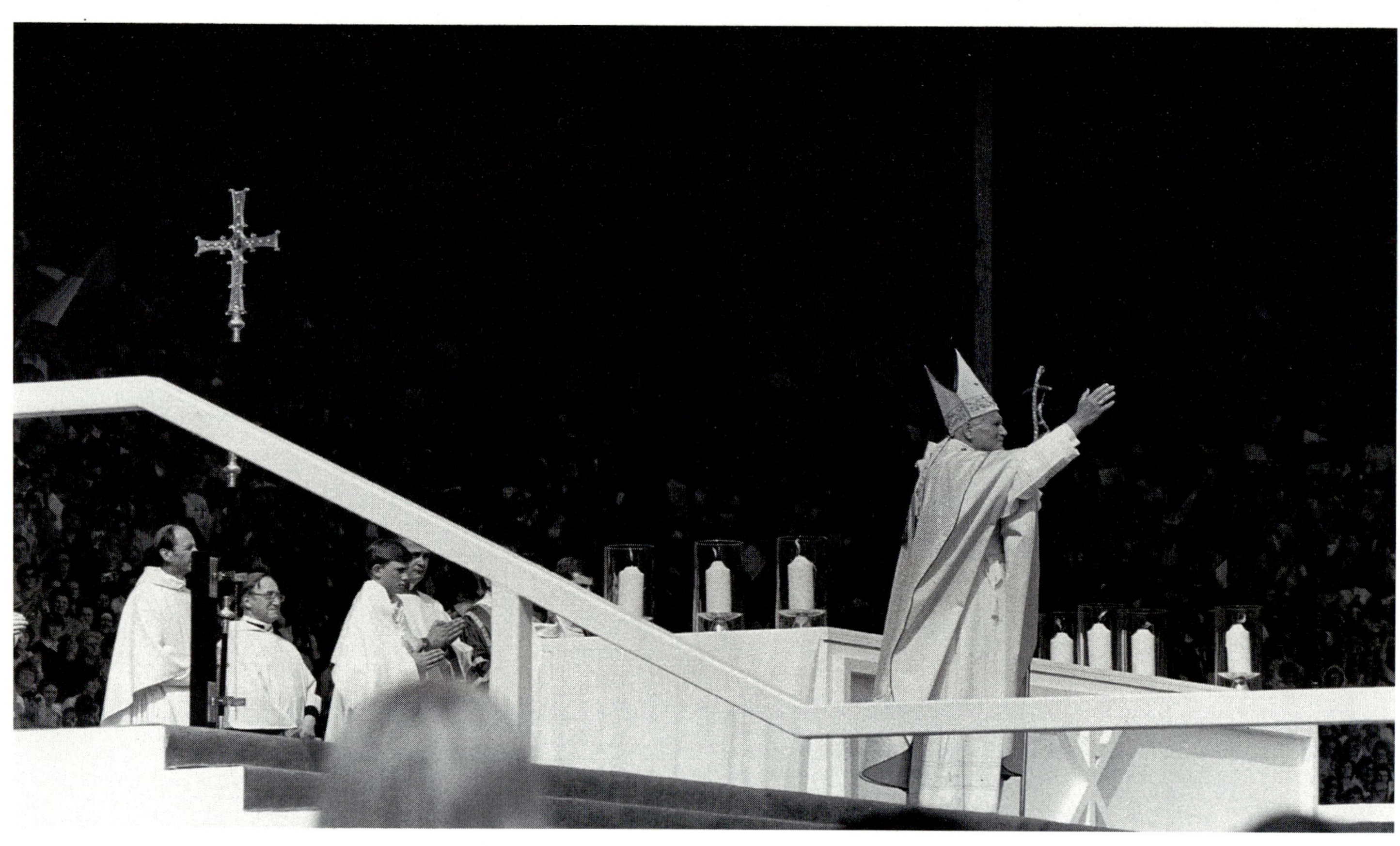

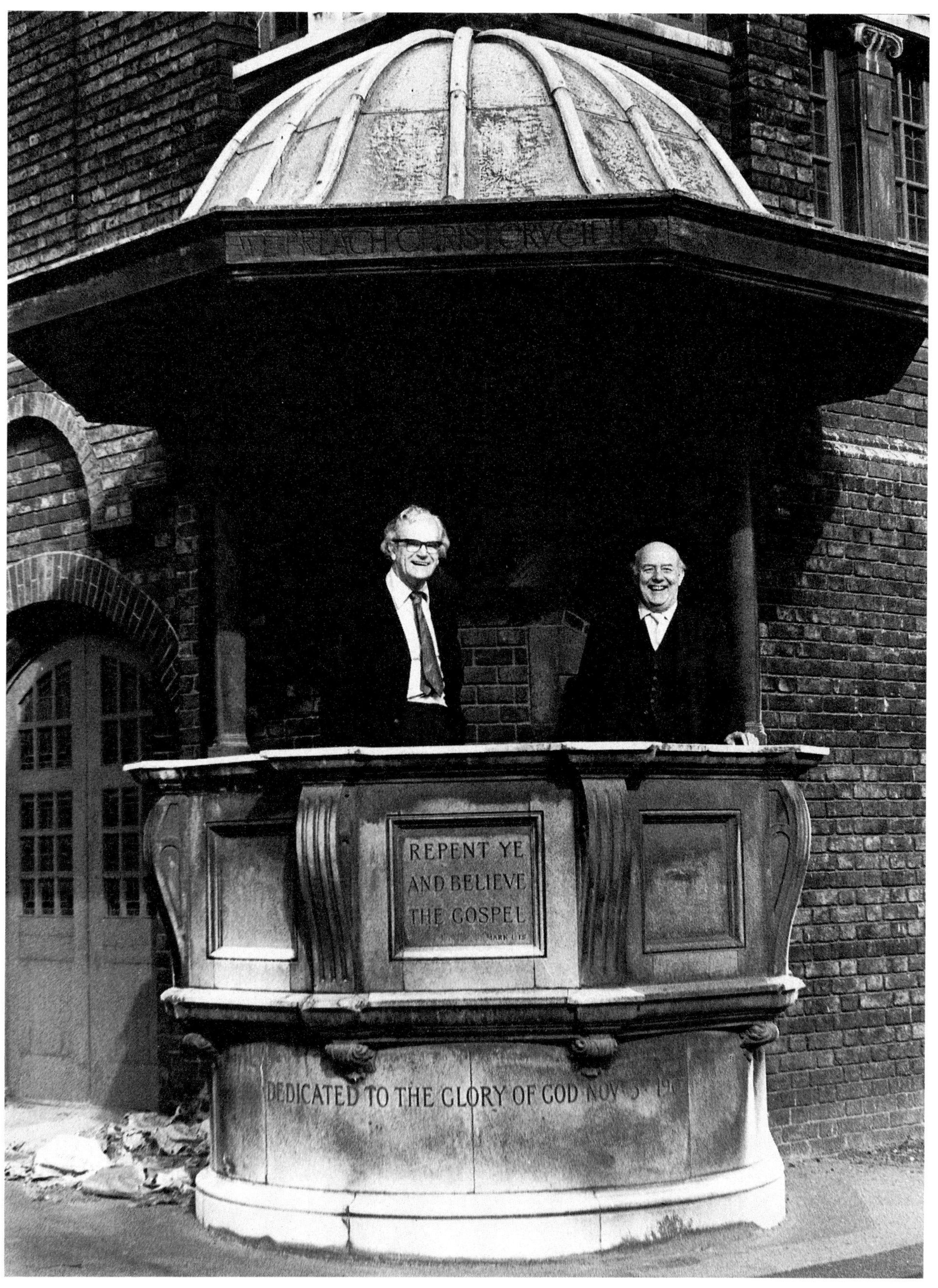

99 – Bishop Mervyn Stockwood and John Betjeman, 1972

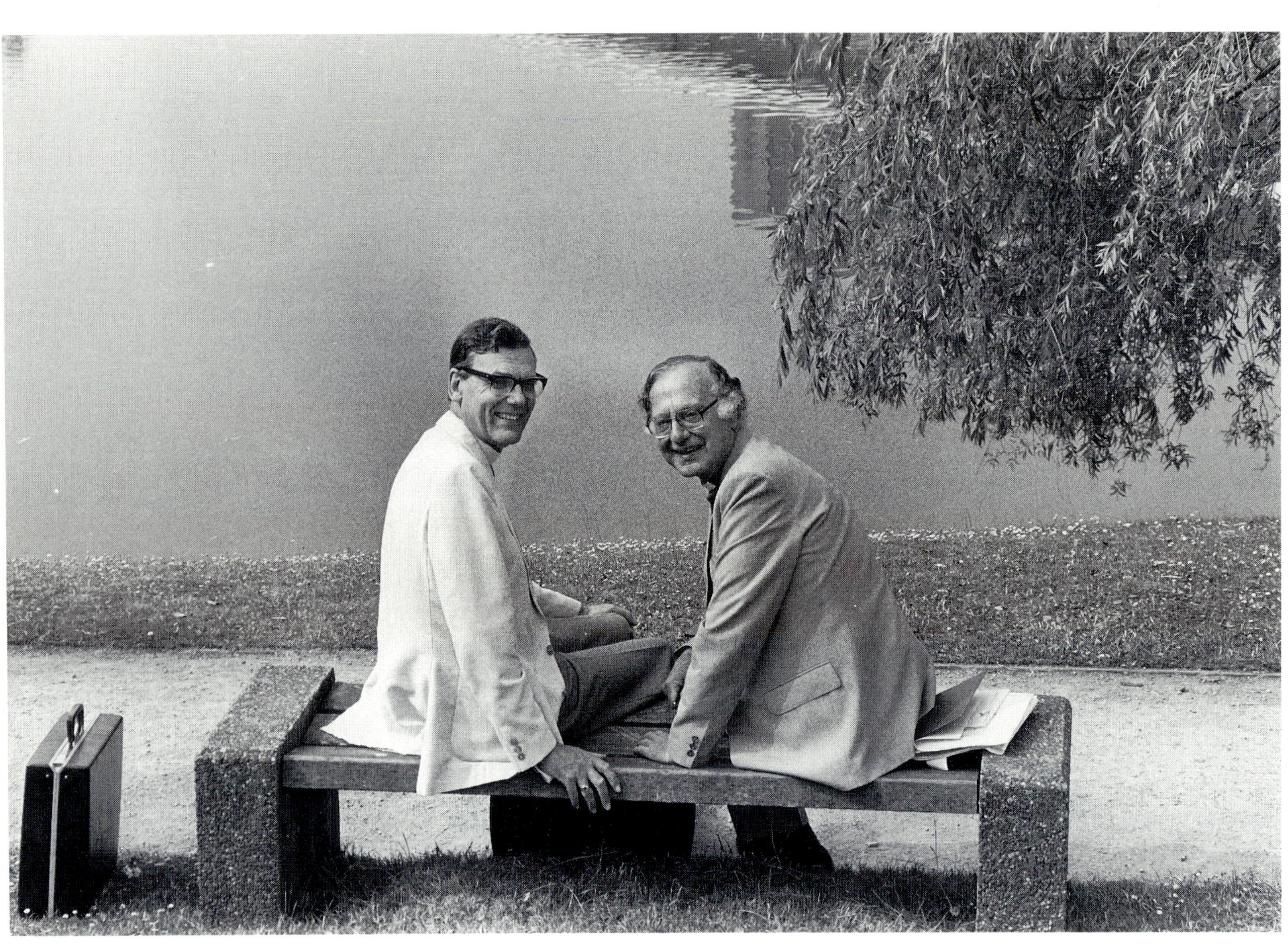

100 – The Archbishops of York and Canterbury, 1983

1 – Jean Paul Getty, 1957
American oil tycoon and art collector, d. 1976
2 – Dr Albert Schweitzer, 1955
French theologian, philosopher, physician and music scholar, d. 1965
3 – General Jan Smuts, 1949
Prime Minister of South Africa 1919–24 and 1939–46, d. 1950
4 – Lord Reith, 1951
Director-General of the BBC 1927–38, d. 1971
5 – Harold Macmillan, 1955
British politician and publisher; Prime Minister 1957–63, d. 1986
6 – William Russell, 1952
Plant breeder and creator of the Russell lupin
7 – The Crazy Gang, 1957
Music hall comedians, at their height in the 1930s and 40s
8, 9, 10, 11 – The Beatles, 1963, Ringo Starr, George Harrison, John Lennon, d. 1980, Paul McCartney
12 – Charlie Chaplin, 1969
British actor, director, screenwriter and composer, d. 1977
13 – Orson Welles, 1951
American director, actor and screenwriter, d. 1985
14 – Edward Kennedy, 1971
American politician and lawyer, brother of John F. Kennedy
15 – Sammy Davis Jnr, 1961
American singer and entertainer
16 – Groucho Marx, 1964
American actor, one of the Marx Brothers, d. 1977
17 – Charles Laughton, 1958
British screen actor and director, d. 1962
18 – Jacob Epstein, 1958
British sculptor, d. 1959
19 – Henry Moore, 1968
British sculptor, d. 1986
20 – Graham Greene, 1957
British writer and novelist
21 – Philip Toynbee, 1961
British journalist, editor, reviewer and author, d. 1981
22 – Sir John Gielgud, 1950
British actor, producer and sometime opera director
23 – George Balanchine, 1960
Russian-born ballet dancer and choreographer, d. 1983
24 – François Mauriac, 1950
French novelist, d. 1970
25 – Jean Cocteau, 1950
French poet, painter, writer and director, d. 1970
26 – Christopher Isherwood, 1970
American novelist and playwright, born in England, d. 1986
27 – W. H. Auden, 1970
British-born poet and writer, d. 1973
28 – Arthur Miller, 1979
American playwright
29 – Gore Vidal, 1981
American author and screenwriter
30 – Henry Miller, 1967
American writer and artist, d. 1980
31 – Robert Lowell, 1967
American poet and playwright, d. 1977
32 – Sir Harold Acton, 1982
British historian and aesthete
33 – Samuel Beckett, 1976
Irish dramatist and novelist, writing in French and English
34 – V. S. Pritchett, 1980
British author and critic
35 – J. B. Priestley, 1980
British writer, playwright and World War II broadcaster, d. 1984
36 – Sir Geoffrey Keynes, 1981
Physician, author and bibliophile, d. 1982
37 – Sir Stephen Spender, 1985
British writer, poet and critic
38 – Kingsley Amis, 1984
British novelist and critic
39 – Bruce Chatwin, 1982
British travel writer and novelist
40 – R. S. Thomas, 1964
Welsh clergyman and poet
41 – Ted Hughes, 1987
British writer and Poet Laureate
42 – Philip Larkin, 1979
British poet and librarian, d. 1986
43 – Sir John Betjeman, 1972
British poet and Poet Laureate from 1972 until his death, d. 1984
44 – Sir Sacheverell Sitwell, 1982
British writer and reviewer, brother of the late Dame Edith Sitwell
45 – Sir William Walton, 1982
British composer, and family friend of the Sitwells, d. 1983
46 – Sir Reginald Goodall, 1982
British conductor

47 – Sir John Barbirolli, 1969
British conductor, latterly of the Hallé Orchestra,
d. 1970

48 – Sir Hugh Casson, 1984
British architect and writer, president of the Royal
College of Arts

49 – Serge Lifar, 1984
Russian ballet dancer, choreographer and writer

50 – Sir Cecil Beaton, 1974
Fashion and society photographer, costume and set
designer, d. 1980

51 – Sir Frederick Ashton, 1970
British choreographer and ballet dancer

52 – Francis Bacon, 1985
British painter

53 – Lucien Freud, 1983
British painter

54 – Brassai, 1982
Transylvanian-born photographer, artist and
author, d. 1984

55 – Frank Auerbach, 1986
British artist, born in Germany

56 – Duncan Grant, 1978
British painter and fabric and furniture designer,
d. 1978

57 – John Piper, 1983
British painter and author

58 – Iannis Xenakis, 1987
Greek composer

59 – John Barton, 1981
Associate Director of the Royal Shakespeare
Company

60 – Sir Michael Redgrave, 1983
British actor, d. 1985

61 – John Osborne, 1986
British playwright, actor and producer

62 – Ian McKellen, 1984
British actor

63 – Simon Callow, 1984
British actor and writer

64 – David Suchet and Ben Kingsley, 1985
Actors, on stage during rehearsals for *Othello*

65 – Alec McCowen, 1984
British actor

66 – Dennis Hopper, 1982
American actor and director

67 – Bernard Pomerance, 1980
American playwright

68 – Quentin Crisp, 1978
Commercial artist and artists' model, author of *The
Naked Civil Servant*

69 – Marty Feldman, 1969
British comedy actor, writer and director, d. 1982

70 – Bob Geldof, 1987
Irish rock singer, founder of Band Aid

71 – Mick Jagger, 1973
British rock singer, songwriter and actor, lead singer
of the Rolling Stones

72 – Bono and The Edge, 1987
Irish rock musicians, members of the group U2

73 – David Knopfler, 1984
Rock musician, founder member of Dire Straits

74 – Richard O'Brien, 1984
British playwright, song and screenwriter, author of
The Rocky Horror Show

75 – Frank Clark, 1985
Author of screenplay *Letter to Brezhnev*

76 – Kit Williams, 1981
Artist, writer and illustrator

77 – John Cooper Clark, 1985
British punk poet

78 – Huw Wheldon, 1972
British broadcaster and one-time presenter of
television arts programme 'Monitor'

79 – Sir David Attenborough, 1985
British broadcaster and writer

80 – Michael Grade, 1986
Director of Programmes, BBC Television since 1986

81 – Jeremy Isaacs, 1980
First chief executive of Channel 4

82 – Rupert Murdoch, 1981
Australian-born newspaper publisher, chairman of
News International Group

83 – Tiny Rowland, 1981
British businessman, chairman of the *Observer* since
1983

84 – Chief Superintendent Newman, 1982
Commissioner of the Metropolitan Police 1982–87,
Chief Constable of the Royal Ulster Constabulary
1976–79

85 – Charles Richardson and 'minder', 1981
Members of London's underworld

86 – Clive Ponting, 1985
Ex civil servant who defied the Official Secrets Act
during the Falklands War

87 – Dr Masud Hoghughi, 1985
Pioneer in the rehabilitation of child psychopaths

88, 89 – 'The Two Davids', 1985, David Steel and David
Owen, joint leaders of the SDP/Liberal Alliance

90 – Arthur Scargill, 1981
British trades-union official, President of the
National Union of Mineworkers

91 – Manny Shinwell, 1981
     British political leader and centenarian, d. 1986
92 – Lord Denning, 1980
     British barrister, Master of the Rolls
93 – Enoch Powell, 1968
     British politician and Ulster Unionist Member of
     Parliament 1974–87
94 – Lord Hailsham, 1981
     British politician and former Lord Chancellor
95 – Edward Heath, 1978
     Conservative MP, British Prime Minister 1970–74,
     musician and yachtsman
96 – Bishop Trevor Huddleston, 1968
     British churchman, President of the Anti-Apartheid
     movement since 1981
97 – George Thomas, 1982
     Former speaker of the House of Commons
98 – The Pope, 1982
     His Holiness Pope John Paul II, inaugurated 22
     October 1978
99 – Bishop Mervyn Stockwood and John Betjeman,
     1972
     Former Bishop of Southwark with former Poet
     Laureate
100 – The Archbishops of York and Canterbury, 1983
     The Most Rev. and Right Hon. John Hapgood and
     the Most Rev. and Right Hon. Robert Runcie.